THE

WAR

ON

WEEDS

IN THE PRAIRIE WEST

An Environmental History

Clinton L. Evans

UNIVERSITY OF
CALGARY
PRESS

University of Calgary Press
2500 University Drive NW
Calgary, Alberta
Canada T2N 1N4
www.uofcpress.com

National Library of Canada Cataloguing in Publication Data
    Evans, Clinton L. (Clinton Lorne), 1960-
    The war on weeds in the Prairie West

    Includes bibliographical references and index.
    ISBN 1-55238-029-7

    1. Weeds — Control — Prairie Provinces — History.
    2. Weeds — Control — Ontario — History. I. Title.
    SB613.C2E92 2001   632'.5'097120904   C2001-911406-0

  We acknowledge the financial support of the Government of Canada through the Book Publishing Industry Development Program (BPIDP) for our publishing activities.

The Canada Council for the Arts
Le Conseil des Arts du Canada

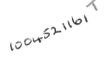

Printed and bound in Canada by AGMV Marquis.
∞This book is printed on acid-free paper.

Page, cover design, and typesetting by Kristina Schuring.

Preface

Any gardener will tell you that weeds are easy to hate. They appear with amazing regularity in your lawn and garden. They mar the appearance of your herbaceous borders and seem to positively delight in pushing through driveways, squeezing between patio slabs, and twisting their way through the wire of chain-link fences. Weeds are a time-consuming nuisance when you assault them by hand; they can cost a small fortune if you prefer to wage chemical warfare. Weeds are diverse, weeds are persistent, and weeds are unavoidable.

I used to hate weeds. I hated them enough to devote four years of university and ten field seasons to seeking their demise. I learned that weeds were "plants out of place" and then was told that they had no place in commercial agriculture. The ultimate goal was to prevent their appearance but, since a plethora of weeds were already here, the immediate goal was to "control" them by the most cost-effective means possible. I learned that ideally weeds could be controlled by tillage in combination with cultural techniques such as crop rotation. Most of my time, however, was spent learning about herbicides — the weed-killing method of choice for farmers and weed specialists alike. Armed with a spray gun and backed by tough-sounding federal and provincial noxious-weed legislation, I then proceeded to eradicate weeds in earnest and I dispatched countless thousands before my career was through.

Towards the end of my career I began to have misgivings. I began to wonder, how is it possible to define weeds as plants out of place and then proceed to treat them as an objective category, as discrete species that can be identified and proscribed by federal and provincial legislation? I began to wonder why weeds are still multiplying and spreading despite the laws enacted against them and why herbicides produce immediate results yet result in little long-term control? I began to hear stories about pesticide companies suppressing the negative results of herbicide field trials and I began to see herbicide-resistant weeds thriving in places where no other vegetation was able to survive. I even began to admire weeds for their toughness, their tenacity, and for their ability to cover the scars caused by human activity with a verdant bandage of green.

This study originated as an attempt to answer some of these questions. Soon afterwards I was introduced to the field of environmental history which further convinced me that weeds had a place in the annals of Canadian history. The story that follows can be read as a conventional history of weeds and weed control in western Canada. It can also be read as an historical primer for weed scientists and other agriculturalists who are seeking new ways to manage weedy vegetation. Generations of farmers, bureaucrats, legislators, and agricultural experts have been engaged in this task and their ideas and experiences shed considerable light on many of the problems facing agriculturalists today. On a deeper level, this study attempts to demonstrate the potential of environmental history by gently parodying the conventional tale of western Canadian settlement and development. Canadian historians have been slow to adopt this relatively new field of historical inquiry and, as a result, they have yet to make a concerted effort to confront their anthropocentric biases, to return to their roots, and to look beyond their current obsession with purely human phenomena. Society and the environment have changed since the days of more environmentally conscious historians such as Harold Innis and Donald Creighton but society and the environment still remain linked even though the linkages are less immediate and far harder to discern.

I wish to thank my ex-thesis supervisor David Breen for allowing me to pursue my interest in the first place and for his quiet support and guidance as the study evolved. Bob MacDonald deserves thanks for much the same reasons as well as for forcing me to address a number of vital questions that I probably would have left unanswered. Publication of this book was made possible by the unflagging efforts of Director Walter Hildebrandt and his staff at University of Calgary Press. Walter was the one who first suggested the possibility of publishing my manuscript and without his patience, persistence, and astute guidance this study would never have gone to print. Last but not least I wish to thank my wife Maureen for her unstinting support and my children Bronwyn, Gwyneth, and Conal for keeping my feet on the ground and my head out of the clouds. Sometimes wiping a runny nose or pushing a kid on a swing is just what a person needs to keep his or her academic life in perspective.

This book has been published with the help of a grant from the Humanities and Social Sciences Federation of Canada, using funds provided by the Social Sciences and Humanities Research Council of Canada.

Introduction

> Weeds are plants which interfere with the growth of crops or lower the profits of farming or mar the appearance of the landscape. In a sense farming is a continual warfare against these intruders, the contending forces being man and crops on the one side and weeds on the other, with nature a neutral onlooker, but one ever ready to lend her aid to the side showing the greatest persistence.
> — Bracken, *Dry Farming in Western Canada* (1921), 211

Like all good politicians, John Bracken, principal of the Manitoba Agricultural College and soon-to-be Premier of Manitoba, had a knack for expressing what most of his constituency believed to be true: Prairie farmers and their vegetative allies were locked in mortal combat with a diverse group of plants called weeds. This study chronicles the war against weeds that raged in western Canada between 1800 and 1950. Farmers were on the defensive for most of this period and, by the close of the Second World War, many people believed that the weed problem alone cast the entire future of Prairie agriculture into doubt. Agricultural experts had long been encouraging

Stinkweed, *Thlaspi arvense*

farmers to abandon grain monoculture and retreat to the relative safety of mixed farming but most chose to stand their ground while waiting for either bankruptcy or deliverance. Fortunately for them, science rode to the rescue with the 1945 release of the first truly effective "selective" herbicide, 2,4-D. This herbicide rapidly supplanted more traditional methods of weed control and within five years 2,4-D had become a standard part of the Prairie farmer's antiweed arsenal. In fact, by then it had become so popular that Prairie farmers bore the dubious distinction of using chemical weed killers "on a larger proportion of the cropland than any other comparable region of the world."[1]

In addition to providing a much needed corrective to the conventional story of agricultural progress on the Canadian Prairies, this study also explores two lesser known subjects: the rise of Canada's large agricultural bureaucracy and the development of a wide array of noxious-weed legislation. Both were dedicated to promoting improved farming methods but their main legacy was to help preserve the ecologically unsound, weed-friendly style of farming that persists on the Prairies to this day. They did so by reinforcing the popular notion that weeds were the "enemy"; by diverting attention away from the fact that the true enemy was the extensive system of grain farming practised by the farmers themselves. The war against weeds was, therefore, somewhat akin to a civil war, pitting farmers against their own unsound practices and the short-term solutions of government experts against their knowledge of the dictates of good husbandry.

The immediate goal of this study is to highlight the shortcomings of current noxious-weed legislation and crop production systems on the Prairies. Legislators are in desperate need of some historical context — context that suggests that today's elaborate and often draconian noxious-weed laws simply do not work. Similarly, in their efforts to lessen herbicide dependency amongst farmers, weed specialists should take note of the sophistication of traditional weed lore and of the difficulties encountered by their predecessors when they attempted to translate this knowledge into practice. Relatively new approaches such as weed "management" and "weed-crop ecology," for example, are often touted as the way of the future yet in some respects they simply represent modern elaborations of very traditional ideas. Historically these ideas have found little favour with Prairie farmers despite their logical appeal to agricultural reformers. Herbicides, on the other hand, have been hugely popular for over half a century. An historical perspective is needed to understand why this is so and to underscore the difficulties facing proponents of nonchemical means of weed management or control.

A less pragmatic but equally compelling reason for investigating the history of weeds and weed control in the Prairie West is simply to draw attention to the fact that weeds are important. Over forty years ago, one federal weed specialist calculated that the annual cost of controlling and not controlling weeds in Canada alone ranged from a conservative low of 200 million dollars to a more realistic figure in excess of 500 million.[2] Today, this figure must be in the billions. While the economic toll is staggering, many people would argue that it only represents the most obvious and immediate cost. The weed scientist LeRoy Holm, for example, has suggested "that more energy is expended for the weeding of man's crops than for any other single human task."[3] Although Holm's contention is impossible to verify it does hint at the scale of our association with these "plants out of place" and at their potential impact on society. Our efforts to eradicate weeds have also had a dramatic effect on the environment. In combination with drought, tillage and other weed-control practices were the leading causes of the Dust Bowl in the 1930s and tillage remains a major contributor to the world-wide problem of agricultural soil erosion. An even greater cost may be borne by future generations because of our present reliance on chemical control and the agrochemical complex that herbicide use helps to support.

Despite the obvious importance of weeds and our efforts to eradicate them, these subjects have received scant attention from historians. There is a substantial body of literature on the history of crop pests and pest control in general but most has been written by agricultural scientists and most is devoted to the study of insects and diseases.[4] Not surprisingly, their emphasis mirrors the distribution of funding and support for crop-protection research in Canada. In Canada, as in most cool temperate regions, "the losses caused by weeds" are believed to be "greater than the combined losses produced by animal diseases, plant diseases and insect pests," yet weeds have traditionally received far less attention than their smaller or more mobile brethren.[5] Weed specialists have long attributed this disparity to the often subtle nature of crop losses due to weeds and to the sense of urgency and drama that attends insect attacks and outbreaks of disease. Historical research appears to have been guided by a similar taste for the dramatic.

Canadian historians also need to be alerted to the following irony in Canadian agricultural and rural history: more attention has been paid to the political and social activities of past generations of farmers than to the practical issues that dominated their daily lives. Take an issue like weeds. Most farmers almost certainly devoted much more time and energy to thinking about weeds and to attempting their eradication than they ever spent reflecting on politics, organizing cooperatives, or socializing at their local farmers' institute. The latter, however, have been the subject of numerous monographs while historiography on the former consists of a handful of comments and the odd footnote. While it is true that rural social activities have played an important role in shaping modern society, historians need to be reminded that the cumulative effect of mundane, practical activities such as weed control are hardly less significant. They are also well documented in the historical record. Utilitarian issues dominate the pages of historical agricultural literature and it is time that historians acknowledged this fact by devoting more attention to the subjects that were of greatest interest to the intended readers.

A history of weeds and weed control on the Canadian Prairies lends itself to a comparative approach. Most of our worst farm weeds are from elsewhere — predominantly from western Europe and Eurasia — and prairie farmers share a common culture with farmers in the northern Great Plains states. Traditional ideas about weeds and weed control have also been imported, first from Great Britain (most British weeds are common throughout Europe) and then from Ontario. A comparative approach, in turn, suggests the need for some judicious borrowing from the field of environmental history. If nothing else, environmental history encourages cross-border investigations by reminding people that biological organisms and ecosystems rarely respect artificial political boundaries. Environmental historians are also committed to the notion that natural phenomena, not just people, can be viewed as independent causal agents in history; as actors rather than merely as something acted upon.[6] Although none of these observations would come as news to weed scientists or even to turn-of-the-century Prairie farmers, they do point to a need to consider the role played by the environment in the development of our relationship with weeds. This is particularly true in North America and other parts of the world where the majority of troublesome species are imported, and hence, free from many of the plant predators and pathogens that serve to restrict weed populations in their countries of origin.

In an effort to avoid lapsing into crude environmental determinism, this study will emphasize both human and nonhuman sources of causation and how the two interact. Topics such as weed biology and ecology will be given roughly equal weight to an analysis of the elements of human society that regularly interact with weeds, and discussions of conflict will pay heed to the triumphs and setbacks experienced by both sides. A sense of parity disappears when the discussion moves on to consider the realm of cognition or conscious thought. It is important to note, however, that weeds are capable of displaying patterns of "learned" behaviour. A familiar example is the ability of dandelions (*Taraxacum officinale* Weber) to shorten their flower stalks in response to repeated mowing. An even more striking example is the recent development of herbicide resistance among a number of weedy species on the Prairies. Dividing the analysis into three main topic areas — biology/society, physical interactions, and cognition — is purely arbitrary as all three are interrelated. They are, in fact, simply different aspects of a larger whole that, for the lack of a better term, can be called "culture."

Culture is an elusive concept that has attracted a great deal of academic attention in recent years. Unfortunately, a great deal of the resulting cultural analysis is laden with esoteric jargon and driven by theories that owe little to sound historical research or to the thoughts, words, and deeds of past generations of people. This study, therefore, makes no attempt to engage in current debates within the field of cultural theory out of the belief that to do so would be both premature and contrary to the goal of making the history of weeds and weed control on the Prairies accessible to an interdisciplinary audience. Readers interested in exploring the deeper social forces and cultural drives that have influenced our relationship with weeds are encouraged to consult Frieda Knobloch's *The Culture of Wilderness: Agriculture as Colonization in the*

American West (1996). Although Knobloch's study provides many insights into the commercial nature of North American agriculture and the way it has shaped our attitude towards unwanted or uneconomic plants since colonial times, readers should be aware that in her effort to critique "western agricultural practices and sciences ... from the domain of the humanities," she presupposes that social forces are mainly if not solely responsible for the way we farm, the development of weed problems, and the emergence of a blindly hostile attitude towards weeds.[7] Her anthropocentric approach, in other words, leads to a foreordained conclusion.

While this book is not intended to advance the field of cultural analysis it does shed light on some of the fundamental linkages between human culture and the "natural" environment. Weeds are, after all, curiously akin to nature. We have striven to control them for centuries yet many of our efforts have been in vain. They still abound in waste areas, towns and cities, along roadsides and in ditches and rarely is a field, pasture, garden, or lawn completely free of their presence. Much of their success can be attributed to their "natural" endowments: their competitiveness, powers of reproduction, and adaptability. Weeds, in short, provide a striking example of what seems to be "nature's" ability to thrive in the face of human opposition.

Weeds are, at the same time, intimately connected with culture. Even though we did not truly create them and they have defied our efforts at classification and control for centuries, they remain dependent on human activities for their habitat and, in a very real sense, for their physical and symbolic existence. Designating certain plants as weeds represents a cultural activity. Similarly, the cultural activities of generations of farmers have inadvertently "bred" weeds through a process that is directly analogous to the breeding of domestic crops and livestock. Weeds are, in other words, both products of and participants in culture. Once this thesis is established the inherent danger of regarding weeds as the "enemy," as something separate from culture, becomes clear. Additionally, if weeds can be said to symbolize "nature" writ large, a logical conclusion is that nature and culture are not separate entities. They are, rather, simply different aspects of a larger phenomenon.

One important phenomenon that receives relatively cursory treatment is the evolution of agrarian capitalism and its influence on the interactions between agriculturists and weeds. There are several reasons why this subject has been deliberately downplayed. The first is to establish the argument that weeds, like other biological organisms, can be regarded as agents of historical change. Weeds are important and their story deserves to be told and to simply assume *a priori* that the development of commercial farming is the main story would automatically impose a narrow, anthropocentric plot on the narrative. Weeds would once again be relegated to the background and some basic insights would be obscured. Consider an issue such as the emergence of a blindly oppositional attitude towards weeds, first in Ontario and then on the Prairies. Was this merely a consequence of growing market orientation and the industrial mindset of Canadian farmers or, as the evidence suggests, is there not a direct correlation between the development of increasingly strident rhetoric and the success of imported weed species? The latter argument may not be sophisticated but it will strike a chord with any home gardener who has witnessed a new weed suddenly appear and quickly take over their lawn, borders, or vegetable patch. Somewhere along the line most people will develop a strong sense of animosity towards these plants even though they are not actively engaged in raising produce for the market economy.

Another way of presenting the same argument is to suggest that capitalism can be treated as a "constant" in order to explore other, more fundamental aspects of the relationship between weeds and the farming community. Is this really all that different from the conventional approach to western Canadian agricultural history where the environment receives but sketchy treatment and the agency of organisms such as weeds are all but ignored? Historians such as Donald Worster have already demonstrated that agriculture on the American portion of the Great Plains was market-oriented from the start and others have suggested that the same is true of farming in Ontario and the Prairie West.[8] As will become apparent in chapter two, British agricultural reformers were staunch advocates of a capitalist mode of production long before settlers began their assault on the virgin forests of Ontario and their influential doctrine of good husbandry was, to a large extent, simply a recipe for maximizing profit.

Additionally, is it not true that key capitalist institutions such as the Winnipeg Grain and Produce Exchange were in place within a decade or so of the start of fully commercial agriculture in Manitoba? They certainly predated the large-scale agricultural settlement of Alberta and Saskatchewan as did a grain grading and handling system that served to draw attention to the undesirability of weeds. Additional features of agrarian capitalism in western Canada that remained a fixture between the 1880s and 1950 include large, owner-operated farms, a shortage of labour, and a severely limited range of market opportunities. Capitalism and the profit motive, therefore, encouraged a negative attitude towards weeds and predisposed farmers to accept the use of herbicides, but a growing sense of desperation and antipathy within the agricultural community and the speed with which herbicides were adopted seems to be more of a testament to weedy success than to an already mature capitalist ethos.

Readers with an interest in pursuing the influence of price fluctuations, marketing boards, or other factors at work in a capitalist economy are encouraged to use this book as a springboard for their own inquiries. They should remember, however, that an essential first step is establish the nature of the relationship between people and weeds in subsistence or non–capitalist societies. This promises to be a difficult and time-consuming task and it may well reveal that farmers in places such as seventeenth-century China or precontact Central America were assiduous weeders who harboured antagonistic feelings towards their unwanted vegetative guests. Whether or not their experiences would have encouraged them to abandon traditional weed-control techniques in favour of chemical weed killers will, of course, remain a subject for conjecture as effective herbicides only became available long after most traditional societies were absorbed by the capitalist economy.

Before proceeding to the study proper, several additional issues need to be clarified. First, the only weeds under consideration are those found on arable land. Farm weeds have received far more attention than weeds in other places and literature on the subject is so extensive that it effectively precludes a consideration of the weedy flora of pastures, rangeland, gardens, and urban areas. Secondly, this study is based upon expert or "elite" sources. It is, as such, a study of only one aspect of our relationship with weeds. This approach can be justified by trotting out the hackneyed excuses that it was the elite who left written evidence or that the wealth of conventional sources dealing with weeds have rarely been consulted. A more convincing justification is to observe that noxious-weed laws were the statutory children of "progressive" agriculturists and agricultural scientists. Whatever the attitudes of the "average farmer," therefore, expert opinion ultimately carried the force of law. Experts also led the way in the use of chemical weed killers but, as their rapid and enthusiastic acceptance by farmers suggests, they were primarily acting in response to the needs and demands of the larger farming public. Technology, in other words, may have served to crystalize attitudes and practices but it was not the engine of change.

A simple lack of space and time discourages an investigation into the role played by agribusiness whereas government experts are assigned a place of prominence. Perhaps this omission can be excused by observing that the creation of a large agricultural bureaucracy is poorly documented, that expert attitudes towards weeds were extremely favourable to the sale of both agricultural implements and herbicides and, that since at least the turn of the century, ties between government experts and the business community have been extremely close. Additionally, in Canada, if not in the United States, chemical companies only began to market and advertise herbicides aggressively in 1945. Prior to this time, Canadian farmers relied almost exclusively on federal and provincial bureaucrats for information on advances in chemical weed control. Beginning in the early 1900s, various government agricultural extension agencies also took the lead in herbicide testing and demonstration as well as in supplying farmers with both chemicals and sprayers.

Finally, readers need to be alerted to the fact that influences from south of the border probably deserve more attention that they actually receive. Having said this, it is important to note that the United States was not the main source of Prairie settlers nor, because of the east-west orientation of our rail system, was it the direct source of most of our imported weeds. Canadians certainly did not take a back seat to Americans when it came to drafting noxious-weed legislation, to developing a massive weed problem, or to using government agencies to promote the sale of herbicides.

Throughout this study I follow the well-established practice of referring to Upper Canada and Canada West simply as Ontario. I have also taken the liberty of substituting the letter "s" for the archaic "f" and generally updating the language in many of the quotations presented in the first few chapters.

I

Weeds and Culture

The seemingly simple question "what is a weed?" has perplexed agriculturists for centuries but they continue to ask it out of a pressing need to distinguish between weeds and more useful or less harmful plants. A history of weeds and our relationship with them must also begin with this question. One reason for addressing this issue is that it serves to identify some of the main features of the disparate group of plants that we call weeds, features that make the term so hard to define. Another is to introduce the study's main cast of characters — both human and vegetative. Having deliberately confused the issue, the chapter then moves on to a brief history of attempts to define the term. Many of these attempts have fallen afoul of the objective and subjective nature of weeds. There is a distinct tension, in other words, between what weeds are and how agriculturists perceive them. The third and final section attempts to reduce this tension by providing a working definition that takes the split personality of weeds into account. This definition leads directly to the study's main thesis.

Quack grass, *Agropyron repens*

What is a Weed?

Even though the English word "weed" has been in everyday use for centuries and represents a concept familiar to most people of European descent, the term is difficult to define with any degree of precision.[1] W. Holzner, a highly respected authority on weeds, believes that this difficulty arises because "the term 'weed' comprises a strongly subjective view of a plant or vegetation, which makes it difficult to find an objective and generally valid definition."[2] Botanists and plant taxonomists have provided little assistance in this search for meaning because they have long been conscious of the subjective and hence, anthropocentric nature of the term and the plants that it describes. Weeds are, therefore, an anathema to these scientists because they are difficult if not impossible to fit into a logical biological classification scheme. Most botanists avoid using the term "weed" and, according to one plant taxonomist, they have traditionally preferred "not even to think about them."[3]

When one does think about weeds, it becomes clear that designating a plant as such is highly subjective since it depends on the person, place, and time. Labelling a plant as a weed typically results from a conjunction of all three. In other instances, a change in one factor is all that is required for a plant to be perceived in a new light. Richard Bradley, an eighteenth-century professor of botany at Cambridge and an active writer on agricultural matters, provides a good example of the influence of the observer. In one of his farmers' calendars, he warns to "take care to weed out the Plant call'd Alliaria or Sauce alone, or by some, Jack in the Hedge" because of its ability to impart a strong onion flavour to the milk of cows that graze upon it. While Bradley, and presumably the farmers that he was addressing, clearly regarded this plant as a weed, he casually observes that it was regarded quite differently by a different class of people: "The Country People in many places eat the Leaves of this with Bread and Butter, making it serve instead of Onions."[4] William Ellis, a contemporary of Bradley, similarly describes "Mustard Seed" as a problem "Weed" on wet ground, only to subsequently remark that it "is annually gathered as a most valuable Thing by the poor People."[5]

More recent examples of how specific plants mean very different things to different people can be provided readily by anyone with experience in the weed-control industry. Irate bee keepers forced the author to recognize this point on a number of occasions while he was engaged in spraying Canada thistle (*Cirsium arvense* (L.) Scop.). Canada thistle is highly regarded by bee keepers for the delicately flavoured honey that it produces yet agriculturists revile it as a very serious weed. On another occasion, while spraying a patch of common toadflax (*Linaria vulgaris* Mill.), a problem on rangeland despite its attractive yellow snapdragon-like flowers, the author observed an elderly gentleman approaching. This man demonstrated the aptness of the old adage, "one person's weed is another person's flower," when he asked: "Why are you spraying the 'butter-and-eggs' that my wife and I planted around our house nearly sixty years ago?"

Place or location is the second factor that encourages people to label plants as weeds. Few people, for example, view wheat or other cereals as anything but valued crops. Yet, when one species of grain is found growing in a field devoted to another, it can present a serious problem. The problem can be so serious, in fact, that weed scientists regard "volunteer cereals" as one of the worst weed problems in grain-producing regions today. Another source of concern for weed scientists is the large weed populations of urbanized areas and disturbed sites. Weeds have been allowed to thrive unmolested in these areas partly because they have ceased to be weeds for many people, including many farmers, by virtue of where they are growing.

Time is the third major factor involved in identifying a plant as a weed. Our views on what constitutes a crop, for instance, have changed considerably over the centuries and many species that were once chiefly regarded as crops have subsequently become widely disparaged as weeds. Purslane (*Portulaca oleracea* L.) and the common dandelion (*Taraxacum officinale* Weber) illustrate this point nicely. Anyone who has gardened in North America is probably quite familiar with the common fleshy-leafed annual weed purslane, or pursley as it is sometimes called, which almost magically appears amongst the vegetables with the heat of July. Dandelion is so ubiquitous as to require no introduction. Today they are generally regarded as nuisances yet in the eighteenth century they were highly esteemed as tasty additions to salads. Ironically, even though we curse them for their prolific nature, they were considered difficult to grow and eighteenth-century gardeners had to expend considerable care and attention to cultivate them successfully.[6] Both species arrived in North America in the early seventeenth century, probably as members of the garden seed collections cherished by settlers, and they were still being sold through seed catalogues in the United States into the late nineteenth century.[7]

While crops can become weeds, the opposite can also occur. Sometimes this transformation takes place gradually. Other times, particularly during periods of crisis, a shift in perception can occur with startling rapidity. Near the end of the First World War, for example, the British Board of Agriculture published an article on the uses of common farm weeds in an effort "to make up deficiencies in supply" of medicines, dyes, animal fodder, and human food.[8] A far more dramatic example is presented by Russian thistle (*Salsola pestifer* Nels.) on the Canadian Prairies. Widely feared as one of the region's worst weeds, this species was transformed into an indispensable fodder plant during periods of drought. Toward the end of a long dry spell in 1924, for instance, the district agriculturist for Medicine Hat remarked:

> The late rains were beneficial in that by furnishing a rank growth of weeds — particularly Russian thistle — they helped out the supply of feed. When the ordinary feed crops are plentiful Russian thistle is not highly valued, but in years of scarcity it is not to be despised as it has been the means when cut at the proper time and well cured of pulling many a herd through the winter.[9]

By now it should be clear that how a plant is perceived is largely dictated by circumstance and personal opinion. Identifying plants as weeds is not, however, simply a whimsical act on the part of an individual. When you think about it, the ability of experts to use the term and be understood, to name and list species widely regarded as weeds, and ultimately, to officially proscribe certain plants through noxious-weed laws implies that many people within a particular society share similar views on the identity of weeds. Suggesting that not all plants are equally regarded as weeds accords well with common sense. It is also supported by the observation that out of the whole world's flora, "only a very tiny fraction, probably amounting to no more than a few hundred species, is composed of weeds."[10] The number of widespread and truly problematic species is even smaller. Of the approximately 250 plant species "regarded as important weeds" worldwide, only about 75 "are thought to be responsible for ninety percent of crop losses attributable to weeds."[11] Similarly, a U.S. Department of Agriculture agronomist estimated that in the United States, of

> about 1,200 species of plants commonly called weeds ... less than thirty are sufficiently aggressive to be able to survive indefinitely on crop-rotated land. These are the superweeds, the so-called noxious species, plants having such extreme tenacity for life that no ordinary good farming measures control them.[12]

Recognizing that only certain plants tend to become weeds further complicates the problem of determining what a weed is. They are, in a sense, plants with a curious split personality or a dual nature. On one hand, they are an anthropocentric category whose identification depends on subjective judgment. On the other hand, they can be singled out as a fairly select, "objective" group of organisms on the basis of a number of peculiar characteristics and a predilection for growing on human-disturbed sites. Although it is possible to objectify weeds, it is important to stress that weeds can only be loosely described as an "objective" class of plants on the strength of their biology or ecological behaviour. Typical "weedy" characteristics are not unique to these species nor can they be used to clearly distinguish weeds from other plants. "Weediness" is, rather, "more a matter of the extreme development of some habit of growth or seeding that is shared by many plants other than weeds."[13]

Much has been written on what makes for success as a weed but, in the context of this study, a brief overview should suffice. Probably the most distinctive feature of weedy species is their ability to compete with crops for the essentials of life: light, water, and nutrients. The idea that weeds reduce crop yields through competition has been around since the eighteenth century but the study of the actual mechanics of competition is still in its infancy. The process of competition, or crop interference as some prefer to call it, is still poorly understood because of the large number of variables involved.

An ability to contend with and, in many cases, outcompete crops for light, water, and nutrients are the function of a wide range of adaptations including deep or extensive root systems and rapid seedling establishment and growth. These adaptations help weeds compete under favourable conditions and often enable them to tolerate a wider range of conditions than domesticates. A high degree of environmental tolerance also appears to be linked to an unusually high degree of interspecific variation within weedy species. Some species are genetically diverse and their populations are "morphologically, physiologically and ecologically very heterogeneous" as a result.[14] This ensures that at least some members of a weed population can survive under specific adverse conditions and that a single species can exploit a number of different habitats. Other species rely less on genetic variation than on phenotypic variability or "plasticity." Phenotypic plasticity is a phrase coined to describe the ability of genetically identical plants to differ quite markedly in terms of size, seed production, and growth habits on the basis of where they are growing.[15]

Weeds enhance their competitive abilities and chances of survival by a number of "weedy" reproductive strategies. A typical strategy, particularly for annual species, is the production of a vast number of seeds after a comparatively short growth period. Shepherd's purse (*Capsella bursa-pastoris* (L.) Medic.), a common weed of arable fields and gardens, can produce up to 38,500 seeds per plant under favourable conditions. Other frequently encountered weeds including broad-leaved plantain (*Plantago major* L.), a tenacious inhabitant of lawns throughout Canada, can produce a similar number and the equally ubiquitous species, purslane (*Portulaca oleracea* L.), has been known to produce in excess of 50,000.[16] In addition to relying on sheer numbers of seeds for survival, many weeds have the ability to produce seeds of varying size and periods of dormancy. This strategy enables them to stagger their germination throughout the growing season and even between years as weed seeds commonly have the ability to lie dormant for decades.[17]

Many perennial species rely on both sexual and asexual modes of reproduction. Anyone familiar with quack grass (*Agropyron repens* (L.) Beauv.), variously known as "couch," "quick," or "twitch" grass, with its tough, spreading rootstocks, will testify to the efficacy of asexual reproduction. Asexual reproduction, whether by creeping rootstocks, stems, or other devices, is a very effective means of short-distance dispersal for long-lived species. Weeds depend on a host of other mechanisms for long-distance dissemination. These frequently involve modifications to the seed or seed coat. Some species produce seeds with unusually thick and hard seed coats which allows them to pass undigested through the digestive tracts of animals. Others, such as the familiar species common burdock (*Arctium minus* (Hill) Bernh.), rely on burs or sticky seed coats and cooperative animals for their travelling. *Bromus tectorum* L., a winter annual native to Europe and known by the aliases downy brome, downy chess, cheat, or cheatgrass, has used both methods to rapidly establish itself on the cattle ranges of western Canada and the United States. Virtually unheard of in 1890, by 1928 it had become a ubiquitous and, in many cases, a dominant component of rangeland vegetation in British Columbia, Washington, Idaho, Oregon, Nevada, and Utah.[18]

Many plants rely on wind and water for their dissemination. Irrigation ditches have long been identified as a major travel route for weeds and most people are familiar with the winged seeds of dandelions and thistles. Some of the most rapidly spreading weeds, notably Russian thistle (*Salsola pestifer* Nels.), prefer to travel in the manner of native tumbleweeds as a complete plant with seeds attached. In the words of an early-twentieth-century weed specialist, they "do not produce any means of flight; but they have slight connection with the earth and soon after the first frost will be off with any good wind which gives them a pressing invitation."[19] The invitation must have been very pressing indeed for tumble mustard (*Sisymbrium altissimum* L.) in the fall of 1893. In that year, not long after the species was first reported in Saskatchewan, Angus MacKay, superintendent of the Indian Head Experimental Farm, wrote,

> We were almost buried yesterday with a neighbour's tumble weed [tumble mustard]. A hurricane blew all day from the North-west, and the edge of the field adjoining the farm is now 10 feet deep with this weed. The trees are full and fences cannot be seen for bank [*sic*] of weeds. The result of yesterday's blow will be to give us many extra days' work next summer, for millions of seeds have been left on the farm. Looking between here and the town while the weeds were galloping along, the prairie seemed like the ocean with a big storm blowing.[20]

Even though "natural" agents spread weeds in diverse ways, natural dissemination is not the most important mode of travel. As one late-nineteenth-century authority observed: "the plants which have become weeds of the farm have spread more through the agency of man than through all the natural agencies combined."[21] Weeds travel as contaminants of seed and animal feed, clinging to domesticated livestock and farm implements; they are carried along by buggies, railway cars, and automobiles. They are accomplished ocean travellers and are known to have frequently stowed away in the ballast of sailing ships. Port cities have, as a result, historically been important sites for the initial establishment of weedy species. During colonial times, weeds often travelled in considerable comfort, safely nestled in packing material or in the straw of mattresses.

Canada thistle (*Cirsium arvense* (L.) Scop.) reputedly used the latter conveyance for its introduction into Upper Canada during the eighteenth century.[22] This species exemplifies the qualities necessary for success as a weed. Like most of the world's worst weeds, this long-lived shiny-leafed member of the composite family is blessed with a multitude of attributes conferring weediness. It spreads both by winged seed and vegetatively through a deep, extensive root system and it is able to regenerate from fragments of root as small as ten centimetres or less. Canada thistle is consequently very difficult to eradicate by mechanical methods and it has been the bane of many a farmer for centuries. Able to tolerate a wide range of conditions, it has spread to all the farming districts of Canada since its introduction into New France from Europe during the early seventeenth century.[23] *Cirsium arvense* has considerable competitive powers that may be enhanced by the release of phytotoxic chemicals from its roots. Finally, researchers have recently attributed much of its adaptability to a marked ability "to alter its morphology in response to environmental conditions."[24]

A Short History of Definitions

While botanists typically solve the dilemma of determining what a weed is by simply ignoring the issue, the importance of weeds to agriculture means that farming experts and agricultural scientists have not had this luxury. Agriculturists have written extensively on the subject of weeds since English-language farming manuals were first published in the six-teenth century. And, from near the outset, they seem to have been aware of the dual nature of weeds and the subsequent difficulty of definition. The earliest writers made little effort to define a term that was, after all, a subject of common knowledge. By the mid-eighteenth century, how-ever, a widespread belief that agriculture was a "science" rather than just an "art" meant that explicit attempts at definition could no longer be avoided.

Jethro Tull, a leading figure in the British "agricultural revolution," was one of the first agricultural improvers to commit his definition to writ-ing. In his influential farming manual, *The Horse-Hoing Husbandry; or, an Essay on the Principles of Tillage and Vegetation* (1733), Tull proposed that "Weeds" are "Plants, that come up in any Land, of a different Kind from the sown or planted Crop." Tull was not noted for either an even temper or a favourable attitude towards labourers and the lower classes, and he appears to have vented some of his irascibility on weeds. For, upon defin-ing the term, he proceeded to rail against them as "hurtful," as "uninvited guests," and as "unprofitable" plants that are guilty of "robbing Legitimate (or Sown) Plants of their Nourishment."[25]

Tull's treatment of weeds is notable for the intense antipathy that it conveys but it differs little in kind from the attitudes expressed by his contemporaries and immediate successors. Most were content with casting aspersions on weeds as useless and unwanted. The few who actu-ally followed Tull's lead and defined the term "weed" simply did so as others described them. Two Scottish reformers, Francis Home and Adam Dickson, argued, for example, that "all such vegetables, as, being of no use to the farmer, are called weeds," and that as plants, weeds "are not only useless; they are also noxious."[26] These early definitions almost solely emphasize the subjective nature of weeds. But, by identifying and naming weedy species and compiling them into lists, commentators implicitly supplied their objective side as well.

Efforts to define "weed" became a standard feature of agricultural literature during the nineteenth century. Linked to this growing need for precise terminology was a concurrent movement to firmly establish agriculture as a "science." Agriculture did eventually become a science in more than just name and, by 1900, it was widely institutionalized in

9

universities, colleges, and government agricultural experiment stations in Europe and North America. Despite these developments, however, many nineteenth-century experts remained content with repeating the weed lore of the previous century.

Eighteenth-century–style definitions emphasizing the inherent differences between weeds and crops can be found in the works of such noted British authorities as John Morton and James Buckman, and in the writings of Canada's first Dominion botanist, James Fletcher.[27] While Fletcher, Buckman, Morton, and others remained content with paraphrasing eighteenth-century expressions, many of their contemporaries were beginning to define a plant as a weed on the basis of where it was growing rather than on the basis of its negative qualities. An increasing emphasis on place may reflect recognition of the ability of crops to act like weeds under many circumstances as can be seen in definitions provided by two of the most popular nineteenth-century British farming manuals: Henry Stephen's *The Book of the Farm* (1844) and J. C. Loudon's *An Encyclopedia of Agriculture* (1825). Both went through multiple editions and the fourth edition of Stephen's book was published as late as 1891. Loudon defined "weed" as "every plant which appears where it is not wanted," and Stephens suggested "that wherever a plant is found to grow where it should not, it is a weed."[28]

Loudon and Stephens were not alone in stressing the role of location in determining how a plant is perceived but during the late nineteenth and early twentieth centuries most British definitions continued to emphasize the useless or undesirable qualities of weeds.[29] In North America, however, location soon became the main feature by which weeds were distinguished from other plants. One definition in particular became so popular that it effectively became the standard definition by the close of the nineteenth century: weeds are plants out of place. The immense appeal of this expression likely stems from the fact that the majority of the most troublesome weeds in North America originate on other continents, most notably Europe. Most weeds in North America, in other words, can be considered out of place regardless of where they are found.

The phrase is usually attributed to William J. Beal, a prominent late-nineteenth-century botanist and weed specialist at the Michigan State Agricultural College.[30] But, while he certainly used and popularized the definition, its origins — like many of the plants it purports to describe — can be traced back to an earlier era in Britain. The expression was certainly not new to the English farmer and newspaper editor, Benjamin Holdich, who wrote in 1825: "The term weed is not definite ... but the best definition seems to be that given by an old botanist, namely, that 'a weed is a plant out of its proper place.'"[31] A little over twenty years later, an American botanist, William Darlington, described the phrase "a plant out of place" as "the best definition that has yet been given" even if it "is the old one."[32] Darlington's book, *American Weeds and Useful Plants*, was first published in 1847 and it probably represents the first full-length North American publication entirely devoted to the subject of weeds.

Federal, provincial, and state departments of agriculture were particularly fond of defining weeds as plants out of place. Farmers were consequently introduced to the concept through widely circulated government weed bulletins.[33] By the turn of the century, rural school children were also being introduced to this concept along with some of the more traditional connotations attached to the term. In Charles James's widely distributed agricultural textbook, for example, the Deputy Minister of Agriculture for Ontario taught his young readers that

a weed is a plant just as much as wheat, corn, or clover. It has all the parts of plant, grows like other plants, and forms new plants. But it is a plant we do not want; it is a plant out of its place, or, rather, it is a plant in the wrong place.[34]

"A plant out of place" or its near equivalent remained the standard definition for "weed" in North American literature well into the 1950s and it can still be seen gracing the pages of some modern weed science textbooks.[35] In 1956, the phrase "a plant growing where it was not wanted" was adopted as the official definition during the inaugural meeting of the Weed Society of America — the first professional association of American and Canadian weed scientists.[36]

Although the expression has proven to be both popular and durable, it has provided a considerable source of unease for some North American weed experts since the 1890s. This sense of unease can be seen in the very publications that popularized the phrase, Canadian and American government weed bulletins. While most preface their remarks with a definition that emphasizes place, they promptly move on to a much lengthier discussion of the undesirable qualities of weeds and, in particular, of the innate characteristics of certain plants that predispose them towards a weedy lifestyle. In 1897, one weed expert challenged the standard definition directly. Speaking before the University of Vermont Botanical Club, F. A. Waugh, an agricultural scientist and botanist at the University of Vermont, complained,

> The common statement that 'a weed is a plant out of place' is by no means satisfactory or final to the student. He is still left to ask how it is that certain species have such pronounced ability for getting out of place. Almost any plant may accidentally get where it is not wanted, but comparatively few usually and persistently get in the way.[37]

Waugh never ventured to offer his own definition but a number of the leading American authorities on weeds were more forthcoming during the 1920s and early 1930s. Their definitions appeared during a time of increasing interest in weed control amongst agricultural scientists — an interest that was sparked by some promising developments in chemical weed killers. These scientists were, like Waugh, dissatisfied with defining weeds on the basis of where they were growing because of the arbitrariness of the phrase and its tendency to obscure the marked propensity of certain plants to get out of place. The definitions that they devised, however, continued to emphasize the subjective nature of weeds at the expense of their objective dimension. A typical definition from this era is that of United States Department of Agriculture (USDA) agronomist A. J. Pieters. Rejecting "the definition which has been pretty generally accepted," he proposed that "a weed is a plant whose potentialities for harm are greater than its potentialities for good."[38]

Pieters and his colleagues were motivated to redefine the term both because of the inadequacies of past definitions and out of a conviction that agronomists and other agricultural scientists needed to "be able to define their concepts as comprehensively and accurately as possible."[39] A need for precision became even more acute in the 1950s and 1960s. Weed science emerged as a distinct field within the agricultural sciences during this period largely as a result of the success of 2,4-D and the development of other selective herbicides following the close of World War II. The enhanced status accorded to the study of weeds and weed control brought with it a pressing need for precise definitions and statements of principle, both to justify and direct the infant discipline.

Attempts to define the term "weed" proliferated during these decades and the activity remains a favourite pastime of weed scientists today.[40] Since the early 1960s, there has been a distinct shift away from purely subjective definitions towards a more "objective" view of weeds. Although this trend clearly represents a response to the irony of basing an "objective" science on the study of a "subjective" class of plants, it is not without some historical precedent. In 1877, for example, E. W. Claypole, a professor at Ohio's Antioch College, told his listeners at a meeting of the Montreal Horticultural Society that by "the term 'weed' we mean those plants to which the surroundings are so suitable that they increase and multiply, year after year, more rapidly than others by which they are surrounded."[41] Two years later, Asa Gray, one of the leading American botanist of the nineteenth century, responded to some of the arguments presented by Claypole and, in doing so, offered his own definition for "weed": "We may for present purposes consider weeds to be plants which tend to take prevalent possession of soil used for man's purposes, irrespective of his will."[42]

Picking up where Gray and Claypole left off, some weed experts took their quest for an objective definition to such lengths in the 1960s that the vital link between weeds and people was effectively severed. A. H. Bunting's oft-repeated definition, for example, simply describes weeds as "pioneers of secondary succession."[43] More typical is Jack Harlan's and J. M. J. De Wet's argument that a weed might be "defined as a generally unwanted organism that thrives in habitats disturbed by man."[44] Preserving a sense of the anthropocentric dimension of weeds while placing considerably greater emphasis on the autonomy and agency of these plants than earlier definitions were wont to do, arguments similar to that of Harlan and De Wet have effectively displaced "plants out of place" as the standard definition in modern weed science literature.[45]

Recent definitions are primarily aimed at identifying the world's worst and most widespread weeds and they do a much better job in isolating, describing, and defining these persistently troublesome plants than did earlier, purely subjective definitions. Unlike earlier definitions, they pay tribute to the agency of weeds and, as argued in this study, they strongly suggest that weeds should be regarded as both victims and aggressors in the complex ecological drama of farming. Unfortunately, the tendency of modern, scientific definitions to objectify weeds suggests that weed scientists have been no more successful in reconciling the dual nature of these plants than were their less specialized predecessors. As weed scientists are well aware, weeds would not exist if it were not for people and their activities. More importantly, they would not exist if people ceased to consider them to be weeds. A few years ago, one weed scientist was forced to concede this point prior to presenting yet another working definition for the term weed: "the only common attributes of weeds are their occurrence in habitats disturbed by man and their undesirability."[46]

Weeds and Culture

By downplaying weeds as a subjective category of plants, weed scientists run the risk of missing a vital point about what weeds are and how they are to be controlled or tolerated. Because weeds are inextricably both products of psychology and ecology, weed problems are best addressed by considering not only the agroecosystems that produce them but also the culture that informs how we farm and think. Recognition of this point is potentially threatening and subversive for it challenges the very social structure of farming upon which the employment of weed scientists depends. They are, in effect, servants of large-scale, single-crop, commercial agriculture and if that were to disappear so too would a large proportion of their jobs.

In order to link weeds with culture and thereby reconcile the two contradictory dimensions of weeds, it is instructive to dwell on the familiar, if usually trivialized, observation that weeds are "the inevitable corollaries of crops."[47] Agriculture, in other words, necessarily implies "the creation of a class of plants which we call weeds."[48] Weeds are concomitants of agriculture because they, or something akin to them, are effectively created by the act of distinguishing between more and less desirable plants. A recent study conducted amongst traditional agriculturists in southern

Mexico suggests that subsistence farmers make this distinction although their views are not as rigid as the simple European dichotomy of weeds and crops.[49] Similarly, several historians have noted that North American Indians were often more conscientious weeders than were European settlers and that weeding represented an important part of their traditional farming systems.[50] The fact that non-European, subsistence cultures distinguish between crops and weeds lends additional support to the notion that there is a direct and, indeed, inseparable structural relationship between arable farming and the creation of weeds; a structural relationship that is common to different cultures and modes of production.

Once weeds are created on a cognitive level, subsequent human activities play a key role in transforming them into an objective reality. Over the millennia, farming has exerted strong evolutionary pressures on both crop and noncrop species which has resulted in the successful adaptation of "weedy" species to human-disturbed environments. One evolutionary strategy has been the development of the weedy characteristics discussed earlier in this chapter. The world's most widespread weeds have found this strategy so successful that they often benefit more from human activities than do the crops that these activities are supposed to favour. Other species have developed unusually intimate relationships with specific domesticates, often as a result of the evolution of weedy strains of crops or through crop-weed hybridization. Many weed species have come to mimic the morphology and life-cycles of crops so closely that they are virtually impossible to eradicate either through the use of chemicals or through more traditional methods of weed control.[51] Some people even suggest that the association between weeds and domesticates has reached the point where the two can only be distinguished by their different "degree of dependence on man for success in permanently disturbed man-made habitats."[52]

While weed scientists are familiar with the argument that weeds are concomitants of agriculture and thus inevitable, they have had little time to explore the implications of this point because of their pressing need to produce practical solutions to all-too-real problems. When the issue is pursued further, however, it becomes possible to deduce a third, broader type of definition for the term "weed." The key to deriving this new definition is to link the word weed" with the equally problematic term "culture." Charles Darwin appears to have been thinking along these lines when he argued that weeds and domesticates evolve in response to similar evolutionary pressures, the only difference being that the latter are deliberately cultured whereas the former are the result of "unintentional culture."[53]

Many decades later, the well-known botanist and plant taxonomist Edgar Anderson updated Darwin's argument by using the word "culture" to mean more than just tilling the land or breeding domesticated crops and livestock. Anderson was one of the first botanists to confront his profession's traditional neglect of the plants that mean the most to people — crops and weeds — and his ground-breaking book *Plants, Man, and Life* (1952) is now considered a classic in the fields of weed science and economic botany. He is most frequently quoted for his powerful yet succinct summary of the age-old relationship between people and their unwelcome vegetative neighbours: "the history of weeds is the history of man." Of even more importance in the context of this study, however, is his explanation for what crops and weeds "really are." They "are artifacts" which by definition are

> something produced by man, something which we would not have had if man had not come into being.... Though man did not wittingly produce all of them, some are as much dependent upon him, as much a result of his culture, as a temple or a vase or an automobile.[54]

Historians familiar with the work of Alfred Crosby will have already encountered some of the concepts expressed above and, at least implicitly, the idea that weeds can be defined as "cultural artifacts."[55] Crosby's work provides an additional insight into the nature of weeds and their relationship with culture by portraying them as unintentional allies in the European conquest of the New World. What he is essentially saying is that weeds are more than just products of culture, they are also active participants in culture.

This chapter has attempted to demonstrate that weeds can be viewed simultaneously as both a subjective and objective group of plants. Weed experts have long been cognizant of this point but they have had little success in reconciling the dual nature of weeds in their attempts to define the term. Since at least the 1890s, authorities on the subject have increasingly emphasized the term's objective side at the expense of its subjective, anthropocentric element. The end result is that weed scientists are in danger of forgetting the intimate link between weed problems and the human cultures that spawn them. A way of reconciling the split personality of weeds as well as for making them a valid subject of study by historians is to define them as cultural artifacts. It is equally important to view them as active participants in culture. Weeds have proven to be quite capable of resisting the hostile attentions of farmers through the centuries and they have probably forced as many changes in human farming systems as people have wrought in weed populations.

2

Good Husbandry and the
Relationship Between People and
Weeds in Great Britain, 1500–1900

The history of British agriculture between 1500 and 1900 has been
extensively cultivated by historians. In an effort to till
such a large and complex field, however, they have
not been able to cover all areas equally and many
specific topics have been neglected. One of these
is the relationship between weeds and farmers. To
some, this relationship may appear trivial and obscure
but it has been of vital interest to agriculturists
for centuries. Their interest is reflected in the
sheer wealth of information on the subject. Such
an embarrassment of riches can prove daunting for
someone embarking upon a general survey of the
history of weeds and their relationship with people
in the British Isles. Perhaps it is fitting, however,
that the task of chronicling what agriculturists did and thought bears some faint
resemblance to the far more arduous task of
keeping the land clean and relatively free of
weeds using traditional tools and techniques.

Filling a void in historical scholarship represents one goal of this chapter; establishing
the breadth and scope of traditional weed lore
represents another. This body of knowledge is

Wild mustard, *Sinapis arvensis*

19

surprisingly sophisticated and it bears more than just a passing resemblance to the modern concept of "weed management." A third goal is to establish the different kinds of weed control options available to farmers in a land with a rapidly maturing capitalist economy and yet one where agricultural markets were diverse, labour was plentiful, and weed populations were essentially part of the native flora. Because much of this knowledge was transported across the Atlantic along with British farmers, their European weeds, and a capitalist approach to agriculture, this chapter can be read as a preface to the development of a distinct relationship between people and weeds in North America. It also can be read in the context of literature on agricultural change in Britain between the sixteenth and late nineteenth centuries. Historians have traditionally portrayed this period as one of rapid and radical change and all or significant parts of it have been dubbed the "agricultural revolution."

The term "agricultural revolution" was widely popularized in the mid-1960s by the publication of two books — J. D. Chambers and G. E. Mingay, *The Agricultural Revolution, 1750–1880* (1966) and Eric Kerridge, *The Agricultural Revolution* (1967) — and the heated debate that ensued between the authors. Chambers and Mingay argue that a revolution in British agriculture occurred between 1750 and 1880 as a result of the "classical enclosure movement" of the late 1700s and the subsequent reorganization and enlargement of production units.[1] Kerridge, in contrast, identifies the agricultural revolution as the period between the mid-sixteenth and early eighteenth centuries and he contends that it involved the widespread adoption of a new crops and farming techniques.[2] A brief study of a single dimension of arable farming precludes making any definitive statements as to the nature of change as a whole but does provide support for the increasingly popular notion that agricultural change over these centuries was more evolutionary than revolutionary.

Before proceeding further, the risks inherent in writing a general overview of any topic need to be spelled out. This chapter, for example, tends to portray British agriculture as an uniform activity even though crops, farming techniques, and ideas about what constituted "good husbandry" varied widely between regions and over time as a result of numerous factors including climate, soil type, labour conditions, animal husbandry, market forces, farming traditions, and landholding regimes. Hopefully the unescapable danger of oversimplification can be reduced by remaining sensitive to these issues and by making qualifying statements wherever necessary.

Weeds and Reformers

Weeds and humans have coexisted in the British Isles for millennia since their arrival as "alien" invaders from continental Europe.[3] Often they arrived together with weeds travelling as seed contaminants or even as crop seeds themselves. In other instances they travelled separately. Pollen evidence indicates that a number of common weedy species such as wild carrot (*Daucus carota* L.), dandelion (*Taraxacum officinale* Weber), perennial sow-thistle (*Sonchus arvensis* L.), lamb's-quarters (*Chenopodium album* L.), and mouse-ear chickweed (*Cerastium vulgatum* L.) were present in Britain prior to human occupation, or at the very least, before the arrival of the first farmers.[4] Successive waves of agrarian settlement added to the ranks of these early weedy settlers. The Romans are thought to have introduced corn marigold (*Chrysanthemum segetum* L.) and the prickly annual sow-thistle (*Sonchus asper* (L.) Hill), and weedy invaders undoubtedly arrived along with their fellow Angles, Saxons, Jutes, Danes, and Normans.[5]

Britain's long history of human and weedy invasions had drawn to a close by 1500. Most of today's widespread and problematic weeds were well established by this date and they had effectively become part of the "native plant population."[6] The weed flora of Britain changed surprisingly little over the next four hundred years, for although new and exotic plants were regularly introduced, very few species succeeded "in establishing themselves as damaging weeds."[7] The ethnic mix of Britain's rural human population was also relatively stable during this period. Historians have written extensively about these people, their activities, and their institutions and there is, as a result, little point in dwelling on them.[8] About all that is required is a brief discussion of the changes in human society that shaped how weedy denizens of arable fields were treated and perceived.

One of the most significant developments was the appearance of a new literary genre and a new way of expressing ideas about and attitudes towards unwanted plants. British farming manuals were first published in English in the early sixteenth century and what began as a trickle of titles became a veritable flood by the late seventeenth century. The more popular works went through numerous editions and many sixteenth-, seventeenth-, and eighteenth-century titles were still being cited by British agriculturists in the opening decades of the last century.

Until the 1960s, British agricultural history relied heavily and, at times, exclusively on farming manuals as sources and agricultural improvers were typically cast in the heroic role of innovators — the great men who shaped and directed the course of agricultural improvement. Lord Ernle's *English Farming Past and Present* (1912), in particular, was an hugely influential book that fits and largely defined this model.[9] Historians have mounted a sustained challenge to Ernle's position and use of sources since the revisionist decade of the 1960s. Today, most scholars believe that while agricultural writers helped publicize and popularize farming improvements, their role as innovators was relatively minor.[10] A number of scholars have even suggested that the true source of innovation and information was none other than the average, well-informed farmer.[11]

Although the reputation of Britain's agricultural improvers has suffered considerably over the past three decades, few historians would deny that many agricultural writers were sincerely committed to farming reform and that their reputations as experts on agriculture in their own times were, and still are, justly deserved. Many were experienced farmers who devoted most of their adult lives to studying their profession, most were well travelled and educated by the standards of the day, and not a few of them were counted amongst Britain's scientific elite. While their writings reflect personal hopes, aspirations, and prejudices, they also contain a wealth of information on standard farming practices and faithfully convey common, if not innovative or revolutionary, knowledge. Farming manuals represent, in other words, a rich and varied source of information on the nature of traditional weed lore in pre-twentieth-century Britain. They are less useful for determining exactly what British farmers were doing although they do provide a sense of the kinds of weed control techniques (or lack thereof) that were commonly employed.

The writers of these manuals were not united by a common background — some were mere armchair farmers while others were experienced, practical husbandmen with keen powers of observation — but, despite their diversity, their works do express several common themes. One is a desire to reform traditional agriculture out of the conviction that a nation's wealth, power, and wellbeing rests on the health and vigour of its agrarian economy. Another is a common audience: the landed gentry and other rural elites.[12] They represented the segment of rural society that combined literacy with the financial resources to purchase books. Beginning in the sixteenth century, they created a large demand for both classical and contemporary agricultural literature. Much of this demand was created by a need for practical advice as more and more landowners began to farm and to manage their own estates actively rather than simply leasing them out as they had done typically during the previous century.[13]

An appeal to the reader's desire for profit represents a third commonality. Most agricultural manuals are prefaced with promises of increased production and profits and specific reforms or innovations are regularly justified on economic grounds.[14] Agricultural reformers, in other words, were prophets of agrarian capitalism. A strong desire to see agriculture, or as one writer described it, this "Noble, though heretofore neglected Science," elevated from the status of a mere art constitutes a fourth theme.[15] Almost all improver literature published after the mid-seventeenth century was dedicated to transforming agriculture into a science and thereby to freeing production from the twin constraints of superstition and tradition.

Agriculture did eventually achieve recognition as a bona fide science during the late 1800s but this new science had only a limited impact on British farming until the early twentieth century.[16] It also had little impact on the physical relationship between people and weeds before 1900, and some might argue, even before the 1940s. Britain's first scientific investigations into weed biology, ecology, and eradication were conducted in the late 1890s, but scientific weed research was not truly institutionalized until much later.[17] Prior to 1900, botany was the only science that had a significant, if decidedly limited, impact on the relationship between farmers and their vegetative adversaries. Botanists and plant taxonomists helped agriculturists achieve a better understanding of general plant taxonomy, biology, and physiology but they had little specifically to say about weeds because of a traditional bias against studying domesticated plants and their weedy competitors. Botany's influence was further diluted by the difficulties of translating general, scientific principles into specific, economically viable practices and conveying new ideas to a largely illiterate farming public.

Although traditional British weed lore is more akin to "common" than "scientific" knowledge, it is surprisingly deep and profound. Centuries of coexistence, observation, hard experience, and countless trial-and-error experiments taught agriculturists a great deal about the unwelcome plants that inhabited their fields, and in many cases, even allowed them to anticipate the findings of twentieth-century science. Agricultural improvers, farmers, and farm labourers were at the very least familiar with the most widespread and troublesome weeds. Sir Anthony Fitzherbert, for example, was not conveying any startling news when he describes "thistyll" as one of the "wedes" that "greue mooste" in *The Boke of Husbandry* (1523), the very first farming manual written and published in English.[18] Fitzherbert's thistle could be any number of species but it was most likely the ubiquitous British weed, *Cirsium arvense* (L.) Scop.[19] *Cirsium arvense* or the "common thistle" was all too familiar to William Marshall, the man who has been described as "the soundest writer and the one with the most comprehensive understanding of agricultural practice" to ply a pen during the eighteenth century.[20] Marshall regularly encountered this prickly member of the Composite Family during his extensive travels and often lengthy sojourns throughout England and he describes it as one of the most prevalent weeds in both pastures and arable fields in districts as diverse as Yorkshire, Gloucestershire, and the Midland Counties.[21]

Wild mustard (*Sinapsis arvensis* L.) or "charlock" is also regularly mentioned in farming manuals and it appears to have been equally ubiquitous throughout most of the British Isles. Numerous provincial names attest to the wide distribution of this species, with one early-twentieth-century authority listing no less than fifty-seven common names in Britain alone.[22] Quack grass (*Agropyron repens* (L.) Beauv.) was another claimant for the title of Britain's worst weed. It too had a host of local identities — "couch," "quick," and "twitch" to name but a few — and in some districts this tenacious, hard-to-eradicate perennial grass was so prevalent that "couching" entered the farmer's lexicon as a distinct farming operation.[23]

Few species are mentioned with such regularity, or are so roundly cursed, as thistles, charlock, and couch. They are not, however, the only weeds identified in agricultural improvement literature. Many species posed equally serious problems but were less widely distributed. The always observant William Marshall was conscious of this point and he regularly comments in his popular *Rural Economies* on the distinctive regional flavour to Britain's weed population. In one, he notes that "wild hemp" or "hemp-nettle" (*Galeopsis tetrahit* L.) was of little consequence on farms in the Vale of Gloucester, while in "Yorkshire it ranks with the more prevailing weeds. In the midland counties it is still more prevalent."[24] Marshall's interest in establishing which weeds grew where prefigures modern, scientific weed surveys and it reflects the importance of tailoring weed eradication measures to suit the species actually present.[25]

Local variations in weed populations are often far more dramatic than variations on a regional scale. Both the identity and density of weeds can differ greatly between neighbouring farms, between fields within a farm, and even between different areas within a field. One of the many causes of this high degree of variation is the type of crop grown and the farming practices that favour both the crop and its associated weeds.[26] Unravelling the genetic and cultural connections between specific weeds and crops is a twentieth-century phenomenon but a basic understanding of the relationship has been part of British weed lore since at least the time of Fitzherbert.[27]

Agricultural writers consistently identified the common weed-crop associations and some even organized their discussions of weeds on the basis of these relationships. The prolific eighteenth-century writer William Ellis provides a typical example of the emphasis placed on the link between specific weeds and domesticates when he begins his description of "Crow or wild Garlick" (*Allium vineale* L.) with the statement that "it chiefly grows among Wheat and Barley, and not so much among Oats and Pease."[28] Comments of this nature reveal both considerable powers of observation and more than just a passing familiarity with different weeds and crops. Sometimes, however, neither was required as many common names include references to the crops that certain weeds tend to associate with. Corn poppy (*Papaver rhoeas* L.), for example, is so named because of its near exclusive tendency to haunt arable fields seeded to grain. The population of this once abundant British weed has declined dramatically over the last century — a decline that can be directly correlated to reductions in the acreage devoted to wheat through much of this period and to the growing popularity of herbicides since the close of the Second World War.

Soil type is another important factor determining the density and species mix of a resident weed population. This too has been a subject of common knowledge for centuries. Gervase Markham, a popular early-seventeenth-century writer, expresses this idea in general terms when he observes that on "hard barren grounds ... weeds, especially great, strong, and offensive weeds" are rarely a problem because they "are the issues of rich and fertile soils."[29] Later writers such as John Mortimer, a Fellow of the Royal Society and author of the popular early-eighteenth-century manual *The Whole Art of Husbandry*, were often more specific. For example, Mortimer writes that "Tine, Poppies, May-weed, etc." were the "natural Produce" of chalk soils whereas on "Black Mould," one could expect to find "Thistles, Docks, and all Sorts of rank Weeds, and Grass."[30] Edward Lisle, a Hampshire landowner, diarist, and contemporary of Mortimer's, was also conscious of the intimate connection between soils and vegetation. On one occasion he noted that "cow garlick was a great whore in corn ... in the dry sandy grounds; and yet it is no whore to them who sow it in the clays; for there it will not grow." On another he observed: "there was an infinite quantity of charlock in cold red clays, both peas-land and barley-land; but in white or lighter land the charlock did not over-run it."[31]

Conflict

Much more could and has been written about Britain's rich and highly diverse weed flora but it is time to move on to a consideration of a third, and probably the most important, factor that determines the weeds of a farm: deliberate human actions. As Lisle's final observation implies, physical interactions between weeds and people have long been portrayed as a form of conflict, both on the part of weeds and their human adversaries. Conflict is inherently dynamic and it suggests at least a degree of reciprocity. This seems to describe the conscious relationship between farmers and weeds quite well. Few if any farms have ever been completely free of weeds, their seeds, or other propagules, and maintaining a "clean" field requires careful vigilance and prompt action. Unwanted plants are constantly mounting new sorties, arriving openly by seed blown from a neighbour's field or stealthily in the hay imported to feed livestock over the winter. Sometimes even the best farmers can see years of hard work undone in a single season because tillage was delayed by an unusually wet spring or through the accidental use of dirty seed. The weed flora of adjacent farms can differ markedly depending on the skill, energy, and resources available to different farmers and it can change dramatically on a single farm over the course of a few years with changes in ownership or tenancy.

The scale of the human conflict with weeds in Britain before 1900 is truly staggering. Arable land seems to have been particularly "dirty" during the medieval period and one economic historian has even suggested that weeds were a "major reason" for the chronically low yields of grain in medieval England.[32] Weeds continued to be "the great Difficulty the Farmer has to struggle with" in the eighteenth century.[33] Jethro Tull, a leading early-eighteenth-century figure in the "agricultural revolution," asked his readers to "Question, Whether the Mischief Weeds do to our Corn, is not as great as the Value of the Rent of all the Arable Lands in *England*."[34] A few years later, one of Scotland's earliest agricultural improvers proposed, "I am quite satisfied that Weeds themselves take more Strength from British Ground, besides the other Mischiefs they do, than all the Dung in Britain gives it."[35] Towards the end of the eighteenth century, William Marshall estimated "that one fourth of the produce of the arable lands of the kingdom is *lost* through a WANT OF TILLAGE."[36] The subsequent growth of weeds and unwanted plants continued to plague British farmers throughout the nineteenth century "wherever a crop will grow."[37]

The ongoing success of weeds between 1500 and 1900 was achieved in the face of regular, and at times rigorous, human opposition. One prominent weed scientist has described this opposition as largely "incidental to crop production," but his contention is not borne out by a careful reading of period sources.[38] Traditional British efforts to combat the growth and spread of weeds were often central rather than merely incidental to crop production and the need to suppress the growth of unwanted vegetation dictated many farming practices. William Marshall's *Rural Economy of the West of England* (1796) provides a graphic example in support of this argument. While in Devonshire, Marshall noted that farmers seeded their wheat one to two months later than elsewhere in England or: "from October to near Christmas." Upon inquiring into the origins of this practice he was told that it was because "early sown crops are liable to weeds."[39]

Late sowing is an example of an indirect, or in the language of modern weed science, a cultural method of weed "control." As such, it represents an example of the most important type of defence traditionally employed by British farmers in their conflict with weeds — discouraging the growth of unwanted vegetation by altering the culture of domesticated crops. British farmers rarely, however, relied on cultural techniques alone and they were usually employed in conjunction with more direct attempts to extirpate troublesome plants. These included hand weeding, digging and cutting, the use of animal-drawn cultivation implements, and, not infrequently, the employment of various biological agents such as domestic sheep and pigs. The more direct methods will be considered first because, in addition to supplementing cultural practices, they often acted as an indispensable component of these practices.

Manual weeding represents the simplest and most direct method of meeting the challenge of weeds on arable land. Virtually all farming manuals refer to this technique and its desirability but there is considerable evidence suggesting that most farmers found weeding, particularly of field crops, more trouble than it was worth. Medieval sources mention regular weeding of cereals and the activity figures prominently in Fitzherbert's *Book of Husbandry* (1523) and Thomas Tusser's *Five Hundred Points of Good Husbandry* (1574).[40] The "old Remedy" for weeds is also discussed at length in eighteenth-century farming manuals.[41] The technology of weeding appears to have changed little over the intervening years and farmers were still being taught that "in the common Husbandry of sowing Grain broad Cast ... the Weed Hook and Hand are the most common Instruments for weeding Corn."[42] William Marshall recorded that in late-eighteenth-century Norfolk, "HAND-WEEDING is ... carefully attended to by farmers in general."[43] Similarly, in Gloucestershire,

THE HOEING OF CROPS IN GENERAL … [is] nearly in full practice. Not only the leguminous crops, which are planted in rows; but WHEAT, which is sown at random, are hoed: not by a few individuals, only; but by husbandmen in general: the wheat crop being hoed, here, as customarily as the turnip crop is in Norfolk.[44]

Hoes, weed hooks, and "thistle drawers" were still being used during the nineteenth century and manual weeding continued to play a part in the human conflict with weeds.[45] Just how important its role was, however, is a subject for debate. Peter Bowden, a contributor to Cambridge University's massive Agrarian History of England and Wales Project, contends that farmers "attached little importance to the practice" during the century and a half following 1500 and he makes a similar claim for the period between 1640 and 1750:

Also of comparatively small consequence as a cost in the cultivation of field crops (as opposed to garden crops) were expenditures on weeding, an activity infrequently undertaken, and then usually by women at about half the normal daily wage rate for men. Juveniles were also employed on this and other suitable tasks.[46]

Bowden's contention seems to apply equally well to the late eighteenth and nineteenth centuries. William Marshall, for one, followed his praise of the farmers of Gloucestershire for their "due ATTENTION TO CROPS WHILE VEGETATING" with the observation that it was, unfortunately, "a species of attention, which, in the management of the kingdom at large, is entirely omitted; excepting, perhaps, what is bestowed on an imperfect hand weeding: In general terms, it may be said, that, in most other districts, crops remain 99/100 in a state of neglect, from seed time to harvest."[47] Marshall's contention was supported by his rival, Arthur Young, who wrote that "nine-tenths of the farmers" in the north of England "treat the idea of hoeing with contempt."[48] Sir John Sinclair, the president of the Board of Agriculture, reached a similar conclusion in 1817: "From a perusal of the County Reports, it appears, that both in England and Scotland, weeding is too often neglected."[49]

Most farmers were probably less than punctilious in their attention

to weeding because of the activity's time-consuming and labour intensive nature. Manual weeding also caused considerable damage in broad-
cast sown crops through trampling and the careless use of weeding tools.
A far more popular and nearly universal method of freeing fields from
unwanted vegetation was to destroy weeds prior to sowing by using a variety of animal-drawn tillage implements. The most important of these was
the plow. Plowing is central to most traditional arable farming systems
and it serves a number of vital functions. These include incorporating
manures and crop stubble, converting pasture into arable, preparing the
soil for seeding, drainage, and last but not least,

> it kills the Weeds by turning up of the Roots to the Sun and Air, and
> Kills not only the Weeds that grow with the last Corn; but wild Oats,
> Darnel, and other Weeds, that sow themselves, and that as soon as
> they begin to peep out of the Ground, so that they have no time to
> suck out any of the Heart of the Land.[50]

Improving the structure or "tilth" of the soil represents the most
important function of plowing but, as numerous writers have argued
since the sixteenth century, it is a mistake to consider eradicating weeds
as merely a secondary benefit of this activity.[51] Some improvers such as
William Marshall even suggested that a need to extirpate weeds should
dictate plow design and how the implement was used. In his *Rural
Economy of the West of England* (1796), for instance, Marshall argues that
the "foul state of the Soil" in much of Devonshire is less a result of "the
small number of PLOWINGS it receives, than to the defect ... in the construction of the PLOW, and the injudicious manner of using it."[52]

Prior to the mid-nineteenth century, British farmers normally plowed
their arable fields once between crops. The timing of plowing varied
widely depending on the nature of the soil, weather, crops, and weeds
present. Plowed fields were usually harrowed shortly before planting or
seeding in order to break down large clods, level the seed-bed, and rid the
soil of both annual and perennial weeds. The various tillage operations
occurring between crops are collectively referred to as "fallowing," regardless of "whether these plowings, &c. be given in two or twelve months."[53]
As William Marshall explained, both the length of the fallow and the
number of tillage operations depended

on the number and the nature of the weeds to be destroyed. If the spring season be found insufficient to effectuate the purgation, — take the summer, and even the autumn, the winter, and the ensuing spring, rather than *crop* an *under-worked fallow*, which is but little superior to a single plowing…. To begin a fallow without continuing it until its *intention be fully accomplished*, is throwing away labour unprofitably.[54]

Fallowing throughout the summer is referred to as a "bare summer fallow" and even though this practice entails the loss of an entire season's crop, it was the single most important direct method used by British farmers in their efforts to rid the soil of weeds. Summer fallowing is doubly important in the context of this study because it was destined to become the preeminent method of weed control in both Ontario and the Prairie West. English farmers were practising summer fallowing during the medieval era and by the sixteenth century it was considered "essential to keep down weeds."[55] Sixteenth- and seventeenth-century farmers usually fallowed a field every second or third year, during which time the field was plowed between two and four times.[56] By the eighteenth century, many agricultural improvers considered this amount of tillage to be inadequate for destroying a number of perennial weeds. Some even advocated extending the fallow for a second year to extirpate wild oats and other annual species whose seeds had an annoying tendency to lie dormant throughout the first year of fallow.[57] By the mid-nineteenth century, the farmers of Essex appear to have taken this advice to heart. James Caird reports that summer fallowing was common in the county and that fallows were "ploughed and harrowed as often during the summer as the farmer thinks it necessary, never less than five or six, and occasionally as often as eight times."[58]

Farming experts continued to advocate summer fallowing throughout the nineteenth century but by then, reliance on cleaning fallows appears to have declined.[59] In the *Code of Agriculture* (1817), Sir John Sinclair attributed the reduced incidence of summer fallowing on light soils to the adoption of new crop rotations and, in particular, to the increasing popularity of turnips as a regular course in rotations.[60] Turnips and other root crops were known as "cleaning" crops because they were rigorously hoed during the growing season. James Caird made a similar comment thirty-five years later, by which time another innovation — row cropping — was further lessening the need for effective but costly fallows.[61] Another factor that probably contributed to the declining popularity of summer fallowing was a profound shift away from traditional long-term leases over the course of the nineteenth century. Britain was a land of tenant farmers and, for a variety of reasons, by the third quarter of the nineteenth century annual leases had become the norm in England if not elsewhere in the British Isles.[62] According to a recent article by Colin Duncan, annual leases discouraged farmers from practising long rotations and there is every reason to suppose that they would have equally discouraged farmers from foregoing a crop for the sake of fallowing.[63]

Seed drilling and horse hoeing, the basic activities upon which nineteenth-century row cropping was based, have traditionally been credited to the Berkshire farmer, innovator, and agricultural improver, Jethro Tull.[64] Lord Ernle describes Tull as the "'greatest individual improver' that British agriculture has ever known" and argues that Tull's book, *The Horse-Hoing Husbandry* (1733), provided the principles "on which was based an agricultural revolution in tillage."[65] Tull's "revolutionary" system involved mechanically seeding or "drilling" field crops in rows and subsequently "breaking or dividing the Soil by Tillage, whilst the Corn or other Plants are growing thereon."[66] The soil between rows was stirred by a "horse-hoe" (essentially a modified light plow) while the more traditional hand hoe was used to cultivate within rows.

Tull argued that the main benefits of drilling and regular tillage were twofold. First, seeding in rows enabled farmers to cultivate their growing crops intensely and, in consequence, greatly increase uptake of finely pulverized soil particles. Tull believed that these particles provided the main source of "Nourishment" for plants and he was confident that his system would largely eliminate the need for crop rotations and regular additions of manure. He also suggested that it would permit farmers to sow the same crop for many years in succession without any significant decreases in yield.[67] Tull was not concerned with the increase in weeds that inevitably accompanies continuous cropping because of the second major advantage to horse-hoeing husbandry: it allowed farmers to kill weeds quickly and relatively easily during the growing season without causing extensive crop damage. Britain's greatest individual improver was so confident in his system's ability to keep weeds in check that he rashly predicted that the "New Hoing-Husbandry in time will probably make such an utter Riddance of all sorts of Weeds, except such as come in the Air, that as long as this management is properly continued, there is no Danger to be apprehended from them."[68]

Tull's soil particle theory of plant nutrition was subsequently proven wrong but his reputation as the father of clean husbandry is justly deserved.[69] Seed drilling and interrow hoeing, however, only came into widespread use during the mid-nineteenth century despite having received considerable attention and publicity. It seems that prior to this time, horse-hoeing husbandry was considered

> suitable only for well-drained and easily cultivated soils, and even there the vast majority of farmers preferred to sow their seed broad-cast and put up with the weeds rather than face the practical difficulties and labour costs of drilling and hoeing.[70]

Other reasons for the slow adoption of Tull's "new husbandry" include the traditional resistance of farmers to new and potentially risky innovations, technological limitations, and a variety of labour-related problems.[71]

A final, direct method of freeing land from weeds required only minimal labour inputs and almost no technology: pasturing livestock on arable fields. It did, however, depend upon the active co-operation of domestic sheep and swine and their ability to selectively graze upon weeds in fields of beans and wheat.[72] This approach seems to have been quite effective and was understandably popular with traditionalist farmers. Some improvers, however, dismissed it as a "slovenly custom."[73] Their primary objection was that it only became practical when fields were heavily infested with weeds and, as such, it was a sure sign of slovenly culture. It was also a tacit admission of the failure of farmers to heed one of the central tenets of good husbandry: "prevention is the better cure."[74]

British farmers employed a wide range of cultural techniques to prevent and suppress the growth of weeds. The easiest in theory, if not in practice, was simply to avoid introducing them into fields in the first place. The use of well composted manure, eradicating weeds on land adjacent to fields, and attempting to sow only clean seed were three of the most heavily promoted preventative measures. Although they seem to have been common practices, they were not always effective, and judging from the volume of complaints by agricultural improvers, they were not always carefully conducted. To compost manure properly, for example, requires a considerable effort in terms of collecting and turning and many farmers found it easier to manure their fields through the expediency of pasturing livestock on fallows, temporary pasture, or stubble. Complicating matters further, the seeds of some weedy species can remain viable in even the most thoroughly composted manure. Cutting weeds in the untilled corners of fields, in ditches, and along fence lines, hedges, and roads also requires a considerable amount of time and energy. This activity was common enough to acquire its own name — discumbering — but agricultural improvers argued that it was all too often neglected.[75]

Agriculturists have stressed the importance of using clean seed since the sixteenth century and seed cleaning appears to have been a common activity for at least as long.[76] For instance, Tusser mentions several methods for cleaning barley:

Some best to winnow, some best to fan,
Some best to cast it as cleane as they can,
for feede go and cast it, for malting not so:
but get out the cockle, and then let it go.[77]

Farmers continued to fan and winnow their seed grain in the eighteenth century and their individual efforts were augmented in the nineteenth century by the advent of commercially cleaned seed and seed-testing facilities.[78] The use of clean seed remains a standard antiweed measure to this day but, as numerous grain drill surveys have shown, modern farmers continue to sow weed-infested seed on an all-too-regular basis. This suggests that despite the best efforts of farmers and improvers alike, the use of dirty seed did much to perpetuate the conflict with weeds in Britain between the sixteenth and nineteenth centuries.

Because farmers were never able to prevent the introduction of unwanted plants into their arable fields entirely, they often cultured their crops in a manner designed to suppress the germination and growth of the weeds that were already there. A very traditional method was to sow heavily because it greatly prevents the Growth of those Weeds, whose Mischiefs seldom are over at the Barn; but too often are known to insinuate themselves into a Growth in the Field.... The Growth of Weeds is often absolutely hindered, by the plenary Furniture that the Ground enjoys from the Roots of the Grain.[79]

Efforts to crowd out weeds were intensified during the eighteenth century through the use of specialized crops such as buckwheat, a plant whose growth "is so rapid as to outstrip and smother almost every species of weeds."[80]

The use of smother crops necessarily implies that the land was also being used for other, more lucrative purposes. Farmers were growing other crops; they were practising crop rotation. Crop rotation was a common practice by the sixteenth century and, as the centuries progressed, the taking of "crop upon crop ... for greediness sake" became a thing of the past.[81] Sixteenth- and seventeenth-century rotation schemes varied widely but they were usually quite simple. Arable fields in the north of England were typically seeded to grains and legumes for two to four years and then were allowed to rest under grass for up to ten years.[82] In the more fertile regions further south, cultivated land was commonly cropped for two years before being fallowed for one, and on the brecklands of Norfolk, farmers followed a four-course system of barley-rye-barley-fallow.[83]

Four-course rotations that included root crops, new legumes, and forage grasses became commonplace during the eighteenth century and the incidence of summer fallowing declined accordingly. In backwards districts, however, and on heavy soils where legumes and turnips did poorly, farmers continued to follow the traditional course of wheat-beans-fallow well into the nineteenth century.[84] Nineteenth-century rotations tended to be more varied, complex, and longer than ever before but they were still designed to fulfill "the principle of keeping the land DRY, CLEAN and RICH."[85] Subduing weeds was not the only function of crop rotation but as one early-nineteenth-century improver observed: "every rotation and course of cropping ought to render the land cleaner and freer from weeds, which it will certainly do in a judicious system with due attention."[86]

Traditional British crop rotations discouraged the germination, growth, and spread of weeds in a number of ways:

The growing of a succession of different crops on a field varied the competitive environment of the weed population. The working of the land in spring, the date of seedbed preparation, the seasonal presence or absence of the crop canopy, the time of harvest and subsequent cultivation all changed from year to year, so that no one weed species could benefit from a consistently favourable environment and thereby gain dominance. In addition 'cleaning' crops such as turnips or potatoes which allowed mechanical weed control during their active growth were balanced against 'fouling' crops (usually the cereals) which did not. An effective rotation struck a balance that involved living with weeds which were never absent but seldom serious and usually under control.[87]

Many agricultural improvers, however, believed that cleaning crops, particularly turnips, were the key to a successful rotation. Rotations were considered, in turn, the key to successfully subduing weeds.[88] By the mid-seventeenth century, turnips were widely grown for fodder in various parts of East Anglia and southern England and by the late eighteenth century they had become a standard course in the Norfolk system and other similar four-course schemes.[89] Unlike the various grains and legumes, turnips were often carefully hoed by hand during the growing season both to thin and space the crop and to reduce competition from weeds. Turnip culture reached its apogee in Norfolk. There, according to William Marshall, turnip hoeing became a way of life: "A boy in Norfolk, by the time he is the height of a hoe, begins to make use of one: consequently, every man who has been bred to country-business is a turnip-hoer; yet not always, even with this advantage, an expert one."[90]

Arthur Young argued that inexpert hoeing or even worse, no hoeing at all, effectively negated the value of turnips in rotations:

Suppose the turnips, which I state as the first crop in the proposed system, are managed after the manner of many whole counties, that is not hoed at all, but left at their utmost thickness, and full of weeds, as such crops mostly are; this management does not affect only the turnip crop, but every one that follow: for the crop of turnips, which is the first in the course, if it is badly managed, will much prejudice even the wheat one, which is the last.… In this manner, every crop is successively injured by the weeds, until the last is almost destroyed by them: and then the circle goes round again upon the same principles, in so much, that every course increases these grand enemies, until at last the ground, however good it may naturally be, becomes quite exhausted, and will yield nothing but trumpery.[91]

Young's analysis of the consequences of failing to hoe reveals that even the most effective techniques for keeping weeds at bay were ineffective when used alone. It also suggests that the conflict with weeds was not a single or discrete activity. Instead, it is best perceived as a highly complex and integral aspect of arable farming, an "essential part of cultivation," and as "one of the most important parts of an improved husbandry."[92]

Determining exactly what combination of techniques most farmers used in their conflict with weeds is difficult because few farmers were able or inclined to record such mundane activities. One that did was William Marshall, and his *Minutes of Agriculture* (1778) provides a detailed account of one farmer's struggle with weeds. In his entries for 1775 alone, Marshall mentions using virtually all of the weed control techniques discussed in this chapter. He may not have been an "average farmer" but it is worth noting that the *Minutes of Agriculture* represents the published version of a journal that he began to keep as a young man after firing an incompetent bailiff in 1774 and assuming the active management of his farm. Marshall describes this period in his life as "an Apprenticeship to farming" and there is, as a result, little reason to regard his activities as particularly unusual or exceptional.[93]

Further Thoughts on Weeds

By now it is clear that the issue of weeds was central to both how farmers farmed and the practical advice offered in improver literature. Agricultural improvers were not, however, solely concerned with immediately practical matters and they devoted considerable space to less tangible issues

37

such as the origin and nature of weeds and of weed problems in general. Their writings on these and other subjects provide intriguing insights into scientific, economic, and religious thought and how these larger cultural contexts helped shape specific ideas about, and attitudes towards, undesirable plants.

Agricultural writers have traditionally expressed considerable dislike for the weedy denizens of cultivated fields. In doing so they probably echoed the prevailing opinion of British farmers. Since at least the sixteenth century, British farmers appear to have drawn "rigid distinctions" between crops and weeds.[94] As one historian explains, to "the agriculturalist a weed was an obscenity, the vegetable equivalent of vermin.... Even today there are few farmers who are cheered by the sight of poppies in their corn."[95] Sixteenth-century writers commonly described poppies, thistles, and other weeds as "ill," "cumbersome," "loathsome," and "noxious" and more than one seventeenth-century writer characterized them as a "great annoyance."[96]

These or similar invectives remained popular during the eighteenth and nineteenth centuries but, by the 1730s, many writers were beginning to express their dislike through the use of far harsher terms. One of the first to escalate the war of words against weeds was Jethro Tull. He described them as "these Enemies," the "spurious Kindred" of "Legitimate (or Sown) Plants" and accused them of "robbing" and "Rapine."[97] Tull's polemics were rivalled and even surpassed by those of his contemporary, William Ellis. Ellis regularly used terms such as "abominable," "stinking," "venomous," and "rampant" to describe some of the more troublesome weeds.[98]

Probably the most inveterate and high-profile weed haters of the late eighteenth and early nineteenth centuries were the president and secretary of the Board of Agriculture, Sir John Sinclair and Arthur Young. They portrayed weeds as "trumpery" and "bad company," they condemned them as "robbers of the soil," and they called for eternal vigilance against this "pertinacious host of enemies to the profitable crops."[99] Sinclair was one of the last of the prominent agricultural improvers to defame weeds in such a colourful manner. His nineteenth-century successors still expressed their dislike for unwanted plants but they did so less often, less violently, and usually through the use of more traditional expressions of antipathy.[100]

The identification of a persistently negative attitude towards weeds and the use of harsher antiweed rhetoric between the opening decades of the eighteenth century and the close of the Napoleonic Wars has a number of important implications. The first is that, despite improvements in tools and techniques, weeds continued to plague farmers and arouse their hostility throughout the period 1500 to 1900. This in turn implicitly testifies to the agency of weeds or, as one essayist lamented, their ability to "hold almost all our endeavours to destroy them at defiance."[101] Agricultural improvers paid grudging tribute to the agency of weeds on a regular basis and in a number of ways. Some emphasized their "Pre-eminence over all other Vegetables" because of their superior hardiness and tenacity of growth, whereas others imbued them with human motives and abilities.[102] The latter was either accomplished through the use of anthropomorphic adjectives or, less subtly, by miscasting weeds as actors in complex and unmistakably human dramas. One early Scottish improver, for instance, warned in a letter to the Earl of Stair that "They, the Weeds, steal in like a Thief in the Night, thrust themselves where Corn would grow, and dwarf it, drawing the Nourishment from it, or they choke and kill what grows beside them."[103]

A third insight that can be drawn from expressions of antipathy is that the strength of feeling that weeds aroused can be linked to a number of more purely human developments. These include changes in the price and supply of labour, a better understanding of weed costs, competition, and eradication, and finally the sheer frustration felt by improvers over the failure of farmers to heed their advice. As outlined in the previous section on conflict, traditional British approaches to weed problems were generally very labour intensive and there is some evidence to suggest that by the eighteenth century the cost of hand-weeding had become prohibitively expensive.[104] It is plausible that higher labour costs discouraged farmers from attending to the finer points of weed eradication and that their neglect, in turn, aroused the ire of reformers such as Ellis and Tull. After all, agricultural improvers had been calling for more attention to weeding since the reign of Henry VIII. It would be hardly surprising if eighteenth-century writers adopted the device of defaming weeds in an effort to impress their readers with the danger that weeds represented.

In the late eighteenth and early nineteenth centuries, long drawn-out wars against France did little to improve the labour situation and it is probably no coincidence that both antiweed polemics and interest in weeds appear to have peaked during this time. During this period, essays solely devoted to weeds and their eradication first made their appearance, as did attempts to estimate the cost of weeds and the economic benefits of weeding.[105] Some improvers were so alarmed over the spread of weeds that they even called for the passing of some form of noxious-weed legislation.[106]

At the same time as the cost of attending to weeds was rising, agricultural improvers were becoming increasingly aware of the fact that weed problems, unlike diseases and other crop maladies, were neither mysterious nor impossible to solve using existing tools and techniques. The causes of plant diseases, for example, were not widely understood until well into the nineteenth century, whereas agricultural writers displayed a fairly modern grasp of the nature of weeds and weed competition by a comparatively early date.[107] By the mid-eighteenth century, earlier notions were being widely ridiculed. These included the idea that weeds could be generated spontaneously from soils, that crops transmutated into weeds, and that weeds and crops did not compete for food because different plants drew upon different types of "juice" in the soil.[108] The early-eighteenth-century farmer and diarist Edward Lisle, for example, dismisses the idea of "equivocal" generation when he writes, "Surely we have great reason to conclude ... that the earth does not produce the most contemptible weed without a seed; and we find that even at the beginning God took not that method."[109] Other eighteenth-century writers were equally adamant that all plants growing in the same soil are "nourished by the same Sort of Food" for

if it were true that every plant drew from the Earth a particular Juice for its Nourishment, which suited its Purpose, and that no other kind, then Thistles Bluebottles, Corn Marygold, and other weeds so frequent among Corn, would do it no Harm; because they would take only such Juices as the Corn would not: but just the contrary is found in Fact.[110]

Agricultural improvers had arrived at an essentially modern understanding of the basis of weed competition by the mid-eighteenth century. Today's weed scientists, for example, would find little to fault in Adam Dickson's 1765 explanation for how weeds act as "impediments to vegetation":

> THEY rob the plants we desire to cultivate of their food; they prevent these plants from branching out from the root, and some kinds of them lessen the vegetable pasture in the land, where they are suffered to grow.... Experience convinces the farmer of the truth of this: for he finds, that his crop is bad in proportion to the quantity and kinds of weeds with which his land is infested.[111]

By the mid-eighteenth century, reformers had also arrived at the conclusion that while weeds presented serious impediments to crop production, "their several Mischiefs" could be overcome by "Care and Diligence."[112] William Marshall added that not only was it possible for the farmer to keep land "in a high state of tillage, and beautifully clean," but that it was "little more than *his* duty as a husbandman."[113]

The frustration of agricultural improvers over the failure of farmers to attend to their duty largely disappeared after the close of the Napoleonic Wars and their antiweed polemics softened accordingly. The first half of the nineteenth century witnessed the reestablishment of a healthy agricultural labour market and the renewed ability of farmers to keep weed populations in check. It also witnessed the widespread adoption of most of the antiweed measures that reformers had been championing for a century or more. Row cropping and the use of cleaning crops in rotations became commonplace, intensive or "high" farming was spreading and farmers simply seem to have become more conscious of the economic benefits of reducing weed populations on their land.

George Rennie, a Scottish reformer, argued that improved techniques were already having an impact on weed populations by 1813. Although his observation is clearly impressionistic, he believed that "by paying due attention" to careful cultivation, drilling, and hoeing, "many farms which, not forty years ago, were a nest of seed-weeds, have now been brought into order, that is to say, the weeds are kept under subjection and easily managed."[114] Four years later, Sir John Sinclair noted that in both England and Scotland "since the introduction of the turnip husbandry, and a more correct mode of fallowing, in several districts the ground is kept much cleaner."[115] Further anecdotal evidence of a relative decline in weed populations can be found in James Caird's comprehensive 1852 survey of agricultural conditions in England in which he frequently praises farmers for keeping "the land very clean and free of weeds."[116] A number of historians have also concluded that from the 1840s onwards, British farmers were generally keeping their land much cleaner than their predecessors had either been either able or wont to do.[117] This conclusion must be considered highly speculative, however, as recent work by Colin Duncan implies that the nineteenth-century trend towards one-year leases resulted in the abandonment of good husbandry until "the great grassing down of rural England occurred" towards the end of the century when the "ecological burden of English seed-eating shifted its place of impact to the prairies of the New World where rapacious soil-miners ripped open pristine grasslands."[118]

Having established the main factors encouraging a hostile attitude towards weeds, it is important to note that even the most inveterate weed haters recognized certain constraints on their rhetorical flourishes. Significantly, most of these constraints were either forgotten or had simply lost their meaning within a generation or two of the establishment of commercial farming in Ontario. One check on the polemics of British improvers was familiarity with a variety of alternate uses for weedy species — uses that made it difficult to portray them as entirely without value. Seemingly against his will, William Ellis concedes this point in his 1744 account of some enterprising hay producers:

A Neighbour of mine ... mistook his Road, which obliged him to arrive late at a single Public-house, near this Village of *Newton*, where he put up his Horse; and when the Landlord came to rack up the Horse for all Night, he brought a Parcel of Hay, to my Neighbour's Surprize, made of Thistles, and other Weeds. On asking the Reason of this, the Landlord said, that several of his neighbours were such indolent People, that they would not sow their Land with Beans, because the Thistle, wild Oat, wild Parsnip, yellow Curlock, Hale-weed, *May*-weed, and other Sorts of Weeds would choke and ruin the Crop; and therefore they let these Weeds grow, in order to mow them for Hay, and, when it was well made, they esteemed it good Hay; for that they took Care to mow the Thistles and Weeds, before they grew too old, rank, and hard; and then they made such good Hay, that they sell it by Weight.[119]

Probably the most comprehensive list of alternate uses for weeds was compiled in 1806 by William Pitt. Pitt was more explicit than Ellis about the value of weeds. He even suggested that their eradication was attended by some negative consequences:

> The plants we term weeds, considered as respecting mankind, are not totally useless; many of them have valuable medical qualities, and some of them may be applied to uses so as to pay something towards the expense of clearing them from the ground: thus, sowthistles are good food for rabbits or hogs: the hog-weed (*Heracleum*) is good for either hogs or cattle: horses are said to be fond of young thistles when partially dried, and the seed may be prevented from spreading by gathering the down, which make good pillows.... Chadlock, when drawn, may be given to cows, who are very fond of it.... It has been observed, that bees have not thriven so well in this island since the extirpation of weeds has been more attended to.[120]

Many agricultural writers were forced to concede that weeds were only relatively, not absolutely, less valuable than crop plants; none could avoid acknowledging that weeds, unlike crops, were natural components of the native flora. Recognition of this point acted as an effective curb to many a slanderous pen from at least the seventeenth century onwards.[121] Jethro Tull may have hated weeds with a passion but even he was unable to deny them occupancy rights in arable fields:

> WEEDS, and their seed, in the Fields where they grow naturally ... are thought to have been, originally, the natural Product of our Climate; therefore, most other Plants, being Exotics, many of them, as to their Individuals, require Culture, and change of Soil, without which they are liable, more or less, to degenerate.[122]

William Ellis also acknowledged the native status of weeds and the advantages this conferred: "Now all are sensible that a Weed out-runs the Corn; because one has its Production naturally from the Earth, while the other is brought forward in some measure by the help of Art."[123]

A traditional awareness of the native status of weeds and their natural advantages led, by the mid-eighteenth century, to the realization that weeds were inevitable. Thomas Hale clearly articulated this idea in his 1756 farming manual:

> Weeds are in this Manner to be expected in all Places; and they will out-grow all Crops. This rises from a plain Reason: they are Natives of the Soil and Climate; and will therefore thrive better in it, than such as are raised by Art.... THE Consideration of Weeds is very essential to the Husbandman, because scarce any of his Land escapes from being abundantly infested with them; and none is ever entirely free.[124]

By the nineteenth century, a sense of the inevitability of weeds had become even stronger. Most nineteenth-century writers impressed their readers with the need to learn to farm profitably in the presence of weeds. They also stressed the impossibility of "complete extirpation" because "the seeds of wild plants constituting weeds are so universally distributed, that ... wherever a crop will grow, there also will weeds flourish, if allowed."[125] Nineteenth-century authorities preferred, instead, to portray conflict as a balancing act or as an exercise in keeping "weeds within bounds."[126]

Religion was the final factor that both shaped how weeds were perceived and curbed rhetorical excesses. On one hand, the Christian tradition encouraged an oppositional view of weeds by stressing the need for humankind to gain ascendancy over nature. This theological emphasis seems to have been particularly strong during the sixteenth and early seventeenth centuries and it left its mark on contemporary agricultural improvement literature.[127] Gervase Markham, for example, began his 1625 treatise on freeing barren ground from unwanted vegetation with the statement that

Thou whom it hath pleased God to place upon a barren and hard soil, whose bread must evermore be grounded with sweat and labour, that most nobly and victoriously boast the conquest of the Earth, having conquered Nature by altering Nature, and yet made Nature better than she was before.[128]

Although the Christian tradition both fostered and justified an antagonistic attitude towards weeds, it simultaneously encouraged agricultural writers to regard weeds as evidence of poor stewardship. Historian Keith Thomas sums up the "deeply ambivalent" nature of the "Judaeo-Christian inheritance" when he argues, "Side by side with the emphasis on man's right to exploit the inferior species went a distinctive doctrine of human stewardship and responsibility for God's creatures."[129] The seventeenth-century improver Walter Blith lends support to Thomas's contention when he writes that God intended "Man to Husbandize the fruits of the Earth, and dress, and keep them for the use of the whole Creation."[130] A century later, William Ellis portrayed weeds "as Beacons to the passing Travelers, to let them know there lives a bad Husbandman in the Neighbourhood."[131] Another William observed in 1806 that

man, possessed of reason, reflection, and intelligence, has powers and abilities to select and cultivate such vegetables as are adapted to his use, and proper for his sustenance, and to destroy and extirpate others; and thus to appropriate to himself what proportion he thinks proper of the earth's surface; which if he neglects to dress and cultivate properly, it will, in some degree, revert to its natural state, producing the hardier and more acrid plants for the sustenance of numberless tribes of insects, and for an infinity of other known and unknown uses.[132]

The passage above illustrates how the Christian tradition reinforced the ideas that weeds were natural and as much the product of human neglect as they were evidence of nature's opposition. These ideas were further reinforced by an explicit statement in Genesis 3.17–18 concerning God's punishment of Adam and Eve: "cursed is the ground because of you; in toil you shall eat of it all the days of your life; thorns and thistles it shall bring forth to you." Agricultural improvers frequently referred or alluded to the Biblical explanation for the origin of weeds and references to God's curse can still be found in modern weed science literature. The unequivocal nature "of the Curse entailed on Man's Posterity, for his Disobedience to his Creator" made it virtually impossible for writers steeped in the Christian tradition to cast weeds as inherently evil because they were, after all, God's creations.[133] Weeds were, instead, generally regarded as symptoms of human failings from the original sin of Adam and Eve to a lack of stewardship and the evil of poor husbandry.

The strength of their religious convictions forced many improvers to search for something positive in God's curse. Some found satisfaction in praising weeds as worthy opponents and as evidence of the superiority of God's design over the vegetable products of human art. Others contented themselves with listing alternate uses for the native species that favoured arable fields. Probably the most ingenious solution, however, was to suggest that weeds existed to stimulate and exercise human industry. This notion was articulated a number of times between 1500 and 1900. According to Keith Thomas, Henry More justified the existence of weeds as a stimulus to human industry in 1655.[134] In 1806, William Pitt described weeds as a check to "the indolence of the human race" and, in 1811, Patrick Brodie speculated that weeds served "to stimulate the industry of man, in so far, that while he is destroying one plant, he may increase the culture of another, more useful to himself or domestic animals."[135] No one, however, expressed this idea more artfully than the farmer, editor, and essayist Benjamin Holdich.

Holdich's 1825 essay, "The Weeds of Agriculture," went through several editions both as a separate piece and part of George Sinclair's *Hortus Gramineus Woburnensis*.[136] The popular and prolific nineteenth-century agricultural writer Henry Stephens describes Holdich as the "first writer of practice" to deal with the issue of weeds and he criticizes earlier essays by William Pitt and others as mere botanical exercises rather than practical guides to "the weeds you may expect to encounter, when cultivating a particular kind of soil, or raising a particular crop."[137] "The Weeds of Agriculture" remained a standard reference article on British weeds for decades and Holdich was still being regularly cited in the early twentieth century by leading weed experts such as H. C. Long and Winifred Brenchley.[138]

Part of the enduring success of this essay can be attributed to the writer's extensive, practical knowledge of weeds and their eradication. It can also be attributed to Holdich's writing ability and his gift for capturing the essential cognitive elements of the relationship between weeds and people in Britain:

> Now, what is the inference from the facts, that couch-grass and thistles can by no means be extirpated? Is it not perpetual exertions, fallowing, and agricultural labour? Some may be inclined to say, "A melancholy reflection!" — But I say *no* — not at all. Providence could not have better contrived than that exertions should be perpetual, and that *success* should be in proportion. There is not a weed that we ought to wish out of our fields, unless we remove and destroy it; because, if there were none, or very few, all fields would be clean, and no praise could light on superior modes of tillage…. Does any man think that our various soils would have been sufficiently pulverized and worked; had there been no enemies of this sort to challenge forth our labour? … The necessity of subsistence produces industrious hands for every department of labour; but the sluggish nature of man requires every stimulus to exertion. The weeds of the fields excite emulation among farmers, and foul fields are always a reproach to the occupier. Thus we are compelled, by an unseen hand, to better habits and more active industry.[139]

Conclusion

Holdich's explanation for the weeds of the fields brings to a close this overview of weeds and their relationship with agriculturists in Britain between 1500 and 1900. Interactions between the two parties on both physical and cognitive levels were dynamic and complex and marked by a great deal of diversity on both local and regional scales. Despite a high degree of diversity, however, it is possible to discern a number of commonalities and long-term trends. One common feature was familiarity with several widespread and particularly troublesome weeds. Thistles, couch grass, wild mustard, and wild oats were, amongst others, ubiquitous throughout much of the British Isles and they enjoyed the dubious distinction of being Britain's worst weeds during the entire period covered by this study. This distinction partly reflects the impressive weedy abilities of the species in question. It also reflects the general failure of foreign weeds to challenge "native" species for the right to occupy arable land.

Indigenous weed populations did not, however, explode in the absence of foreign competition and it seems likely that field densities declined significantly between 1500 and 1900. Most of this decline probably occurred after the close of the Napoleonic Wars although there is some evidence suggesting that weeds may have enjoyed a brief resurgence just prior to the conversion of much of Britain's arable land into pasture during the last quarter of the nineteenth century. During the first half of the nineteenth century, many of the antiweed measures that agricultural improvers had long agitated for were finally being adopted and farmers seem to have been more conscious of the deleterious effects of weeds. Economic considerations probably had more to do with the adoption of these measures than did the efforts of agricultural reformers but proponents of improved husbandry do deserve credit for increasing public awareness and for publicizing practical methods aimed at suppressing the growth of uneconomic or less desirable plants.

The basic nature of the tools and techniques used to discourage the growth of unwanted vegetation changed surprisingly little over the centuries. For example, of the ten general methods for "suppressing" weeds that are discussed in a 1904 Board of Agriculture and Fisheries leaflet, only one — the use of chemical sprays against charlock — would have been considered new to agriculturists in the eighteenth, seventeenth, or even sixteenth centuries.[140] This conclusion may be somewhat new to historians but as early as 1947 agricultural scientists were arguing "that from the time when the plough was invented up to half a century ago there were no radical changes in the techniques available for killing weeds."[141] Even Tull's "new husbandry" cannot be described as a radical innovation, for it was simply a refinement of a cropping technique that gardeners had employed for centuries and one that farmers had used in certain crops for generations.

Throughout the period 1500 to 1900, British farmers generally employed a combination of direct and cultural practices in their struggle with weeds and the design of most arable farming systems at least took weeds into account. From the late eighteenth or early nineteenth century onwards, however, the intensity of conflict increased considerably.[142] A greater emphasis on weeds and their destruction can be linked to the classical enclosure movement that was underway during this period and to the era of intensive, commercial farming that it ushered in. Involving longer, more effective rotations, seed drilling and horse hoeing, deeper plowing and more frequent tillage operations, intensive farming was greatly facilitated by concurrent improvements in the design and construction of plows, harrows, and cultivators.[143] These developments may not represent revolutionary changes but they certainly enabled British farmers to eradicate weeds with greater vigour, speed, and efficiency than ever before.

Cognition, like the other two levels of analysis, also displays a pattern of continuity and change over time. That it does so is not surprising as all three are simply different aspects of culture. An understanding of weed biology and ecology, for example, helps explain both their survival in the face of human opposition and the persistence of a hostile attitude towards weeds on the part of agriculturists. The hostility of agriculturists was further aroused by the deleterious effect of weeds on production and profit. It even received a certain amount of religious sanction from a theological emphasis on the need for humanity to contest with, conquer, and improve upon nature.

Agricultural improvers had a tendency to carry expressions of dislike to extremes during the eighteenth and early nineteenth centuries. A heightened sense of animosity towards weeds was partly linked to the negative impact of rising labour costs and war-related labour shortages on the ability of farmers to keep weeds in check. Agricultural improvers also appear to have been guilty of fanning the flames when, frustrated over a lack of response to their advice, they adopted the device of dramatizing the deleterious effects of weeds in an effort to remind farmers of their duty. Their frustration was also increased by the slow rate of agricultural reform, knowledge that weed problems were not insurmountable, the growing force of the capitalist imperative, and a better sense of the impact of weeds on the pursuit of agrarian profit.

Improved labour conditions and the widespread implementation of long-called-for antiweed measures after the close of the Napoleonic Wars resulted in a softening of attitudes towards weeds and a return to the use of traditional invectives. Even when antiweed rhetoric was at its height, however, most agricultural writers recognized that there were distinct limits to the aspersions they were able to cast. Familiarity with a host of traditional uses for weedy plants, for example, discouraged them from describing weeds as completely worthless or without value. Similarly, because weeds clearly meant different things to different people in different places, they could only be portrayed as an "evil" or "the enemy" in the context of the farm.

Agricultural improvers could not even deny weeds occupancy rights in arable fields out of respect for their native status and natural advantages over crops. Weeds, in short, were seen as undesirable but generally regarded as inevitable. The Christian idea of stewardship and the biblical explanation for the origin of weeds helped agriculturists accept the presence of unwanted plants in their fields. Both also reinforced the traditional idea that weeds were not inherently evil. Rather, they were best seen as the expression of a human evil — both the original sin of Adam and Eve and the evil of poor husbandry. Strong religious convictions and a belief in the superiority of God's design even led some improvers to posit an eminently positive role for weeds: weeds were Providence's device for countering the natural indolence and sloth of humanity by compelling farmers to farm better and more industriously.

Traditional British agricultural literature conveys a surprisingly sophisticated view of weeds. Weeds were portrayed as being both active agents and acted upon; as an identifiable category of plants and yet one with a large subjective dimension. Although they were consistently vilified, their vilification was usually described as the consequence of poor farming and calls for the extirpation, extermination, or destruction of weeds were countered by the admission that weeds were inevitable and that farmers had to learn to live with them.

The physical relationship between weeds and people in Britain from the sixteenth to the nineteenth centuries was far from harmonious, but it too appears to have been marked by a rough degree of balance. Over the short term, particularly on the level of the farm, this balance frequently tipped in favour of one side or the other as a result of changes in weather, land tenancy, ownership, and management. Over the long term, however, no clear winner emerged from the ongoing conflict. Weed populations may have declined somewhat but the weed "problem" remained a serious one and the success of British arable farming continued to depend on the observance of time-honoured, cultural rituals that had evolved alongside the plants that they were designed to suppress.

As we will see in the chapters that follow, the traditional relationship between people and weeds in Britain was subtly transformed when it was transported to North America. The new social setting was unfavourable to the application of many of the techniques that made a precarious balancing act possible in Britain. In combination with a weed-friendly environment, this soon led to an unprecedented problem with European weeds. The sheer success of immigrant plants by the late nineteenth century encouraged North American agriculturists to adopt a harsh, and at times blindly oppositional, attitude while agricultural scientists and government authorities frantically searched for immediate solutions to an ever worsening problem. Their search often obscured the need for fundamental changes in North American farming systems, in part because they were forced to downplay the culpability of farmers in an effort to enlist their active co-operation. The advent of effective herbicides in the 1940s simply entrenched the notion that weeds were the enemy and it is only within the last decade or so that North American weed scientists have begun to pay serious attention to the traditional British insight that the true enemy to profitable farming is a style of agriculture that actively cultivates weeds.

3

From Colony to Nation:
The Transformation of Immigrant Culture in Ontario, 1800–1867

An experienced British farmer who immigrated to southern Ontario in 1867 would have found much that was familiar and much that was not. Most of the resident farmers were of British descent and they lived in a land that had been transformed into a rough facsimile of rural Britain. Few surprises awaited in terms of the crops being grown and the tools and techniques employed in their culture. The observant immigrant would even have noted that the weed flora of Ontario was dominated by species that had troubled British farmers for centuries.[1] Upon closer observation, however, subtle but significant differences would become apparent. Farming, for example, was backward by British standards with techniques such as summer fallowing acting as a substitute for a more mature system of husbandry. The immigrant farmer would be struck by the absence of many weeds that were common back home and, conversely, by the unusual abundance of others. The common field thistle of Europe (*Cirsium arvense* (L.) Scop.), in particular, flourished to such an extent that it had acquired the name of its adopted country. Many people even believed that it was an indigenous rather than imported species.

Many of these impressions would be confirmed by a glance at

Canada thistle, *Cirsium arvense*

a local agricultural newspaper. Further reading would reveal that local farmers were aware of the danger that weeds represented. The strongly oppositional view of weeds that the local press presented, however, would have appeared foreign to someone steeped in the British tradition of good husbandry. So too would news of the recent passage of legislation that effectively outlawed Canada thistle (*C. arvense*) and demanded that land owners attend to its destruction prior to the setting of seed. A particularly perceptive reader may also have detected the irony of harsh antiweed rhetoric in a land where traditional British teachings were known but apparently ignored. Local agriculturists, in other words, tended to blame weeds for the problems they posed while downplaying the fact that they were largely responsible for the creation and maintenance of a weed problem in the first place.

This chapter chronicles the evolution of a distinctive relationship between people and weeds in Ontario between 1800 and the time of Confederation in an effort to highlight the intimate connections between human culture and the environment. More specifically, it explores how the environment acts in conjunction with ecological and social factors to bring about cultural change. Within the context of the entire study, this chapter serves to introduce the reader to many of the factors that shaped the war with weeds in the Prairie West. As will become apparent in chapter five, it also represents a case study of some of the cultural ties between agriculturists in Canada and the northern United States.

The "Rough Era," 1800–1865

Weedy immigrants arrived in Ontario alongside their human compatriots as unwanted but integral components of their cultural baggage. There are no accurate records on when and how most were introduced but we can be confident that they travelled as contaminants of seed, clinging to livestock and implements and, not infrequently, in the packing material protecting human settlers' more fragile possessions. Some species arrived directly from Europe while others availed themselves of a convenient ride north in the company of late-eighteenth-century Loyalists and American settlers.[2]

Another important route of entry was in seed, animal feed, and packing materials harvested from the well-established weed colonies of Lower Canada. The history of imported weeds in New France is a long one — Champlain, for example, reported a problem with portulaca (*Portulaca oleracea* L.) in grain fields near Quebec in 1632 — and by the early nineteenth century, even the most sympathetic critics of Lower Canadian farming were moved to chastise the habitants for allowing weeds to grow "unmolested."[3] With reference to Lower Canada, one observer commented that it was impossible to estimate "the produce from a farm" because the sheaves of grain "are frequently composed of one half weeds," while another noted "that the character of Canadian wheat is proverbial in the English market for foulness."[4]

Agricultural reformers and British travellers attributed the foul, weed-infested state of Lower Canadian fields to a number of causes. J. E. Burton, an Irish Catholic priest and resident of Lower Canada during the 1820s, believed that the problem was mainly the result of widespread ignorance of the economic consequences of weeds.[5] In 1828, he was moved to write,

In every country where agriculture has arrived at any degree of per-fection, particular attention is paid, to the extirpation of weeds. In England, Ireland, and Scotland, you seldom or ever see a weed, annual or perennial, in field of grass or corn. The industrious farmer, deems it the greatest disgrace, to have the curse, of his great progenitor, constantly reproaching him, face to face, for his frailty. It is not so however, with the Canadian; for he seems to exult, in that placid phi-losophy, which makes him overlook altogether, the thing and its con-sequences. If you ask, why he allows such nuisances unmolested to *infest the land* his own and his neighbours. He will say with a smile, indicative of the contempt he holds you in for your particularities. *Mon Dieu, il me coute trop, a les toucher, avec les doigts....* I have seen a meadow so much overrun with thistles and golden rod in Canada, that it was not worth cutting; altho' the crop of hay would have been good, in case, those vegetable leeches had been prevented, from sucking the blood of the land.[6]

Critics more commonly attributed the prevalence of weeds to poor

plowing techniques, crude and ineffective tillage implements, and the continuous cropping of wheat in the absence of a proper crop rotation. While
on a reporting mission for the Highland and Agricultural Society of
Scotland in the early 1830s, Adam Fergusson compared Lower Canadian
farming to "the old Scottish practice of infield and outfield, taking crop
after crop of grain from their fields, until nothing but weeds remain, and
looking to Nature for the renovation which their own industry ought to
have effected."[7] His comments echo those made a decade earlier by C. F.
Cresinus who described the prevalent practice of alternating wheat with
an unattended fallow as "this alternate rotation of grain and weed crops."[8]
Yet a third critic quipped that in the vicinity of Montreal in 1832, "The
agriculture cannot be said to have been reduced to a system, if we except
the alternation of wheat and thistle pasture."[9]

Farmers in the earliest settled districts of Ontario may have been critical of Lower Canadian agriculture but, by the 1830s, the state of their
fields would seem to have conferred little in the way of bragging rights
over their French-speaking neighbours. Patrick Shirreff, for example, the
same British traveller who decried the farming practices near Montreal,
was equally scathing in his assessment of the farms along the shores of the
Bay of Quinte near Kingston:

> Crops were inferior and crowded with thistles, apparently the common
> perennial way-thistle of Britain. My friend D___ and I, walking
> on deck, remarked a field bearing a dense-looking crop with purple
> coloured flowers, which one pronounced clover, the other pease, but on
> nearer approach it was seen to be pasturage intermixed with thistles.
> This was an unfortunate mistake for those having some pretensions
> to a knowledge of practical agriculture, and perhaps the thistle-grower
> may esteem our discernment as lightly as we do his management.[10]

Shirreff's remark suggests that European weeds were already flourish-
ing in parts of Ontario by the 1830s. By the 1840s, what scanty evidence
exists indicates that a problem with weeds had become widespread. In
1847, W. G. Edmundson, the editor of Ontario's first "successful" farm
newspaper, *The British American Cultivator*, urged his readers to diligently
cultivate their summer fallow and for the "bush farmer" to use clean seeds

and eradicate weeds upon their "first appearance." He warned that the consequences of failing to implement these measures were only too evident "on land that has been long under a state of cultivation" where "we know scores of careful cultivators who find it a very difficult task to rid their farms of injurious weeds."[11] Later in the same year, the paper's co-editor and the future holder of the first chair in agriculture at the University of Toronto, George Buckland, remarked: "The loss occasioned by weeds is too notorious to need but a bare mention — and notwithstanding, the many great improvements that have lately been made in the best cultivated districts, the loss and anxiety to the farmer occasioned by these unwholesome intruders are far from being removed."[12]

Lists of these unwholesome intruders include many plants that had troubled British farmers for centuries. Canada thistle, for instance, was none other than Shirreff's "common perennial way-thistle of Britain." This species seems to have been equally common in Ontario where it topped all the 1840s lists of the most problematic and widespread weeds. Ontario's first agricultural textbook, *The Canadian Agricultural Reader* (1845), describes Canada thistle as "the great enemy that the wheat grower in a large part of our country has to contend against" and more space was devoted to it in the local agricultural press than all other weeds combined.[13] Canada thistle may have been considered Ontario's worst weed in the 1840s but it was not the only species singled out for dishonourable mention. Other common weeds included charlock or wild mustard (*Sinapsis arvensis* L.), common milkweed (*Asclepias syriaca* L.), ox-eye daisy *(Chrysanthemum leucanthemum* L.), couch grass (*Agropyron repens* (L.) Beauv.), burdock (*Arctium* spp.), shepherd's purse (*Capsella bursa-pastoris* (L.) Medic.), lamb's-quarters (*Chenopodium album* L.), and chess (*Bromus secalinus* L.).[14] Milkweed is the only native species on this list while the rest are of western European origin.

All of the main participants were in place in Ontario by the 1840s but a distinct relationship between people and weeds had yet to develop. Another way of looking at this issue is to argue that the relationship that did exist was a curiously disjointed one, marked as it was by a lack of conscious interactions between participants and by tension, if not outright contradictions, between practice and prescription. Shirreff and other British observers regularly criticized Ontario farmers for their slovenly tillage and inactivity towards weeds. One of the better informed visitors, University of Durham Professor James F. W. Johnston, a leading authority on scientific agriculture in mid-nineteenth-century Britain, was appalled by the apparent lack of "knowledge of improved agriculture" and he warned that unless farmers mended their ways, they would suffer the same fate as the farmers of Lower Canada and New York state where the soil was close to exhaustion and the wheat lands were overrun with weeds such as corn gromwell (*Lithospermum arvense* L.).[15] Similar general criticisms can be found in Ontario's infant agricultural press although it too was largely guilty of ignoring the weed issue, only publishing a handful of articles on the subject through the 1840s and early 1850s.

When the subject of weeds was addressed in a Canadian publication, traditional British solutions were invariably prescribed. Farmers were advised to use properly cleaned seed, to exercise constant vigilance, and to pull, cut, or root out weeds whenever and wherever they appeared.[16] They were told the value of summer fallow, impressed with the need for timely, careful, and frequent tillage, encouraged to grow root crops as part of a proper system of rotation and, finally, asked to contemplate drill husbandry and horse-hoeing even though it "is in advance of the age in Canada."[17]

A tendency to parrot British advice is hardly surprising considering the colonial status of Upper Canada, its largely British population, and the Mother Country's long tradition of agricultural improvement. Nor is it surprising given that the "farmers who dominated the agricultural literature" and provided its main readership, Ontario's relatively small number of "improving farmers," almost all hailed from England and lowland Scotland.[18] Early Canadian farming journals were essentially patterned after British improver literature and newspapers. Canadian editors also regularly reprinted British articles and relied heavily on British authorities for information. The few books on agricultural improvement published in Canada before 1850 — most notably William Evans's *A Treatise on the Theory and Practice of Agriculture* (1835) and *The Canadian Agricultural Reader* (1845) — are virtually indistinguishable from contemporary British publications.[19]

Both Canadian and American agriculturists continued to look to Britain to provide leadership in agricultural science and expertise into the

1860s and North American literature bears the unmistakable stamp of the British movement for agricultural reform well beyond that decade. Two Confederation-era Canadian publications that testify to this point are Sir John Dawson's *First Lessons in Scientific Agriculture* (1864) and Egerton Ryerson's *First Lessons on Agriculture; For Canadian Farmers and their Families* (1870). Both share the style and assumptions of the British improver tradition. These include the belief that agriculture provides the basis of a nation's wealth and social well-being, a deep faith in the promise of science, an emphasis on education, the idea that farming brings one closer to God, and a tendency to equate "agriculture" solely with "capitalist agriculture."[20]

While Canadian reformers continued to seek inspiration in British improvement literature, their advice was increasingly at odds with the measures that were actually taken to eradicate weeds by the more conscientious segment of the farming population or by most farmers when weed infestations simply became too serious to ignore. By far the most popular technique for dealing with weeds in wheat, Ontario's pre-eminent field crop, was the naked summer fallow.[21] Summer fallow has been described as "an integral part of Upper Canada wheat-farming down to 1850" and as practised in Ontario, it involved alternating fields between a crop of grain one year and fallow the next.[22] Fields were typically plowed three times during the fallow year.[23] Multiple tillage operations encouraged annual weed seeds to germinate and permitted their subsequent destruction and it was effective in disrupting the growth of many perennial species through starving their roots. As noted above, Lower Canadian farmers also followed a wheat-fallow-wheat rotation but their "system" was considerably more weed friendly because it lacked the crucial tillage operations during the fallow year.

The style of naked summer fallowing employed in Ontario was virtually identical to British practices of the sixteenth and seventeenth centuries and it may well reflect the influence of British immigrants.[24] By the late eighteenth century, however, British agricultural improvers such as William Marshall considered three plowings over the course of the fallow year to be hopelessly inadequate for keeping weeds in check. He warned that even in areas where farmers practised crop rotation and rigorously hoed their field crops, "this small quantity of tillage" too often resulted in wheat stubble being "knee-deep in couch and thistles."[25] As indicated in chapter two, nineteenth-century British farmers seem to have taken this advice to heart and they generally tilled their fallows far more frequently than their predecessors. By then, however, summer fallowing had fallen out of fashion because of the loss of production that it entailed and the development of more cost-effective methods for subduing weeds.

Colonial agriculturists were well aware of these developments and how they contrasted with the situation in Ontario. There, bare summer fallowing had become increasingly central to the cropping system and, by the mid-nineteenth century, it represented a standard and near universal practice. The practice had become so widespread that some commentaries such as D. Christie's 1855 Presidential Address to the Agricultural Association of Upper Canada even suggest that it provided the basic distinction between agriculture in Ontario and Britain:

> Our mode of farming differs essentially from that now pursued in Britain. We have no course of rotation of crops, which there is generally practised. Their system is the four years' course — turnips, barley or oats, clover and wheat. Summer fallowing is seldom resorted to, as it is considered that the land can be sufficiently freed from weeds and grass by the hoeing and working of the land required for the turnip crop.[26]

Christie's address was delivered in the middle of an anxious decade for Ontario's farmers. One source of anxiety was the unusually low price of wheat during the early 1850s. Another was the need to profit from the veritable wheat "boom" ushered in by the Crimean War. Heady optimism over the strong market for wheat was tempered during the last half of the decade by increasingly serious outbreaks of the Hessian fly and wheat midge and there is some evidence to suggest that it was also tempered by the first signs of widespread soil exhaustion. Contemporary accounts frequently refer to the deleterious effects of continuous wheat cropping without compensating additions of manure or fertilizers and it seems that for many farmers, "their land was becoming so hard and weedy that it would scarcely produce ten bushels to the acre."[27]

The 1850s also witnessed a growing recognition of the unprecedented scale of the weed problem facing Ontario farmers and the first indications that new attitudes towards weeds were developing. Newspapers such as the *Canadian Agriculturist* and publications by the Board of Agriculture of Upper Canada were beginning to devote significant attention to the issue of unwanted and aggressive vegetation and, over the course of this decade, weeds became the target of increasingly violent rhetoric. Henry Youle Hind was amongst the first to sound a note of alarm. In 1850, while a lecturer in chemistry and natural history at the Normal School of Upper Canada, he presented a lecture on agriculture to a number of teachers' institutes in which he warned,

> The growth of weeds among cultivated crops, is an increasing and serious evil.... The use of clean seed, the practice of clean cultivation, of draining, and of rotation of crops, can alone eradicate these hurtful vegetables, which, from past neglect, seem now to be successfully struggling to gain exclusive possession of many fertile tracts of country.[28]

A similar cautionary note can also be found in the conclusion to Christie's 1855 annual address, "The great enemy to wheat is spear or couch grass, and it is a very difficult one to get rid of; if not checked it bids fair to take possession of our best wheat lands."[29] Any gardener who has attempted to do battle with this perennial species would probably agree with Christie's assessment of the threat that it poses. Like Canada thistle, it spreads through underground rhizomes and, once established, it is virtually impossible to eradicate through cultivation alone.

Severe outbreaks of the Hessian fly and wheat midge over the next four years tended to divert attention away from a growing weed problem but weeds were not completely overshadowed by these more dramatic pests. At the height of the insect scare in 1858, for example, the editor of the *Canadian Agriculturist* devoted a long editorial to weeds in which he argued that the best way of dealing with them was to keep the land in "a clean state of cultivation." Unfortunately this was "a matter not very easily accomplished in practice, especially in this climate where annual weeds are so numerous, prolific, and of so remarkably quick growth." To make matters worse, clean seed "is seldom to be procured ... no wonder, then, that we hear such constant complaints of the difficulty and expense of keeping land even tolerably clean."[30]

James Croil expressed a similar concern and unwittingly acted as a spokesman for an emerging subculture while speaking before the Dundas County Agricultural Society in 1859. Ironically, he paused in the process of extolling the virtues of British farming and agricultural science to exhort his audience "to wage a war of extermination against the weeds."[31] His passionate plea marks a significant departure from conventional British polemics and it ignores the traditional insight that the "complete extirpation" of weeds is impossible.[32] It did, however, have considerable rhetorical appeal in a land being overrun by unwanted vegetation and it subsequently became the standard rallying cry for agriculturists in Ontario, western Canada, and the northern - tier states.

The distinctive relationship between people and weeds that emerged in Ontario in the 1850s crystallized in the 1860s. Aggressive European plants continued to enjoy unprecedented success and Canada thistle, the "great enemy" of the wheat grower in the 1840s, now had a "strong hold" on "thousands of acres in this Province" and it had "literally overrun ... some of the older settlements of this Province, particularly in the Eastern sections."[33] Articles on weeds appeared in the farm press with increasing frequency and antiweed polemics became even more heated. Farmers were berated for their "slovenly farming" and weeds were well on their way to being considered an "unmitigated evil."[34]

The editors of the *Canadian Agriculturist* launched their 1863 volume by proclaiming the end of "the rough era, the chopping and clearing of the forest."[35] The "rough era" may have been drawing to a close, the editor warned, but the farmers' struggle with unwanted vegetation was far from over. In a March 1863 editorial, weeds supplanted the Hessian fly and wheat midge in the estimation of the paper's editors as the most serious problem facing agriculture in the colony. The editorial describes weeds as "the greatest barrier to agricultural improvement, and the profitable employment of farm capital" in Ontario and adds:

Some of the best yielding wheat soils twenty years ago, both in Canada and the neighboring States, have, in consequence of over cropping and negligent culture, become so much exhausted and filled with the seeds of the different varieties of weeds, as to be wholly incapable of yielding a remunerative crop; and no inconsiderable portion of such lands may now be regarded, for all practical purposes, as in a state of wilderness; not occupied, unfortunately, with stately forest trees, but with various species of pestiferous weeds, the bane of all successful cultivation.[36]

Later the same year, James Elliot, a farmer from King Township, proclaimed 1863 "a year of weeds" on the basis of the infested state of farms in the vicinity of Toronto and the paper ran yet another editorial on the weed menace under the title "WAR AGAINST THE THISTLES."[37]

The subject of this final editorial was the introduction to the Assembly of a bill aimed at preventing the spread of Canada thistle. While this bill was unique in proposing an act aimed solely at curbing the spread of weeds, it was not without precedent, for several earlier Ontario statutes contained weed eradication clauses. The earliest was a 1793 act for regulating public highways and roads. Section 9 required overseers to "direct all persons performing labour on the said highways and roads, to destroy as much as may be in their power, all burrs, thistles, and other weeds, that are hurtful to the purposes of husbandry."[38] In 1849, municipalities acquired the right to pass bylaws for "destroying or suppressing the growth of weeds detrimental to good husbandry."[39] Four years later, they also received the authority to force road and railway companies to comply with these bylaws on "all cleared land or ground belonging to such Company."[40]

Although these tough-sounding clauses remained on the books through the 1860s and beyond, they seem to have been as widely ignored by people as they were by weeds. One farmer commented in 1863, that in York Township, "a Bye-Law in existence some time ago seems to have become obsolete, as weeds abound to an alarming extent through the township, not only on waste land partially cleared, but on farms and lots under ordinary cultivation."[41] Contemporary comments by the editorial staff of the *Canadian Agriculturist*, Ontario's leading farm newspaper and the official organ of the Board of Agriculture of Upper Canada, suggest that in addition to being poorly enforced, weed eradication bylaws were poorly publicized. They were so obscure, in fact, that the paper's editors seem to have been unsure of their existence let alone their precise wording. For instance, in one 1861 article on Canada thistle they suggested that "clean culture and not allowing thistles to seed in waste places and on road sides against which we believe there is a statute, involve the general principles of prevention."[42] The phrase "we believe" and the lack of knowledge it implies reappears two years later in an editorial calling for stricter antiweed legislation:

> In Canada, we believe, enactments have been issued against allowing thistles to ripen on the road-sides and exposed public situations, both from the legislature and township corporations; and it is passing strange that such important and beneficial regulations on the proper observance of which both private and public wealth is so closely dependent should in many districts become practically inoperative.[43]

Agitation for stricter antiweed measures bore fruit in 1865 with the passage of The Canada Thistle Act of Upper Canada (see Appendix 1).[44] Under the terms of the act, land owners or occupiers were annually required to cut down or destroy Canada thistle prior to the setting of seed or face fines ranging from two to ten dollars. Highway overseers were charged with similar responsibilities on lands under their jurisdiction. Additionally, if overseers observed thistles on adjacent farm land, they were directed to notify the land owner of the presence of weeds. If no action was taken within five days of said notice, the overseer could enter the property and cut down the thistles without fear of prosecution. Municipal clerks had similar powers plus the right to enforce the act on railway companies. People who "knowingly" sold seed contaminated with the seeds of Canada thistle faced fines ranging from two to ten dollars and all officers who refused to enforce the act could be fined ten to twenty dollars. Finally, a refusal to pay fines could result in a unspecified prison sentence at the discretion of the local justice of the peace.

The new relationship between people and weeds in Ontario received government approval with the passage of the Canada Thistle Act of 1865. It was the first noxious-weed act in British North America and it effectively established a foundation and pattern for subsequent weed legislation in Ontario and the Prairie West. In common with many other features of the emerging relationship, it does not represent an absolute break with the British tradition — several of Britain's leading agricultural improvers in the late eighteenth and early nineteenth centuries had agitated for some form of weed legislation, and legislation was eventually passed by the British Parliament in 1920.[45] It does, however, represent a significant shift in emphasis and strong evidence of cultural change.

If Ontario's 1865 thistle act can be said to represent a clear expression of the human side of the distinctive colonial culture that was emerging in Ontario, the plant that it singles out equally symbolizes the culture's nonhuman dimension. *Cirsium arvense* was a common problem in Britain but it acquired a new identity and an enhanced significance in the New World. As mentioned in chapter one, this perennial member of the composite family is thought to have been introduced to New France sometime during the seventeenth century and, because of its adaptability and numerous attributes conferring weediness, it has subsequently spread to all the farming districts of Canada.[46] Exactly when the common field thistle of Britain acquired a new North American identity is unknown but as early as 1814 farmers in northern New York State were cursing "Canada thistle" as an unwanted import from the land bearing the plant's name.[47]

Cirsium arvense probably owes its common name to its early success in the fields of New France. By the 1830s, however, it was equally at home in both of the Canadas.[48] By the 1840s, it was regarded as the worst weed in Ontario and it held this dubious distinction until the early twentieth century. The successful colonization of Ontario by this European immigrant can be attributed in part to the fact that it is very difficult to eradicate using mechanical methods, particularly if it is allowed a period of grace in which to establish an extensive root system. Some peculiarities of the climate or environment also seem to have contributed to its impressive spread. According to one late-nineteenth-century Ontario weed expert, something about the North American environment encourages Canada thistle and some other European weeds to "flourish to a greater extent than even in the lands whence they came."[49] *Cirsium arvense* flourished to such a degree that by the late nineteenth century, it was widely regarded as Canadian in more than just name. One agricultural writer wryly observed that Canada thistle was commonly considered to be "indigenous to our soil and climate.... It has indeed obtained such a foothold upon Canadian farms, that we blush to think that outsiders may be readily excused for the assumption that it is a Canadian pet."[50]

Canada thistle and the act aimed at halting its spread figure prominently in J. C. Rykert's 1865 presidential address to the Agricultural Association in Upper Canada. His speech seems to capture the essence of the emerging relationship between people and weeds in Ontario in much the same manner as Benjamin Holdich does for the British tradition as described in chapter two:

> Another great source of evil to the farmer, and one which could readily be removed were proper efforts to be made, is the increasing growth of that scourge, the Canada thistle, which seems particularly indigenous to our soil. Year after year we are compelled to witness its gradual increase and in many parts of the country we find it has become master of the soil. It is needless to attempt to point out a remedy for the extirpation of so great an evil, which so long as it can find one farmer in a community who will not wage war against it, is sure to increase and multiply. Nothing but Legislative enactments with unlimited power will check its onward progress. It is to be hoped that the Act lately passed will be rigidly enforced by every friend of the farmer.[51]

By the mid-1860s, interactions between people and weeds in Ontario can be distinguished from their British equivalents on all three analytical levels. In nineteenth-century Britain, there was a rough, if far from harmonious, ecological balance between people and weeds. Contemporary sources indicate that this stability was tenuous and easily upset — weed populations, for example, may have increased during the French and Napoleonic Wars because of the acute labour shortage that attended it — but they give little indication that weed populations changed dramatically over the century as a whole. This contrasts sharply with the situation in Ontario where weed populations are described as increasing at phenomenal rates. In the absence of hard data, it is impossible to accurately determine just how severe the weed problem had become but most mid-nineteenth-century accounts strongly suggest that the weed populations per acre of farmland in Ontario were far in excess of those normally encountered in Britain.

Nineteenth-century British farmers usually employed a multitude of weapons in their conflict with weeds. Some techniques such as weeding and hoeing were solely aimed at extirpating weeds while others, including frequent tillage and crop rotation, served a number of functions in addition to subduing unwanted vegetation. For most farmers in Britain, eradicating weeds was not a discrete activity. Rather, responsibility for this task was spread throughout their entire arable farming system. Some farmers in Ontario did weed and rotate their crops and most practised some form of cultivation prior to sowing or after harvest. The vast majority, however, relied on a single procedure — a naked summer fallow — to keep their farms clean and relatively free of weeds.

Whether out of ignorance, choice, or circumstance, farmers were ignoring a number of the central tenets of good husbandry by relying heavily, and at times exclusively, on summer fallowing to keep weeds at bay. Had they read such popular works as William Marshall's *Rural Economy of Yorkshire* (1788), the specific consequences of their neglect would have been made clear. Writing on the topic of Canada thistle or the "COMMON CORN THISTLE," as he called it, Marshall noted, "Nature has been singularly attentive to the preservation of this species of plant.... Neither FALLOWING alone, nor WEEDING alone, will prevent its mischief: their joint efforts are necessary to keep it within bounds."[52]

Farmers were not the only people to exhibit a disregard for venerable British traditions. By the 1860s, the more articulate or literary-minded members of Ontario's agricultural community were regularly portraying weeds as foreign aggressors who were rapidly wresting farmland away from their human adversaries. Individual farmers were cast as helpless in the face of this evil onslaught and hope for the future was pinned on a general call to arms enforced by the legal might of the state. Emphasizing the aggressive, human-like qualities of weeds and their impending occupation of Ontario's farmland may have served to impress farmers with the need for immediate and vigorous action but it drew attention away from the vital role humans play in fostering the spread of weeds. British writers also used anthropomorphic terms to express their dislike for weeds but they rarely if ever carried their rhetoric to such fearful and oppositional extremes. Nor did they let their polemical flourishes obscure the point that weeds were inevitable and that they only presented a serious problem when farmers failed to follow the time-honoured measures aimed at suppressing their growth on the soils of the British Isles.

Explaining Cultural Change

The rapidly crystallizing relationship between people and weeds in Ontario was the product of a complex interplay between a number of ecological and social factors acting in conjunction with the environment. Some features of this relationship are relatively easy to explain; others are considerably more difficult. Included in the former would be explanations for the development of an unusually fearful and hostile attitude towards weeds and the subsequent passage of Canada's first noxious-weed act: both were mainly a response to the thriving state of Ontario's weed colonies. Determining why weeds were thriving to a degree unprecedented in Britain, however, definitely belongs to the latter category. Any attempt to resolve this issue is further complicated by the need to explain why it was European immigrants and not native species that ultimately challenged Ontario farmers for possession of their fields.

The predominance of European or Eurasian species in the weed flora of mid-nineteenth-century Ontario was not a unique phenomenon. Rather, it was something Ontario shared with all the British colonies in eastern North America and with the former colonies south of the border. The weed ecologist R. J. Aldrich, for example, estimates that about two-thirds of "the problem weeds in the United States" are introduced species, most notably from Europe.[53] Botanists and agriculturists have long been aware of this curious fact and its corollary, that relatively few North American species have become problem weeds in Europe, and they have proposed a number of mechanisms to explain it.[54] One of the earliest and most obvious explanations is that well into the nineteenth century, goods and people predominantly moved westward across the Atlantic.[55]

Although this argument has long been popular and still finds expression in weed ecology literature, it has rarely been presented as the only explanation for the preponderance of European weeds in North American fields and the relative absence of North American species in the fields of Europe. One weakness of this argument is that, while the flow of people and goods may have been mainly from east to west, it has never been unidirectional. Another is its failure to adequately explain why native species are relatively poorly represented in the weed flora of North America, particularly in the eastern sections of Canada and the United States.

E. W. Claypole, a lecturer at Antioch College, Ohio, was one of the first scientists to attempt a more comprehensive explanation for the dominance of European species in the weed floras of both Europe and North America. In an 1877 paper presented to the Montreal Horticultural Society, Claypole speculated that the successful naturalization of European plant species in North America was the result of a greater degree of adaptability or "plasticity" on the part of European flora.[56] Claypole's interpretation still has some merit but it too suffers from some serious weaknesses including a failure to adequately address the issue of why European flora is more adaptable than its North American counterpart.

Asa Gray, the leading American botanist of the nineteenth century, raised this very point two years later. Gray agreed with Claypole that the predominance of European weeds in North America could be partly attributed to a much heavier westward migration of plants across the Atlantic but he added that because eastern North America "was naturally forest-clad, there were few of its native herbs which, if they could bear the exposure at all, were capable of competition on cleared land with emigrants from the Old World."[57] The idea that European weeds have prevailed over native species in North America because of preadaptions to agriculture has stood the test of time surprisingly well and Gray's paper is still cited in scientific literature, even if modern explanations prefer to cast the argument in terms of preadaptions to ecological niches.[58] It has even been introduced to historians through the work of the noted American environmental historian Alfred Crosby who argues that the successful transplantation of European weeds and other "portmanteau biota" to North America and the other "Neo-Europes" was primarily the result of preadaptions to a "Europeanized" environment. More specifically, European weeds were better able to endure the harsh, exposed conditions found on arable fields because of their coevolution with farming.[59]

Preadaptions to agriculture explain the preponderance of European species on mid-nineteenth-century lists of the worst weeds of Ontario. While these species clearly deserve a great deal of credit for their own success, credit for their ability to flourish to a degree unprecedented in

Britain belongs to the environment and the settlers who attempted to transform it. The environment aided the cause of immigrant plants by providing a climate that was congenial to the activities of many species and yet, one that was too harsh to allow all the representatives of Britain's weed flora to migrate successfully.[60] Plants such as Canada thistle must have benefited significantly from reduced competition for space and resources. According to recent weed science literature, it would also seem that they benefited at least as much from an absence of the predators and parasites that kept weed populations in check in Europe.[61]

The historical geographer Kenneth Kelly once commented that "in terms of effect on agricultural development the forest cover was the prime physical characteristic of Ontario."[62] In terms of the influence of the environment on the culturing of weeds, this comment certainly rings true. Between 1800 and the 1860s, settlers waged a relentless war against forest species: plants out of place in the eyes of farmers. British travellers were often appalled at the ferocity with which settlers conducted their assault and, as early as the 1830s, they were struck by the "nakedness" of the cleared portions of Ontario and the adjacent United States and the prevalent idea that "wood is a nuisance" even in areas that had been effectively denuded.[63] The idea of forest as enemy was so powerfully ingrained in the minds of settlers that it was still being expressed in the 1860s. For example, James Johnson ignored a growing trend to regard the forest as a valuable if depleted resource when in 1864 he encouraged the members of the Agricultural Association of Upper Canada to avoid human strife and "confine our warfare to the subjugation of the forests."[64]

The forests of Ontario acted as both a physical and cognitive impediment to the recognition of weed problems. In physical terms, forest clearing demanded a great deal of labour which left little time or energy to attend to weeding amongst other niceties of good husbandry. Even when the trees were felled and burned, their stumps, roots, and regrowth were "so thickset as in many places to bid defiance to the plough and preclude any mode of cultivation except sowing and hand-raking the seed."[65] Historians estimate that it took between five and ten years after initial clearing before roots and stumps were rotted sufficiently to permit anything but the most cursory tillage.[66] This, in combination with the use of improperly cleaned seed and the protracted nature of carving a farm from the forest, meant that European weeds enjoyed years if not decades of relative freedom in which to establish themselves.[67] Freedom of action during these crucial establishment years was further guaranteed by the recolonization of clearings by forest species, the "first and greatest of the 'weed' problems encountered by the pioneer farmer."[68]

The sheer challenge of subduing the forest tended to divert attention away from a growing problem with imported weeds, the result being that many settlers were quite simply unable to see the weeds for the trees. In 1858, George Lawson, a newly appointed natural history professor at Queen's University, cautioned against making this very mistake:

> No sooner are the trees hewn down and the soil turned up, than the herbaceous weeds assert their place and power.… In your march forward into the woods forget not that the enemy comes in behind; and forget not that it is less honourable to make the conquest of new territory than it is to hold and defend that which has already been won.[69]

European weeds would probably have become a serious problem in Ontario even if the majority of farmers had engaged in a spirited defence against weedy aggression. Most farmers, however, were either unwilling or unable to mount such a defence. Instead, they practised a style of farming that was, in many respects, more favourable to culturing weeds than to culturing crops. British travellers, the local farm press, and historians alike have criticized Upper Canadian farmers for their extensive style of agriculture and failure to attend to the essential details of good husbandry. They have been described as "land butchers" who eschewed mixed farming in favour of "wheat mining," a term used to describe the wheat-fallow-wheat rotation described previously.[70] High initial soil fertility and an abundance of land were the environment's contribution to this "system" — a system that one critic in the 1850s argued "is better defined as the absence of any system at all."[71] He continued:

> There is however one redeeming qualification in regard to our agriculture, for which, if for nothing else, we may claim credit, and I am bound to accord it, and that is consistency — O yes, we are very consistent. We pay no attention to any regular rotation of crops; we regard

thorough cultivation as a matter of secondary importance, therefore we are quite consistent in giving ourselves no uneasiness at all, either to the accumulation or the application of manures.[72]

Historians have traditionally argued that this style of farming ultimately led to its own demise in the 1860s through widespread soil exhaustion and a resulting decline in wheat yields.[73] That an emphasis on wheat in the absence of a proper farming system led to a serious decline in soil fertility can be debated but there can be little doubt that it was very conducive to the growth and spread of weeds.[74] For a healthy stand of weeds was, in the days before the invention of herbicides, the inevitable consequence of inadequate cultivation and the overcropping of grain. A general decline in soil fertility would only have compounded this problem as weeds are generally more able to tolerate poor soil conditions than their domesticated brethren.

Some farmers chose to practice an extensive, weed-friendly style of farming out of inexperience, ignorance, expedience, or outright greed. Others chose it because it made sense in a country where land was cheap, abundant, and covered by trees. Summer fallowing, for instance, was highly effective in subduing forest regrowth even though it was costly and far less effective against farm weeds than a combination of weeding, rigorous cultivation, and growing hoed crops as part of a systematic rotation.[75] The majority of farmers, however, had little choice in the matter because of a number of socioeconomic constraints.

The first was the high cost and scarcity of labour. Most traditional British methods for eradicating weeds are very labour intensive and, as such, they simply were not feasible in a land where labour was both scarce and dear. Male labourers were not the only ones whose scarcity was felt for as the president of the Agricultural Association of Upper Canada observed in 1860, "The high standard of farming which obtains in Great Britain cannot so easily be arrived at with us in Canada, on account of one sort of labor, such as is done there by women and children, who are chiefly employed in weeding, hoeing, hay-making, and other light work of the farm."[76]

Ontario's weed problem was further exacerbated by a driving need to produce a cash crop. Most farmers lacked the necessary capital or outside sources of income to forego an immediate return from the land during the lengthy process of establishing a farm. They were forced, as a result, to produce a crop that could be sown within a year or two of initial clearing, one that could bear the expense and rigours of travel by road and one for which a large, ready market existed. During the first half of the nineteenth century the only crop that met these criteria was wheat.[77]

Poor roads and a severely limited market for produce other than wheat made it unprofitable and impractical for cash hungry farmers to diversify their operations. Until the 1860s or 1870s, these factors also precluded "any regular rotation of crops."[78] Through their inability to apply a systematic crop rotation, Ontario farmers were denied the use of a tried and trusted tool for maintaining soil fertility. More importantly, they were denied the use of the single most important cultural technique that British agriculturists had devised for maintaining weed populations at acceptable levels.

Ontario farmers were severely criticized by British travellers and the local farm press for their failure to implement a system of crop rotation. Centuries of British agricultural literature and experience informed this criticism and much of it was reasoned and valid. But, like many aspects of British advice regarding the treatment of weeds, it was difficult if not impossible to apply in the environmental and social context of Ontario. Poorness of fit between traditional British advice and local conditions represents a final social factor that aided and abetted the spread of weeds in Ontario. Agriculturists in Ontario did eventually cease to look to Britain for expert advice on weeds. The development of locally suitable recommendations for eradicating weeds, however, only occurred during the closing decades of the nineteenth century. By then, it was far too late to prevent immigrant weeds from posing an effective challenge to human immigrants for possession of the soil.

Conclusion

The relationship between people and weeds in Ontario began as a colonial offshoot of British culture. Most of the farmers were British as were many of the weeds, and Britain supplied virtually all of the expert advice on how relations between the two groups were to be conceptualized and governed. This body of advice had taken centuries to develop and it was beautifully tailored to restrain the activities of familiar plants that had long been part of the native flora and whose populations were regulated by a number of natural constraints. British recommendations for the eradication of weeds were also predicated on the availability of a cheap, plentiful supply of labour, the presence of long-cleared, easily tilled fields, and the ability of farmers to practice crop rotation in order to avoid the build-up of certain weeds that are particularly well adapted to growing with specific crops. In the opinion of the British weed scientist J. G. Elliot, "the tradition of abundant labor" in Britain until World War II was particularly important as it represents one of the chief historical differences between agriculture in Britain and North America.[79]

Fortunately for weeds, if not for farmers, none of these conditions applied to Ontario. Labour was expensive and scarce, the presence of stumps, roots, and rocks precluded all but the crudest of cultivation, and rotation was prohibited by a driving need to produce a cash crop. A lack of markets and inadequate transportation facilities further inhibited the ability of farmers to rotate their fields between crops of wheat, vegetables, and pasture. Forest regrowth, an abundance of land, and low labour requirements encouraged most farmers to practice a bare summer fallow but this technique alone was unable to halt the development of unusually healthy weed populations in comparison to Britain. Weedy immigrants found all of these conditions very much to their liking. Those that were able to adjust to Ontario's climate discovered a land of opportunity that was free from many of the cultural and natural constraints that governed their lives back home. Would-be native competitors posed little problem once their ranks were decimated by the weedy colonists' human associates and potential adversaries were too busy pursuing their own territorial ambitions to prevent European weeds from putting down roots and establishing thriving New World colonies.

The unprecedented success of immigrant weeds evoked a harsh response from their human adversaries — a response that ultimately culminated in the passage of Canada's first noxious-weed law in 1865. Britain provided little precedent for the passage of the Canada Thistle Act of Upper Canada and this statute represents a clear expression of an emerging national identity. Although it represents a milestone in the development of an essentially modern relationship between agriculturists and weeds in Ontario, this piece of legislation is, nevertheless, far too obscure to qualify as a symbol for a new nation. A far more appropriate symbol is the plant that it legislates against: *Cirsium arvense*, "the thistle 'of Canada' *par excellence*."[80]

4

Dominion of the West,
1867–1905

This chapter presents the story of the further evolution of colonial culture in Ontario, its westward migration and subsequent flowering on the broad expanses of the Canadian Prairies. During the period between Confederation and the creation of two new western provinces in 1905, the roots of the ongoing conflict between people and weeds in the West were planted as were most of today's educational and statutory antiweed measures. The era was one of paper diplomacy and intense propaganda and it witnessed the entrenchment of a blindly oppositional view of weeds in response to the rapid advance of aggressive immigrant vegetation. This tide of weedy invaders met some human resistance but the period is best portrayed as one of relatively peaceful territorial expansion by immigrant plant and human populations and as a prelude to the inevitable conflict to come.

The chapter begins with a section on developments in Ontario between 1867 and the turn of the century. During these years, state-funded, professional weed experts supplanted British authorities as the main source of information on weeds and their suppression. They tailored their control recommendations to fit local conditions, and through the application of a thin gloss of science, added a new lustre to violent antiweed rhetoric. The teachings of this first

Tumble mustard, *Sisymbrium altissimum*

generation of Canadian agricultural scientists were soon being transmitted to farmers in Manitoba and the North-West Territories. Both began as colonies of Ontario from whence they initially drew the majority of their settlers, not to mention a weed-friendly style of farming and a large number of weeds. The second section deals with these issues as well as with Ontario's influence on the early development of western noxious-weed legislation. The section concludes with a discussion of how eastern experts spread the rhetoric of war to a land where the need for conflict was still only dimly perceived.

The final portion investigates a process that was underway at the same time as the West was being won: the development of a distinct western identity. Prairie governments had, by 1905, instituted a number of unprecedented policies in response to an equally unprecedented problem with weeds. Some of these weed problems were familiar to farmers in Ontario but many were not, and if Canada thistle (*Cirsium arvense* (L.) Scop.) can be said to symbolize the subculture of weeds in the East, the same is true of Russian thistle (*Salsola pestifer* Nels.) in Manitoba and the North-West Territories. A little-known immigrant from the steppes of eastern Europe, Russian thistle spread so rapidly on the Northern Plains that, in the words of Dominion Botanist James Fletcher, it almost seemed to have "partaken of the conquering spirit of the West."[1]

Weeds and Weed Experts in Ontario, 1867–1900

The period between 1867 and 1900 was one of great change for the farmers of Ontario.[2] In the 1870s, improved market conditions, declining yields, and growing western competition encouraged a general shift away from wheat production towards a pattern of mixed farming. This meant that summer fallowing was largely abandoned in favour of crop rotation and more intensive cultivation.[3] The following decade saw the Ontario government beginning to take a more active role in fostering agricultural improvement.[4] At the start of the decade, the government sponsored a commission to inquire into the state of agriculture in the province. The commission's findings were subsequently published and made widely available both as a complete report and as a practical guide to farming.[5] Towards the end of the decade agriculture received full ministry status.

During the 1870s and 1880s, farmers also gained greater access to agricultural education from local sources of advice and expertise. In 1874, after decades of agitation for a college of agriculture and a failed attempt to establish agricultural studies at the University of Toronto, the Ontario Agricultural College and Experimental Farm (OAC) was officially opened at Guelph.[6] The college initially suffered from a lack of resources and poor attendance but, by the late 1880s, under the able leadership of President James Mills, the OAC was well on the way to becoming the leading agricultural college in the Dominion and the main research and extension arm of the Ontario Ministry of Agriculture. Beginning in 1880, the research and extension activities of the college were expanded through the creation of the Ontario Agricultural and Experimental Union (OAEU). Comprised of the faculty and alumni of the OAC, the OAEU provided the college and the provincial government with the ability to conduct field trials throughout the province, and it was soon involved in a wide range of practical research and demonstration programs.

Both the OAC and the Experimental Union co-operated closely with yet a third source of expertise that was made available in the late 1880s: the staff of the Central Experimental Farm at Ottawa. The Dominion Experimental Farms System was created in 1886, and it has been the dominant agricultural research institution in the country ever since its inception.[7] With the establishment of divisional specialists in Ottawa and well-staffed experimental farms at Nappan, Nova Scotia, Brandon, Manitoba, Indian Head, North-West Territories, and Agassiz, British Columbia, it was not long before the system also emerged as one of the leading sources of information for the farming community.

The establishment of the OAC and the Dominion Experimental Farms System provided the context for the further evolution of the relationship between agriculturists and weeds in Ontario. Both contributed to the creation of a new breed of weed expert — the government-funded agricultural scientist — decades in advance of similar developments in Britain, and both created experts who drew their authority from a combination of science and the state.[8] Much of their knowledge continued to be drawn from British farming literature but, unlike their amateur predecessors, the practical farming experience of these new professionals was firmly rooted in Ontario.

The weed experts at the OAC — J. Hoyes Panton, Thomas Shaw, Charles A. Zavitz, and F. C. Harrison — all spent their formative years on southern Ontario farms. Shaw, who held the positions of farm superintendent and professor of agriculture between 1888 and 1893, was largely self-taught while Panton, the college's natural history and geology professor, held a bachelor's degree from the University of Toronto.[9] Their assistants and later professors in their own right, Zavitz and Harrison, were graduates of the institution that later employed them.[10] Even James Fletcher, a man who gained a reputation as Canada's leading "apostle of clean farming," drew most of his first-hand experience from Ontario and later, the West.[11] Born in England where he trained as an accountant, twenty-two-year-old Fletcher arrived in Canada in 1874.[12] He soon entered the civil service as an assistant parliamentary librarian in Ottawa, and it was there that he taught himself the elements of botany and entomology. Fletcher was so successful in his studies that he was appointed honorary Dominion entomologist in 1884. Two years later, he became the head of the entomology and botany division of the Dominion Experimental Farms System.

Fletcher, Panton, Shaw, Zavitz, and Harrison learned about farming in a land where a serious weed problem persisted despite significant structural changes in agriculture. In 1884, for example, the nation's most prominent botanist, John Macoun, wrote that many "country roads in Ontario are almost impassable in summer owing to the prevalence" of Canada thistle (*Cirsium arvense* L.).[13] He also noted that between Brighton and Toronto, "on the line of the G. T. R., many fields during June are quite yellow with the flowers" of wild mustard *(Sinapsis arvensis* L.).[14] A decade later, Thomas Shaw complained

the extent to which certain varieties of noxious weeds have been allowed to multiply is simply alarming. Some of them are, in a sense, taking possession of the land. Notably is this true of wild mustard, the Canada thistle, and the ragweed in Ontario.... In several sections of Ontario, the seeds of the wild mustard are so numerous in the soil that, though no more seeds were allowed to ripen during the present generation, there would probably still be a few left to grow plants for the next generation to destroy.[15]

Shaw and his colleagues at the OAC suspected that not only was the weed problem serious but that "weeds [were] on the increase in Ontario, both in number and species."[16] Their suspicions were subsequently confirmed by an 1898 questionnaire distributed to the members of the Ontario Agricultural and Experimental Union. In response to the question, "Are the weeds in your neighborhood more numerous and more troublesome than they were ten years ago?" the majority of the correspondents reported that "weeds are far more numerous than they were, and … the injury done by them is far greater."[17] Most of the injury was still resulting from long-standing problems such as Canada thistle, wild mustard, and wild oats *(Avena fatua* L.) but new species were also making their presence felt.[18] These included stinkweed (*Thlaspi arvense* L.), field bindweed *(Convolvulus arvensis* L.) and, in particular, perennial sow-thistle (*Sonchus arvensis* L.).[19] According to at least one expert on the subject, the latter had displaced Canada thistle as "the worst weed in the Province of Ontario" by the first decade of the twentieth century.[20] Looking a bit like a dandelion on steroids, perennial sow-thistle is noted for its ability to spread rapidly following its initial introduction into an area, and while it lacks the prickly nature of Canada thistle, it more than makes up for this deficiency by its sheer fecundity.

The ongoing success of immigrant plants in turn-of-the-century Ontario bears mute testimony to the difficulty of eradicating weeds once they have become firmly established. Given time, improved farming techniques did have the potential to make significant inroads on existing weed populations but even the most progressive farmers appear to have had difficulty adjusting their practices fast enough to deal with the steady arrival of new weedy species. There is also a possibility that farmers simply placed too much faith in the power of legislative enactments to halt the spread of weeds. The Canada Thistle Act of 1865 was amended at least twice between the time of its passage and the close of the century but, as the Ontario Agricultural Commission intoned in 1881,

> in noticing the cultivation of various crops it would hardly be proper to omit allusion to some of the eminently prolific species of spontaneous or voluntary productions that appear with a degree of certainty and regularity in too many sections of country. Among these the Canada

thistle as it is termed, stands conspicuous. Its increase is even alarming in some districts, and its tenacity in holding its own and propagating itself defies even the power and authority of the Legislature to restrain or suppress it.[21]

The failure of Ontario's early noxious-weed legislation can be attributed to a number of factors. Weeds, for one, simply refused to recognize the power of human laws to govern and regulate their actions. Farmers also appear to have been uncowed by the coercive power of the state both because Ontario was so heavily infested with Canada thistle and other weeds that it made a mockery of a zero-tolerance law and because the act was essentially unenforced. Nearly every late-nineteenth-century reference to the weed statute describes it as "a dead letter."[22] In 1898, about ninety-five percent of the respondents to an OAEU questionnaire answered "*No* most emphatically" to the question: "Are the provisions of the weed law enforced in your township?"[23] The reasons provided for this lack of enforcement include a fear of losing votes on the part of township councils, municipal pathmasters wishing to avoid "incurring the enmity of neighbors," and the difficulty of enforcing the act on "rented farms, especially such as belong to loan companies."[24]

The inability of Ontario's weed legislation to stem the tide of weedy aggression led the government to place increasing emphasis on education rather than on coercion. This shift in emphasis began in the late 1880s and the task of educating the farming public primarily fell on the shoulders of the staff of the OAC. Most of the burden was borne initially by J. Hoyes Panton. A highly respected teacher, researcher, and scientist, his activities included lecturing on weed identification and biology, regular speaking engagements at various farmers' institutes and agricultural society meetings, and writing articles on weed biology and ecology for distribution to agricultural newspapers in both Ontario and the Prairie West. He directed the planting of a demonstration weed garden and, as his annual reports to the college reveal, he was constantly on the alert for the arrival of new plants to add to his growing collection.[25] Panton's reports also mention that he acted as an unofficial provincial botanist and entomologist. By the mid-1890s, he was complaining that because of the time spent "answering correspondence relating to injurious plants and insects," he had little time for research or for preparing his lectures.[26]

Panton was also kept busy as the author of several government pamphlets on weeds. The first was issued in 1887 under the auspices of the Ontario Department of Agriculture and with it an enduring tradition was born. Over the next decade or so, Panton and his OAC colleagues authored at least five practical guides to weed identification and control and the college staff still bears this responsibility in Ontario today. OAC professor J. F. Alex's book *Ontario Weeds* (1992), for example, is the direct descendant of Panton's small five-page pamphlet *Weeds* (1887).[27] These bulletins were freely available upon request and they were issued in the thousands long before the first government weed bulletin made its appearance in Britain.[28] By 1900, F. C. Harrison's *Some Common Ontario Weeds* weighed in at an impressive eighty pages of pictures and text. The size of the bulletin hints at both the severity of the weed problem in Ontario and the relative ignorance of Ontario farmers in comparison to their British counterparts. Harrison himself alluded to both of these distinctive features of Ontario agriculture when he reported that

a leading educational authority lately said he did not believe that one farmer in a dozen could give the generally accepted common names of twenty of our common weeds. Whether this is so or not, one thing is certain, viz., that noxious weeds are spreading very rapidly in the Province of Ontario, and farmers need all the information they can get to assist them in preventing further loss from this very serious hindrance to successful agriculture.[29]

The federal government began to issue its own weed bulletins during the 1890s and by the first decade of the twentieth century these pamphlets had become full-fledged books.[30] It is impossible to estimate the proportion of Ontario's farmers who were exposed to this weed-related literature but, judging from the number of bulletins issued and the volume of requests for information received by Panton, Fletcher, and others, their numbers must have been substantial.[31]

Even adult illiteracy was not a bar to the spread of the antiweed message. Aware that farmers could be informed through their children, James Mills and Thomas Shaw were asked to co-author a school book on *The First Principles of Agriculture* (1890). Charles James, the deputy minister of agriculture for Ontario and a former professor of chemistry at the

Ontario Agricultural College, published a similar textbook in 1899 that was widely distributed "for use in the Public, Separate and High Schools of Ontario."[32] Both books devote considerable space to the issue of weeds as does a final source of information that became available during the 1890s: Thomas Shaw's independent venture, *Weeds, and How to Eradicate Them* (1893).

Shaw's book anticipates similar British publications by over a quarter of a century and it provides one more small piece of evidence of the cultural change underway in Ontario.[33] Change is also evident in the specific messages delivered by Shaw and his provincial and federal colleagues. For example, they regularly prefaced their discussion of weeds by defining them as "plants out of place," whereas no single definition dominated contemporary British writings on the subject.[34] The appearance of a standard definition for the term probably reflects the greater degree of bureaucratic control over weed literature in Ontario. As Shaw reminded his readers, it also reflected the simple fact that most of the province's "troublesome and aggressive weeds are foreigners."[35]

As mentioned in chapter one, the origins of this definition can be traced back to Britain. So too can the general antiweed measures advocated by government weed experts. Their specific advice, however, increasingly took the labour, market, and growing conditions of Ontario into account. In his 1900 bulletin, for example, Harrison advocated the use of "Indian corn" as a hoed crop, urged farmers to remove "all obstacles to cultivation," and argued that "snake fences" should be "got rid of as soon as possible" because of their tendency to provide places of refuge for weeds.[36] None of these specific recommendations can be found in contemporary British literature. There, cool summers precluded the economic production of maize, fields had long been cleared of obstacles such as roots and piles of stones, and weeds found refuge in places such as ditches and under hedge-rows rather than in the angles of log snake fences — a style of fencing that was effectively unknown in Britain.

Most of these adaptations represent the product of a growing body of experience rather than the fruits of scientific discovery. As was the case in Britain, Canadian agricultural scientists only began serious scientific investigations into weed biology, ecology, and eradication long after the nineteenth century had come to an end. Nineteenth-century investigations were limited to an attempt by Thomas Shaw to determine the cost and effectiveness of various techniques for ridding the college farm of weeds, to two minor experiments by Panton on the root growth of Canada thistle and on different methods for killing field bindweed, and finally, in 1899, to a series of trials by the OAC and Central Experimental Farm on the use of iron and copper sulfate sprays for the eradication of wild mustard in grain.[37]

The most striking evidence of a departure from British conventions in the late-nineteenth-century weed literature of Ontario is the entrenchment of violent antiweed rhetoric and a near complete absence of the traditional British sense of restraint. Ontario weed specialists were undoubtedly aware of the link between poor husbandry and the development of weed problems but they chose instead to focus on weeds as an external enemy rather than as evidence of the enemy within. Thomas Shaw's 1893 book, for instance, begins with a reference to the biblical curse and portrays the "alarming" spread of weeds in Canada as "a stigma on the agriculture of any country, and a withering criticism on the defectiveness of the modes of cultivation that are practised in it."[38] The remainder of the treatise, however, decidedly downplays the culpability of farmers, emphasizes the "necessity" for waging "a war of extermination" against weeds and is dedicated to staying "the progress of the great tide of weed invasion and weed aggression."[39]

In their government weed bulletins of 1893 and 1897 respectively, J. Hoyes Panton and James Fletcher also berated farmers for their carelessness and neglect but they took most of the sting out of their criticism by praising farmers for paying more attention to weeds during recent years.[40] Panton followed his brief critique of past practices by urging farmers to press their "warfare against weeds" and by suggesting "that weeds must be classed with such enemies as parasitic plants and insects."[41] Fletcher adopts a similar rhetorical stance when he describes weeds as "aggressive enemies" against which the farmer "should be constantly on the alert."[42] Even school children were being taught that weeds "can be subdued" and that "every weed should be considered an intruder, a thief, and a murderer of other crops."[43]

A Colony of Ontario

At the same time as government experts were emerging as leaders in the war on weeds in Ontario, large-scale agricultural settlement was well underway in the Prairie West. Between Confederation and the late 1890s, this process was largely driven by Ontario with Manitoba and, to a lesser extent, the North-West Territories effectively representing colonies of the central province.[44] As British immigrants had done one or two generations before, Ontarian settlers brought a great deal of cultural baggage with them — baggage that included agricultural techniques and ideas about farming, crop seeds, and their weedy contaminants. They were also accompanied by Ontario-style noxious-weed laws and, before the century had ended, by a deluge of eastern weed lore and expert advice.

The 1870s and early 1880s witnessed the establishment of "fully-commercial agriculture" in Manitoba.[45] Like pioneer farming in Ontario, it was based on the production of a single cash crop — wheat — and the ability of virgin soils to provide adequate yields with minimal inputs. At the height of Manitoba's settlement boom in 1882, botanist John Macoun enthused that "the fertility of the ground" in the Red River Valley was so great that it could "be considered as practically inexhaustible ... bad husbandry has little effect on the crop for many years."[46] A visiting agriculture professor from England, Henry Tanner, made a similar claim in 1883 and he was equally untroubled by the current system of "rough culture."[47]

Tanner's rough culture generally consisted of a single spring plowing followed by broadcast sowing of wheat and harrowing to cover the seed.[48] Period sources frequently comment on the subsequent lack of tillage, the use of dirty seed, an absence of manuring, the continuous production of wheat, and the fact that other "approved" practices such as "rotations are almost unknown."[49] In 1900, the Manitoba Department of Agriculture and Immigration criticized the first generation of farmers in the province for their "tendency to crop the land for all that can be got out of it, leaving posterity to shift for itself."[50] Manitoban farmers were, in other words, being condemned for "wheat mining" just as their predecessors had been in Ontario.

Even summer fallowing was little practised before 1885, although the technique was apparently used during the 1820s by some of the Red River settlers.[51] By the mid-1890s, however, a regular summer fallow was considered "absolutely necessary in the West to ensure a crop" and it remained "a commonplace in the methods of practical western farmers through the 1920s."[52] The significance of summer fallowing to Prairie agriculture is clearly indicated by statistics collected by Manitoba's Department of Agriculture and Immigration: in 1893, just under twenty percent of the cultivated farm land in Manitoba was devoted to fallow and the mean for the period 1890 to 1905 is over fifteen percent.[53] Angus Mackay, the superintendent of the Dominion Experimental Farm at Indian Head, is often described as the "father" of summer fallowing on the Prairies, but although he clearly publicized and improved the technique, its origin remains obscure.[54] A more likely if only partial explanation for its origin and subsequent popularity is the influence of farmers from Ontario.

The specific operations undertaken when summer fallowing a field will be discussed in the following section on adaptations to the western environment. Before proceeding further, however, it is important to note that in the West, summer fallowing served two main functions: killing weeds and water conservation. According to S. A. Bedford, the superintendent of the Dominion Experimental Farm at Brandon, the former usually took precedence over the latter: "No doubt the *main* object, and with many the only object, is to destroy weeds."[55] Summer fallowing may have helped to keep down weeds but as developments in Ontario had already shown, fallowing by itself was incapable of halting their spread or long-term increase.

Imported European weeds almost certainly made their first appearance in the West as companions to the vegetables sown by fur traders and by the 1860s familiar species such as Canada thistle and wild mustard were well established around posts such as Fort Garry.[56] It was not until the late 1870s wheat boom in Manitoba, however, that weedy colonization began in earnest. By the early 1880s, wild mustard was "prevalent" in the Red River Valley and Old World species such as lamb's-quarters (*Chenopodium album* L.), wild buckwheat, Canada thistle, and wild oats were said to "abound" in various parts of Manitoba.[57] The predominance of annuals in this list of pioneering weeds reflects their ability to multiply faster than less prolific but more tenacious perennials such as Canada thistle. Not surprisingly, all of these annual species are well adapted to life in a grain field and have long been associated with the production of wheat.

Preoccupied with other concerns, early settlers seem to have over-looked this weedy invasion. As late as 1894 one commentator remarked that the "farmers of Manitoba, as a whole, have not as yet been much troubled by noxious weeds."[58] Farmers in general may not have been much troubled by weeds up to this time but, as other contemporary reports imply, they probably should have been. According to a farmer from Brandon, imported weeds, "notably Canada thistle and wild mus-tard, which all who came from Ontario know as old enemies," were, by 1892, already "thriving" in "some parts of the country."[59] A year later, Angus Mackay reported that another familiar "enemy," lamb's-quarters, was causing "great loss" to farmers in the vicinity of Indian Head, North-West Territories.[60]

Exactly from where, when, and how these weeds arrived is poorly doc-umented but many appear to have migrated from Ontario in the company of their human counterparts. The editor of the popular Winnipeg news-paper the *Nor'-West Farmer* clearly identified Ontario as a major source of weeds in 1890 when he warned,

> it is now nearly time to look out for the noxious weeds that the care-lessness and culpable neglect of past years have contributed very much to make [*sic*] a certain and unfailing crop for long years to come. It will be a very pertinent matter for observation to take note of the consequences of importations of Ontario oats during the last winter. That province has got so overrun with weeds of too many sorts, and especially with thistles that the 'Canada thistle' has come to be a great deal more known than admired over half this continent.... There must have been a considerable addition to the stock of wild oats here also from this season's importation, and wherever the manure from this sort of feed has been left either on cultivated or wild land there is pretty certain to be a good showing of those very obnoxious immigrant weeds this fall and this spring.[61]

Eight years later, a widely distributed federal government weed bulletin noted that Canada thistle had spread "right across the continent to the Pacific;" in the North-West Territories, it "seems to have come to stay and is very plentiful along the northern branches of the railway."[62]

Ontario-style noxious-weed laws had, by the 1890s, also come to stay. Manitoba's Canada Thistle Act of 1871 was enacted during the first session of the province's first parliament and it represents a simplified version of the 1865 Canada Thistle Act of Upper Canada.[63] The striking resemblance between the legislation of the two provinces was further enhanced in 1882 when Manitoba amended its weed act to include nearly all of the original provisions of the Upper Canada statute that had been left out eleven years previously. Just as in Ontario, municipal authorities were charged with enforcing the legislation, they were given the right to destroy weeds on private land at the owner's expense, and explicit reference was made to the responsibilities of railway companies.[64] A similar ordinance was passed by the North-West Territories in 1888, and, in 1890, Manitoba weed legislation was again brought into line with current Ontario laws.[65] Like the Ontario statute of 1884, Manitoba's 1890 Noxious Weed Act expanded the designation "noxious weed" to include several plant species and it enabled municipalities to designate other species as noxious through the passage of municipal by-laws.[66]

Prairie antiweed laws were initially greeted with considerable optimism. William Fream, a leading British agricultural scientist who toured the Prairies in 1884, certainly saw their potential:

> It is easier to prevent the spread of noxious weeds in a new country than in one where the soil has long been under cultivation, but in a new country it is difficult unless there is concerted action over a wide area. This, however, is the case in Manitoba, and it may perhaps surprise English farmers to know that every owner or occupier of land must cut or cause to be cut down, or otherwise destroyed, all wild mustard, wild oats, and Canada thistles growing thereon.[67]

Initial optimism, however, soon gave way to increasingly harsh criticism of the manner in which the law was enforced. A correspondent to the *Nor'-West Farmer* suggested in 1887 that the average municipal noxious-weed inspector in Manitoba was "only a needy hanger on of the party in power, with nothing but his impecuniosity to recommend him for the position."[68] A few years later, the paper's editor called for municipal authorities to be supervised by the Ministry of Agriculture if "the law is not to be a dead letter."[69] By the mid-1890s, even the government of Manitoba was publicly acknowledging the inadequacy of existing legislation. In the province's first official weed bulletin, "Carelessness on the part of officials in carrying out the provisions of the law" was cited as one of the main obstacles hindering recognition of a growing weed problem.[70]

An even greater obstacle was a lack of knowledge on the part of settlers. Many had little experience with farming in general and most were inexperienced when it came to farming on the Prairies. Western governments began to address this problem seriously in the 1890s when, lacking weed experts of their own, they dipped into the pool of expertise that had developed in Ontario. James Fletcher was particularly influential. He was "one of the principal sources of material for numerous provincial publications on weeds" and was directly responsible for the preparation of the first comprehensive weed bulletins published by the governments of Manitoba and the North-West Territories in 1896 and 1898 respectively.[71] Demand for the first edition of Manitoba's *Noxious Weeds and How to Destroy Them* (1896) was so great that all 12,000 copies were quickly distributed and the government was forced to issue a new edition the following year.[72] This edition was also heavily indebted to the work of Fletcher and it bears the unmistakable stamp of attitudes that had developed earlier in Ontario. The first paragraph begins by suggesting that farmers have "been slow to learn that the battle with weeds is after all a serious matter." It then proceeds to soften this criticism by applauding farmers for showing more interest in the subject of "weedy plants and the best means of destroying them" before concluding with a strongly worded version of the standard definition:

Weeds are often tersely defined by farmers as dirt. It is a good definition, for dirt is matter out of place, and weeds are plants in the wrong place; namely, where they may do harm.[73]

Government bulletins were not the only means by which western farmers were introduced to an eastern view of weeds. Between 1891 and 1893, the widely read western edition of the *Farmer's Advocate* ran a lengthy series of weed articles by J. H. Panton and, by 1904, the editorial staff of both the *Advocate* and its cross-town Winnipeg rival, the *Nor'-West Farmer*, were headed by recent graduates of the OAC.[74] Both newspapers and many prairie dailies also introduced farmers to the antiweed gospel of the East through their extensive coverage of James Fletcher's western weed tours.[75] Beginning in 1896 and for many years afterwards, Fletcher spent one or two months each summer touring the West and lecturing on the subject of weeds and injurious insects. Accompanied by provincial officials and provided free transportation by the railways, he managed to address thousands of farmers in hundreds of communities over the years.[76] At each stop he provided farmers with detailed descriptions of the weeds "most to be feared in each locality," prescribed remedies for "the common species of aggressive weeds occurring on their land" and, as reported in the *Leader* (Regina), warned them against the danger of complacency in a land still relatively free of this terrible scourge:

To be forewarned was to be forearmed, and if they knew about the weeds before they got strong hold among them then they could the more easily fight them when they came. The fact that weeds were growing around the elevators and along the railway tracks ought to make them not only interested but frightened. To play with these weeds was playing with fire.... Let them all therefore learn to recognise the enemy as soon as it made its first appearance.[77]

The adversarial view of weeds promoted by Fletcher and his eastern colleagues soon became a standard part of public discourse in the West. Farmers such as Edmund Drury, of Rapid City, Manitoba, learned to define a weed as "simply a plant out of place" and a host of articles warned that the "enemy" was not easily "annihilated," stressed the importance of "eternal vigilance on the part of every individual farmer," and cautioned that even after a few years of relatively clean crops, the "battle with noxious weeds is only well begun."[78] By the turn of the century, weeds were almost always portrayed in a negative, oppositional light. As an editor of the Regina *Leader* stated, "That noxious weeds are an unmitigated evil is pretty generally admitted."[79]

Shaping a Western Identity

Fletcher was once again in the West in 1903, and during an address to the newly formed Natural History Club of Manitoba, he made yet another passionate plea for prompt action: "There is a time in the history of weeds ... when they are new in the land and weak. That is the time to attack them."[80] Unfortunately for Fletcher's antiweed crusade and western farmers in general, this time had already passed. The discussion that follows represents a continuation of the story that began in the previous chapter and chronicles the emergence of the main features of the relationship between weeds and agriculturists that survives on the Prairies to this day. Immigrant species found that the West provided a social and physical environment that was even more congenial to their growth and spread than conditions in Ontario. It took time for farmers and agricultural scientists to adapt their techniques to these new conditions and to put rigorous antiweed measures in place. By then a host of familiar and not so familiar weeds were already well established.

Prairie weed culture was destined to diverge from its Ontario counterpart even before the first sod was turned. The Prairies were home to many plants that had evolved in an environment marked by frequent animal disturbances, drought, and a lack of tree cover. These species were, as a result, already well equipped to take advantage of the conditions that accompany arable farming.[81] In 1884, for example, William Fream was struck by the near complete absence of European weeds in the massive fields of the recently created Bell Farm near Indian Head. He did report, however, that "in the case of one field, the prairie rose (*Rosa* sp.) seemed to have acquired undisputed possession at the beginning of June."[82]

By the close of the nineteenth century, it had become clear that while "it is usual to look to other countries" for the "origin of noxious weeds," many indigenous western species "have found in cultivated soil very congenial homes, and have become troublesome pests."[83] This fact is well documented in James Fletcher's 1898 pamphlet, *The Worst Weeds of the North-West*, where fully eleven of the twenty-seven weeds listed are native and nine are uniquely western species.[84] Some of these were locally "stigmatized as 'the worst weed[s] in the country,'" and a number of them such as common pepper-grass (*Lepidium densiflorum* Schrad.) and povertyweed (*Iva axillaris* Pursh) are still considered problem weeds under certain conditions.[85]

As troublesome as these native plants were, alien species had, by the 1890s, effectively usurped indigenous plants as the worst weeds on western farms. The big advantage enjoyed by recent immigrants was relative freedom from a range of predators and pathogens that restricted their populations in Europe. Another advantage was their preadaptation to an agrarian lifestyle, or more specifically, their ability to compete with crops and complete an entire life cycle between the time of seeding and harvest. Unlike their native competitors, almost all imported species had seeds that were difficult to remove from grain using the relatively crude seed-cleaning techniques employed by most farmers. Also unlike their native counterparts, imported perennials were used to having their roots disturbed by cultivation and some even seemed to welcome this rough form of attention.

A number of these imported weeds had been troubling farmers in Ontario for decades but, as one observer noted in 1893, the imported weed flora of the West was not identical to that of the East: "there are many weeds, such as mullein, yarrow and Mayweed, which, though troublesome in Ontario, are harmless in Manitoba, and several of the most common Manitoba weeds are almost or entirely unknown in the east."[86] Even Canada thistle and wild mustard were considered "far less troublesome than many other weeds" on the Prairies whereas several minor eastern nuisances flourished on "prairie soils" like "nowhere else."[87]

Prominent amongst the latter was stinkweed (*Thlaspi arvense* L.). Stinkweed, or "pennycress" as it is commonly called in Britain, hails from western Europe where it has long been considered a nuisance on pastures and fallow. Able to taint meat and dairy products when grazed by livestock, this pungent-smelling, annual member of the mustard family probably crossed the Atlantic at an early date — one account suggests that it was first introduced to New England in woolen goods from Britain whereas another maintains that it "was imported originally from France to Quebec" — and, by 1818, it was reported as "common" in the vicinity of Detroit.[88] Stinkweed was collected at Fort Garry in 1860, and, by 1883, botanist John Macoun described it as "abundant in many parts of Quebec; scarce in Ontario; but a real pest in Manitoba and around all the Hudson Bay Co. Posts in the North-west Territory."[89]

T. arvense's connection with Quebec and French-speaking settlers is suggested by another of its common names — "French weed." In both Quebec and Ontario, however, it remains "mainly a weed of waste places," while it has long been regarded as a "serious pest in the areas of intensive grain growing in Western Canada."[90] One early commentator speculated that French weed was "peculiarly adapted to the nitrogenous soil of Manitoba" and that it spread rapidly in the vicinity of Winnipeg and along the Red River because "little notice was taken of it, as it was a new weed, and no one thought it to be of any consequence."[91] More recent literature suggests that stinkweed flourishes on the Prairies because it is well adapted to grain culture, matures and sheds its seed prior to the harvesting of wheat, easily tolerates cold and drought, and can compete successfully with crops for a "limited moisture supply."[92]

Stinkweed was so successful in Manitoba by 1890 that it "alone [had] for all practical purposes of cultivation lowered the value of the old river lands at least one half, often very much more."[93] Within a few years Winnipeg newspapers were describing it as "ten times as bad as yellow mustard or Canada thistles."[94] James Fletcher's 1895 annual report describes stinkweed as "undoubtedly the most abundant weed in Manitoba, the peculiar greenish yellow colour of the unripe pods in infested crops in many parts of the province at once attracting attention of travelers on the railway."[95] By the close of the century he was referring to it as "the curse of Manitoba."[96]

Manitoba's curse was beginning to trouble farmers in the North-West Territories by 1892, but by then they had their own unique problem to contend with.[97] Tumble mustard (*Sisymbrium altissimum* L.) arrived in the vicinity of Indian Head sometime in the 1880s. Unlike stinkweed, this annual species was completely unknown in the East and Thomas Shaw of the OAC speculated that it immigrated directly from central Europe in the company of "certain Austrians employed in the construction of the Canadian Pacific Railway."[98] "Tumbling mustard" capitalized on its drought tolerance and ability to roll before the wind to such an extent that by 1892 it had "infested the whole country around Indian Head, within a radius of from ten to twenty miles."[99] Some fields within this area were so densely occupied that it was thought likely they could produce "seeds enough to infest a whole state if properly distributed."[100] Even the Dominion Experimental Farm at Indian Head fell prey to this windborne pest as reported by Farm Superintendent Angus Mackay in 1894:

> I can safely say that one half of this farm was literally covered with plants of the **tumble mustard**, *Sisymbrium sinapistrum*, Cranz, blown in from adjacent farms on November 14, last. By good luck, the greater part of this was fallowed last summer, and I hope not many plants will appear next year in the crop. In 1893 there was not a plant in this whole lot. This year when we ploughed the field for the first time, it was a mass of flower, and the plants were so thick that every foot was covered with the weed. The tree plots, garden plots and all places of that nature were filled up, and continued so till the frost came.… If something is not done soon, this whole country will be overrun.[101]

Mackay was so concerned over the spread of tumble mustard that he compared it to an even greater tumbling menace: Russian thistle (*Salsola pestifer* Nels.). Russian thistle was first introduced to North America in about 1877 on a farm in South Dakota.[102] This eastern European immigrant appears to have arrived as a contaminant of imported flax seed and, by 1894, it had "spread over an area of 30,000 square miles" and was costing the farmers of Iowa, North and South Dakota and Minnesota an estimated three to five million dollars annually.[103] Extremely drought tolerant, Russian thistle thrived on the dry, windy plains of central North America. As James Fletcher warned in 1893, it was only a matter of time before it arrived in Canada.[104]

Fletcher's warning was seconded by a number of Prairie newspapers including the *Farmer's Advocate* and the Regina *Leader*. In late 1893 and early 1894, the former published several articles on the subject in which pictures and a complete description were provided. Farmers were told to "be on the *lookout*" for "this fearful pest" so "that it may not get a foothold on this side of the [border]."[105] The *Leader* employed even stronger language:

The Northwest papers are calling attention to a danger of no ordinary magnitude which threatens that country. This new foe is a Russian weed, which, for lack of a better name is called a thistle, and if all that is said of it is true it casts all other agricultural pests into the shade. The Canadian variety of the Scottish emblem is a comparatively unobtrusive plant compared with this fresh terror of the husbandman.... Its spread has been remarkably rapid.... Whole countries [*sic*] in South Dakota are overrun with the weed. Minnesota is similarly cursed. It has crossed into North Dakota and is now rolling towards the Canadian border ... thousands of acres of land in the three states mentioned above have been practically abandoned, the cultivator retiring before an enemy that he cannot subdue. It is clear that if it is to be kept out of Manitoba and the other western provinces the greatest vigilance must be maintained. It is a battle that must not be left to Governments alone. It is one in which every inhabitant must bear a hand. Wherever the pest is seen it must be extirpated. Forewarned is forearmed, and with a knowledge of the enemy it may be possible to keep it out, even though, as it has been pointed out, it will be rolled into the country on the wings of every chance wind from the south.[106]

Russian thistle's imminent arrival so alarmed the federal government that North-West Mounted Police "officers in command of the various posts in Manitoba and the Territories" were ordered "to be on the watch and to report the appearance of the weed in districts under their supervision."[107] The Department of the Interior also "officially" drew Fletcher's attention to the matter and his own department subsequently ordered him to prepare the first in a long line of federal noxious-weed bulletins.[108] Before the ink was even dry on *The Russian Thistle or Russian Tumble-Weed* (1894), however, Fletcher received intelligence that the would-be colonist had definitely been sighted in Manitoba the previous July.[109] Further inquiries revealed that one of Manitoba's municipal weed inspectors had actually reported the weed on the farm of "one Peter Rhimer" in 1889 and that the same inspector had also found "surprising quantities" on other parts of the Mennonite Reserve east of Morden.[110]

During the summer of 1894 reports of the arrival of Russian thistle began to flood in. Plants were found along the track of the

Morris-Brandon branch of the Northern Pacific Railway in August, and in October further infestations were discovered on the Mennonite Reserve.[111] These and other infestations were subsequently destroyed by Manitoba's Department of Agriculture and Immigration. James Fletcher and the local farm press praised the provincial government for taking such vigorous, unprecedented actions and for alerting the public through distributing pressed specimens of Russian thistle "to all the Farmers' Institutes and Agricultural Societies in the Province."[112]

Fletcher and his associates were also quick to praise the actions of the immigrant farmers upon whose land the new pest was first reported. The Russian thistle invasion of the United States contained "ugly social undertones" because of "the widespread belief that the weed was deliberately introduced by Russian Mennonite emigrants in revenge for social injustices they were receiving on the agricultural frontier."[113] The following account of an 1899 speech by Fletcher indicates that similar tensions may have existed in Canada:

The Russian thistle over-ran the Mennonite farms. They thought nothing of it. Indeed they fed it to their pigs, as it was the kind of food they gave their pigs in the old country. But, mark you, as soon as they were told it was a noxious weed they set to work and got rid of it, and now their farms were clean. He (Prof. Fletcher) would like to see every man in Manitoba and the North-West become a Mennonite for two or three years. He had watched these Mennonites pulling up Russian Thistles and pulling them up properly; not merely pulling them up and then leaving them on the land for the seeds to ripen. He had seen the father, mother, and family walking across their fields, drill by drill, and pulling up every weed that was a bad weed, putting them into a sack or bag and taking them away. Thus they got rid of them and their lands were cleaned.[114]

In attempting to clear Mennonite farmers of charges of duplicity, Fletcher also inadvertently highlighted several of this chapter's main themes: the way in which western settlement can be seen in terms of parallel immigrant streams, how weeds are inextricably bound to culture, and how culture changes in response to changing circumstances.

By 1897, Fletcher was confident that,

so much attention has been drawn to this plant by the Manitoba
Department of Agriculture since its discovery in Manitoba, that … it
is very unlikely that this weed will be allowed to propagate and spread,
now that its dangerous capabilities have been made known.[115]

His optimism was well placed and within a few years, Manitoba's noxious weed inspector was "glad to report that the much dreaded Russian
thistle is almost a thing of the past."[116] Governments were quick to claim
credit for the weed's demise, but as observed in an 1898 *Nor'-West Farmer*
article, "nature" rather than human actions deserved most of the credit for
the dramatic collapse of Russian thistle populations in the Canadian and
American northwest.[117] Rapid expansion of this weed occurred during
years of prolonged drought and, with the return of heavier precipitation in
the late 1890s, the species lost its competitive advantages and its populations plummeted accordingly. By 1909, Russian thistle was abundant only
"in the dryer parts of southern Alberta and Saskatchewan," and by the
1940s it had effectively ceased spreading although its range continued to
expand and contract depending on the annual precipitation.[118]

Although Russian thistle failed to live up to its advance billing, it had a
profound effect on the development of attitudes towards weeds in western
Canada. As Fletcher told the farmers of Moosomin, N.W.T.,

the Russian Thistle was one of the greatest blessings that ever came to
the west…. It awoke Manitoba up to the question of noxious weeds.
Very little attention had been given to the subject until the Russian
Thistle asserted itself and then the eyes of the people were opened.[119]

It opened their eyes to the fact that the Prairie West was facing an
unprecedented problem with weeds — unprecedented in terms of the
origin of invading species, their rate of spread, and the potential scale of
weed infestations.

The unusually rapid spread of new or previously minor weeds was
the product of a unique combination of circumstances. These include
an open, wind-swept environment, the existence of fast, efficient modes

of transportation prior to large-scale settlement, the importation of new types of seeds and their weedy contaminants from new sources in an effort to develop crops suitable to Prairie conditions, a near universal use of dirty seed, and a general lack of seed-cleaning facilities. Extensive farming, poor husbandry, and the ease in which land was brought into production further aided and abetted the rapid advance of noxious plants. More importantly, it provided them with a wealth of disturbed sites upon which to establish their colonies. The speed with which this new ecological niche was created, in other words, is a testament to the hard work and enthusiasm of prairie settlers. The speed with which it was filled is largely a testament to the ecological superiority of weeds.

Manitoba school children were taught in the 1890s that,

> among the many advantages that Manitoba has for the farmer is the ease with which the soil, which has been lying for centuries untilled and unoccupied, is brought under cultivation. In the Eastern Provinces before a farmer could begin his work a heavy growth of trees was to be chopped and logged, the stumps were to be burnt or uprooted, and the progress was very slow. On the prairies, a single year is all that is required to bring the land into use.[120]

Trees may have screened the activities of weeds in Ontario, but because a dense forest cover imposed a check on the rate of agricultural clearance, it also checked the rate at which weeds could spread. On the Prairies, in contrast, the absence of trees meant that the soil could be brought into production at an unprecedented rate. Before long, settlers were farming more land than they could properly manage and weeds benefited accordingly.

Just as it was in Ontario, extensive farming was also the product of greed, inexperience, generous land grants to settlers, and the need to achieve a reasonable income from the sale of relatively low-value crops such as wheat. Prairie farmers were largely compelled to grow wheat because of a lack of alternative markets and marketing facilities. This was partly due to technological limitations that restricted the storage and transportation of certain types of produce. It also reflected a lack of large urban centres on the Prairies and the aims of the national policy. Under the logic of the national policy, the role of prairie farmers was to grow wheat for export and, by doing so, to strengthen the national economy. Differential freight rates ensured that their grain flowed east and high tariffs designed to protect eastern industry ensured that manufactured goods flowed west. Western urbanization and industrialization were not on Ottawa's agenda nor was the development of large, diverse markets for a wide range of western agricultural commodities. To make matters worse, western producers faced additional physical constraints imposed by the harsh Prairie climate. Cold winters, short summers, strong winds, and a dearth of precipitation placed severe restrictions on the range of commercially viable crops and, in the 1890s, many farmers complained that even hardy forage grasses and legumes such as timothy and red clover were difficult to grow.[121]

These physical restrictions acting in concert with various economic constraints and incentives encouraged farmers to produce wheat on a continuous basis while discouraging both a movement towards mixed farming and all but the crudest of rotation and tillage schemes. They also forced farmers to rely on summer fallowing as the main defence against weedy aggression. As one Manitoba farmer observed in 1899,

> there is no rotation of crops that I have heard of that can take the place successfully of summer-fallowing. Things are very different here from what they are in Ontario and in many other countries. There the farmer on fifty or a hundred acres has a piece of land in hay, some in pasture, some in wheat, oats and barley, and a considerable acreage in potatoes, turnips, and corn; then they may do without summer-fallow-ing; but when we consider that many of us have more summer-fallow than many an Eastern farmer has land altogether, it will be easily seen that while that system of rotation may do for the East, it is not adapted for this country.[122]

Other sources emphasized that "summer fallowing is essentially necessary in Manitoba and the Northwest Territories" because "the farms are large, labour is scarce and the time for preparing the land in autumn and spring is very short."[123]

By the late 1890s, summer fallowing had become the primary defensive manoeuvre against weeds on the western plains. Eastern immigrants initially attempted to implement the same style of fallowing then "in vogue" in Ontario — three plowings followed by repeated harrowing — but as one pioneer recalled,

> the result was that our land was in very loose condition, and a great deal of it moved over with the wind to our neighbors, also some of the seed. We had a very rank growth of straw which lodged badly, and the yield was disappointing. A great many of us, when we were newcomers to the Province, thought nothing was properly done unless we followed the methods practiced in the East. We soon learned that the conditions, soil, and climate were different and required different treatment. Many of us found we had a good many things to learn and some to unlearn.[124]

Settlers soon learned to avoid more than one plowing because multiple operations tended to promote delayed maturity and lodging in subsequent crops. They also learned to adjust the timing of tillage operations to better suit the prairie climate and weed flora and that the land only needed to be fallowed once every three to five years rather than every second year as had been the practice in mid-nineteenth-century Ontario.[125]

Although summer fallowing proved effective against Russian thistle, the threat of this weed did little more than enhance the popularity of an already established technique. The threat of Russian thistle was, however, largely responsible for governments assuming a more active role in the conflict with weeds. The *Farmer's Advocate* applauded the "energetic measures" taken by the Manitoba government in ordering and overseeing the destruction of "the Russian cactus" and the paper's editorial staff expressed the wish "that now the Government has become alive to the importance of the weed business, they will 'stay by it.'"[126] In 1898, the Manitoba government expressed their willingness to do so through the appointment of Charles Braithwaite as the first provincial noxious weed inspector.[127] Braithwaite was charged with coordinating and directing the actions of municipal inspectors and ensuring enforcement of the provincial noxious-weed act. Within a year, T. N. Willing was appointed to a similar position in the North-West Territories. Together, they represent the emergence of a uniquely western source of weed expertise.[128]

The statutes that Braithwaite and Willing operated under were also significantly affected by the Russian thistle scare. The *Farmer's Advocate* reported in 1894 that a "very lively interest was taken in the [Manitoba] Legislature when the Noxious Weed Act was under consideration."[129] This interest subsequently resulted in the passage of legislation that was forty years in advance of similar enactments in Ontario. Russian thistle was added to the list of Manitoba's noxious weeds and more importantly, weed inspectors could if "necessary, cut down all and every such growing crop" in which a serious weed problem existed.[130] North-West Territory inspectors received similar powers in 1897, the same year as the territorial weed list was expanded to include "hedge mustard, hare's ear mustard, black mustard, common mustard, any other variety of mustard and ragweed, tumble weed, red root, Canada thistle, Russian thistle, wild oats and French weed."[131] Amendments to the North-West Territories Noxious Weeds Ordinance in 1899, 1900, and 1903 expanded the weed list to include even more species, gave the government the right to appoint inspectors to enforce the ordinance, banned the sale of contaminated elevator screenings, and ordered that threshing machines were to be cleaned before moving to new sites.[132] The 1903 version of the Territorial Weeds Ordinance was adopted virtually intact by the new governments of Saskatchewan and Alberta and it still provides the framework for their current noxious-weed legislation.[133]

Government officials such as G. H. V. Bulyea, the commissioner of agriculture for the North-West Territories, felt that the passage of increasingly "stringent" noxious weed laws and giving "arbitrary powers" to inspectors was justified in light of "the nature" of the weeds gaining a foothold in the Prairies.[134] Past experience in Ontario and Manitoba, however, made it clear that enforcement was not going to be easy. Bulyea himself noted "that it was obvious that there were not sufficient botanists in the country" to properly fill all the district and municipal weed inspector positions and during his third and final year as Manitoba's noxious weed inspector, Charles Braithwaite was forced to admit,

I have again to report, as in the two previous years, that I have not deemed it prudent to prosecute any one under the Act. It is true that there have been apparent infractions of the existing law, but there have always been extenuating circumstances of such a nature that to have enforced the Act would have brought the Act and its authors into contempt and accomplished no good.[135]

Braithwaite's successor, R. G. O'Malley, was more aggressive in applying the act but as he remarked in his 1903 Annual Report,

weeds are ever spreading, and in many districts have gained such a foothold the carrying out the provisions of the Act is no easy problem. The majority of the municipal councils in the Province are interested in suppressing weeds, and take active measures in carrying out the provisions of the weeds Act, but some councils find it a difficult task to enforce the Act in opposition to public opinion. Education in this, as well as in many other matters, is better than coercion.[136]

A massive government weed-education program represents the final legacy of the Russian thistle affair. Considerably more ambitious than the program in Ontario, the prairie campaign was launched with the publication of Manitoba's first government weed bulletin in 1894 and the Carmen Hill Convention on Noxious Weeds in July of the same year. Held in conjunction with the annual meeting of the Central Farmers' Institute of Manitoba, the Carmen Hill Convention was intended to address the "dangers" of weeds and "consider ways of destroying them."[137] Speakers from both the federal and provincial governments delivered lectures on weed identification, biology, and the "general principles of extermination," and delegates were urged to make weeds a "matter of earnest thought," for it "is ignorance alone that prevents farmers declaring war against these enemies."[138]

James Fletcher's western weed tours were also largely an outgrowth of the concern sparked by Russian thistle and his work was augmented by similar speaking engagements on the part of provincial and territorial officials. Fletcher's 1898 tour of Manitoba, for example, was only part of a much larger lecture series arranged by the Department of Agriculture and Immigration. In addition to Fletcher's address on "Noxious Weeds," farmers were also treated to weed lectures by H. S. Maclean of the Winnipeg Normal School and by Hugh McKellar and Charles Braithwaite of the provincial agriculture department.[139] Provincial officials such as Braithwaite regularly addressed between twenty and thirty farmers' institute gatherings annually and they augmented their formal speaking engagements by numerous conversations with individual farmers, inspectors, and municipal councils.[140] Manitoba's Department of Agriculture and Immigration established a "Weed Tent" at the 1898 Winnipeg Exhibition. Providing plant samples and expert advice, the tent was "thronged by inquiring farmers" and it proved so popular that the minister was called upon "to have a weed exhibit at all the leading fairs throughout the province."[141] By 1900, government weed exhibits had become fixtures at the Winnipeg, Portage, Brandon, Carberry, and Neepawa fairs and fair managers were said to look upon them "as a distinct feature of their attractions, a useful education and an object lesson to the farmers."[142]

Prairie governments' efforts to educate farmers were avidly covered and actively supported by the agricultural and daily press. The press was also one of the staunchest supporters of adding courses on weed identification, prevention, and suppression to school curriculums.[143] Teachers in the schools of both Manitoba and the North-West Territories were sent copies of the 1894 federal pamphlet on Russian thistle, and as the Regina *Leader* reported, "specimens of the thistle will be sent out wherever required, so that the children may become thoroughly acquainted with these deadly enemies to agriculture."[144] Manitoba children were further familiarized with "eleven of the plants found most hurtful to agriculture" through the school book *Our Canadian Prairies*, published in 1895.[145] Two years later, the Department of Education distributed coloured plates of various plants as "a means of making our younger people familiar with the weed pests most likely to give future trouble."[146]

James Fletcher was pleased to report that, by 1903, school nature studies had proven their worth: "As I have gone up and down in the Province [Manitoba] for the last ten years, I have repeatedly met with farmers who have told me they have been saved hundreds of dollars by their children knowing how to recognize noxious weeds."[147] A few years earlier, the

Nor'-West Farmer had similarly reported that the "average Manitoban has already become familiar with the noxious weed fiend through the medium of farmers' and other papers."[148] Governments and the press appear to have done their job in alerting farmers to the danger that they faced. Now all that remained was the far more difficult task of translating knowledge into action.

Conclusion

By 1905, both weeds and humans could confidently proclaim their dominion over the western prairie. The human triumph was heralded by the creation of two new western provinces; that of weeds by the passage of the first federal weed legislation. Created in response to the alarming success of alien weeds on the Prairies and the need for the federal government to protect the vast tracts of public land under its jurisdiction, the Seed Control Act of 1905 was designed to curb further weed advances and introductions by prohibiting the commercial sale of contaminated seed. It outlawed thirteen species including tumbling mustard and stinkweed throughout the Dominion, made provisions for government seed inspections, and instituted fines for various offences such as obstructing government officials and knowingly vending weed-infested seed.[149]

The passage of the Seed Control Act brought a period of rapid change to a close. Beginning around the time of Confederation, this period was marked by the rise of professional weed experts — first in Ontario and then in the Prairies — who soon supplanted British authorities as the main source of information on weeds and their suppression. Close ties with various levels of government enhanced their influence and gave them the ability to address a wide audience. Their views also gained credibility through their connections with the new science of agriculture in combination with considerable practical experience with Canadian farming and farming conditions.

This new breed of experts did not really deserve the title of "weed specialists," nor did they significantly advance the study of weeds as a science. They did, however, publicize and promote a range of weed control techniques that had proven effective in Ontario and regions further west. Most if not all of these techniques represent modifications of traditional

British practices, but unlike their amateur predecessors, the state-funded weed experts of the late nineteenth century were conscious that many British techniques were difficult if not impossible to implement under contemporary Canadian conditions. The one thing that they did share with an earlier generation of experts in Ontario was an overtly hostile attitude towards weeds; a near universal tendency to depict these plants as aggressive enemies to farmers rather than as evidence of unsound farming practices.

The advice and prejudices of eastern experts were soon being transmitted to Manitoba and the North-West Territories. They were inadvertently transported by the region's largest single group of nineteenth-century immigrants — settlers from Ontario — and deliberately disseminated by western governments with equally strong eastern ties. By the time the first large-scale wave of Prairie settlement was drawing to a close in the early 1880s, Ontario-style noxious-weed laws were in place. So too were many eastern weeds. Most farmers were also practising a style of farming that bears a striking resemblance to the "wheat mining" of mid-nineteenth-century Ontario.

But, even as the first wave of Ontario settlers were arriving, the relationship between people and weeds on the Prairies had already begun to evolve into something new and distinctive. The first sign that change was underway was the appearance of many troublesome native species that were far better suited to life in arable fields than were their woodland counterparts to the east. Close on the heels of these native weeds came a host of immigrant plants. Some were present but posed little problem in eastern Canada whereas others were entirely new to farmers of western European descent.

Species such as stinkweed, tumbling mustard, and the dreaded Russian thistle were beautifully adapted to the vagaries of western life and the broad, wind-swept Prairies provided them with an ideal setting within which to pursue their territorial ambitions. Their spread was so rapid and their population growth so great that, by 1898, Manitoba was "generally conceded to be the dirtiest province in the Dominion"; by 1905, the "question of weed destruction and control" was being described as "the all but universal problem" in the province.[150] Weedy dominion over the North-West Territories took longer to develop because of the later settlement of the region. Nearly all of the respondents to a 1954 question-naire distributed to Saskatchewan pioneers, for example, "stressed" the "absence in the early years of settlement of a later hazard, the noxious weeds.... Many report no weeds at all when they arrived; others recall only one or two."[151] By the time that Alberta and Saskatchewan were cre-ated in 1905, however, "many of the larger farms" were already "foul with weeds of all kinds."[152]

The shocking success of immigrant weeds on western homesteads did not escape the attention of federal and western officials. Rather, as a 1904 editorial in the *Farmer's Advocate* observed, it prompted a number of unprecedented government actions:

> Weed infestation has provoked legislation to stamp out weeds; has caused theses to be written by the Department of Agriculture on weed identification and suppression; has induced a campaign of education through the institutes regarding weeds, and has been the result of call-ing into being a weed inspectorship.[153]

The passage of increasingly stringent noxious-weed laws, giving arbitrary powers to inspectors, direct government intervention, and a massive pub-licity campaign did not, however, do much to stem the tide of weedy aggression. For as the *Farmer's Advocate* editorial concluded, "with all this formidable armament, it remains for the farmer to do the practical work of weed extermination."[154]

Prairie farmers were hampered in their antiweed efforts by a combina-tion of environmental and social factors. Many arrived with little practi-cal knowledge of farming and only a few had any experience with farming under Prairie conditions. The early establishment of railways facilitated the rapid spread of both human and weedy populations and the broad, treeless Prairies further aided the dissemination of wind-borne plants. Widespread use of dirty seed, a general lack of seed-cleaning facilities, and the ease in which land was brought into production added even more impetus to the rapid colonization of prairie soils by both native and alien plant species. The prevalence of continuous grain cropping ensured their subsequent success.

Grain monoculture, particularly that of wheat, was encouraged by the national policy, by a lack of markets and marketing facilities for other commodities, and by the narrow range of commercially viable crops suitable to the harsh prairie environment. In combination with an acute labour shortage and the large size of prairie farms, these factors effectively precluded the implementation of crop rotations. Farmers were forced instead to rely on a modified version of summer fallowing to keep their fields clean. Farmers in Ontario had already discovered that summer fallowing alone was not able to keep weeds in check, so it should come as no surprise that even with the most careful system of fallowing, prairie farms gradually became home to an ever-increasing number of vegetative homesteaders.

By 1905, therefore, all of the basic elements of modern prairie weed culture were in place. Governments had assumed command of the war on weeds by providing weed experts and weed police, through the enactment of increasingly draconian noxious-weed laws, and by launching a massive propaganda campaign. Extensive, ecologically unsound farming was well on the way to becoming entrenched and the majority of today's problem weeds were already proclaiming their presence. Violent, antiweed rhetoric had reached new extremes of purple prose and even the "average" prairie farmer was finding it difficult to dismiss warnings about the danger of weeds as merely "the children of a dyspeptic or pessimistic mind."[155] The conflict that numerous newspaper editors and government experts had foretold could no longer be avoided, and as the next chapter will show, the relationship between human and weedy newcomers soon degenerated into a war of attrition for possession of Prairie Canada's arable land. Like purely human conflicts of this nature, the outcome remained in doubt for years. Determining the eventual winner has taken even longer and there are signs that the contest may never be truly resolved.

5

War on the Western Front, 1906–1945

If the period between 1867 and 1905 can be portrayed as one of territorial expansion in the West, the following forty years are best described by the term conflict. Relatively peaceful coexistence ceased to be an economic option as weed populations exploded and as the ability of farmers to practice avoidance declined in direct proportion to the availability of previously unbroken land. As the first section will demonstrate, the battle between farmers and weeds for possession of the soil was continental in scope as it raged on both sides of the border. The "unique" relationship between agriculturists and weeds in the Prairie West is, in other words, simply a regional expression of a common culture shared by Great Plains agriculturists in Canada and the northern United States.

The study's focus returns to events on the northern front in sections two and three. Frequent use of war-like metaphors in these sections serves to emphasize the adversarial manner by which the human-weed relationship was universally portrayed by governments, agriculturists, and the farm press during the first half of the twentieth century. Military metaphors also provide a surprisingly accurate picture of the drama that was

Leafy spurge, *Euphorbia esula*

unfolding. Section two implicitly draws an analogy between the creation of a Canadian general staff to fight the two world wars and the roughly contemporary creation of a massive, centralized weed control bureaucracy charged with coordinating the war on weeds. The sheer size of this military-style chain of command testifies to the seriousness of the situation. So too does the passage of noxious-weed legislation that, by the early 1940s, rivalled various war measures acts in terms of the emergency powers they granted to the state.

Antiweed propaganda from this period is even more jingoistic than the weed identification and control literature issued during the pioneer era. As time progressed, however, it became tinged by a growing sense of desperation and by more than a hint of defeatism. Hard-pressed farmers were told that weeds were here to stay, that "eradication" was no longer a feasible goal, and that they must learn to "control" unwanted vegetation if farming was to remain profitable. Beginning in the late 1920s, the weed control high command even took the much overdue action of initiating serious research into weed biology, ecology, and control. This research, however, had little impact on the course of the war until after 1945. As it was intimately connected with the development of chemical weapons, the entire subject has been relegated to chapter six.

Section three demonstrates that an increasingly pessimistic assessment of the weed situation is less of a testament to the inactivity of farmers than to the territorial gains made by the armies of immigrant weeds. Faced with a serious challenge to their economic survival, Prairie farmers had begun to fight weeds with considerable vigour and ingenuity by the close of World War I. Seed cleaning had become a near universal activity by this time and tillage implements and techniques underwent a series of important changes over the next quarter of a century. One change that did not occur, however, was a general shift to mixed farming. Weeds were, in consequence, more than able to hold their own in the face of escalating human aggression. Pioneer species, primarily annuals, continued their inexorable march westward and their territorial gains were consolidated by the perennials that brought up the rear. The weed situation had become so serious by 1945 that Prairie agriculture was on the verge of collapse and the way was paved for the chemical "revolution" that followed.

Allies to the South

The relationship between agriculturists and weeds in western Canada has, up to this point, been treated as something unique in an effort to emphasize the influence of the environment on human culture. A sense of uniqueness vanishes, however, when a comparison is made with relations between people and weeds in the northern United States. Settlers on both sides of the international boundary were confronted with a similar environment and social setting. They shared a common background and responded in much the same ways to the opportunities and limitations they faced. Their weed problems were similar, as were their responses to the rapid spread of immigrant plants, and information, farming techniques, weeds, and agriculturists moved freely across the border. Cultural exchange between the Prairie West and the United States was not unidirectional, although it is probably safe to state that the northward flow of people, plants, tools, and ideas was greater than the flow to the south.

Like Upper Canada, early-nineteenth-century agriculture in the northern United States was heavily influenced by British farming. The majority of the farmers were of British descent and, as an 1830 Ohio farming manual noted, Great Britain was responsible

for our best breeds of horses and neat cattle, for many of the implements of agriculture, and for the best written treatises upon farming. The agriculture of the United States, says a distinguished writer, may be considered as entirely European and chiefly British.[1]

Similar arguments have been made by twentieth-century historians, although few fail to add that American practices were heavily influenced by the maize husbandry of native peoples and the need to adapt to New World conditions.[2]

These conditions include a dense forest cover, cheap land, scarce labour, and limited marketing opportunities on the frontier. Farmers in the northern tier states reacted to these conditions in the same way as their counterparts in Ontario: "they mined the land by cropping it continuously to its most promising staple."[3] For most this staple was wheat. Continuous cropping of wheat "broken only by summer and occasional year-long fallows" was the "rule" in western New York until the 1850s and it remained the standard practice in Ohio, Indiana, Michigan, Illinois, Iowa, and Wisconsin well into the following decade.[4] The steady westward movement of settlement encouraged farmers to "take what Nature yields spontaneously, and when she makes the first suggestion of exhaustion move onward to new and fertile lands."[5] This common observation goes a long way towards explaining why continuous grain cropping survived as the dominant production system in Minnesota, North Dakota, and Montana well into the twentieth century.

The inevitable consequence of this style of farming was an increasingly serious problem with imported weeds. As early as 1814, the author of a farming encyclopedia published in Albany, New York, reported that "there is a species of thistle gaining ground in the northern parts of this state, called Canada thistle, being imported from Canada, which threatens to become a serious evil to our soil."[6] By the early 1840s, *Cirsium arvense* L. was described as "extremely troublesome" in many arable "fields of the Northern and Middle States."[7] Over the next two decades, Canada thistle gained the reputation of being "the most execrable weed that has yet invaded the farms of our country" and one authority estimated that it was responsible for "decreasing the annual products [of the soil], when abundant, from *twenty-five to fifty per cent.*"[8]

Early-nineteenth-century observers noted that Canada thistle was not the only weed common to both the Old World and the New World. One botanist commented in 1832, that the "worst enemies of the farmers, at least in the northern states, are all foreigners."[9] He added that most "derived from Great Britain and the North of Europe ... testimony to the fact, that this country received its culture of every description from thence."[10] By mid-century, it had become clear that the

number of plants indigenous to our country, that are entitled to rank as pernicious weeds, is comparatively small ... the majority of the plants to be met with along the lanes and streets of villages, and upon farms, are naturalized strangers, who appear to be quite at home, and are with difficulty to be persuaded or driven away.[11]

American agriculturists reacted to this weedy threat in an entirely predictable fashion. William Darlington, the author of the earliest North American book on weeds, *American Weeds and Useful Plants* (1847), regarded the relationship between unwanted plants and farmers as a "constant struggle."[12] He argued that weeds represented a serious "evil" and encouraged farmers to respond to them in "the spirit of the Western savages who kill the women and children of their enemies, as a tolerably sure way of preventing the multiplication of warriors."[13] Darlington's polemics supports geographer Daniel Gade's contention that weeds "acquired a new meaning in the middle of the nineteenth century."[14] While his observation specifically refers to the situation in Vermont, a general hardening of "attitudes towards weeds as noxious plants without redeeming qualities" seems to have occurred throughout the northern states and Canada during this time.[15]

Attitudes had hardened to such an extent by the close of the nineteenth century that an uncompromisingly hostile view of weeds had become the norm. A typical example can be found in the opening paragraph of an 1894 state weed bulletin from Wisconsin:

> There are good reasons why the farmers of Wisconsin should be especially interested in the subject of noxious weeds at the present time. Three of the most aggressive and tenacious weeds that have ever harassed the agriculturist in any country have already invaded our borders, and are slowly, yet most vigorously pushing their campaign of conquest. I refer to the Canada thistle, the sow thistle and the Russian thistle.[16]

There is even evidence that this intense antipathy was shared by farmers. Wheeler McMillen, for one, remembers how his father "waged relentless war on weeds" from the time he purchased his small farm in northwestern Ohio in 1891 to the time of his death nearly forty years later.[17] The senior McMillen "hated weeds; hated them intensely" both because they insulted his sense of what constituted good farming and because they "challenged his possession and use of the land."[18]

Many state governments responded to the spread and proliferation of immigrant weeds by passing various forms of noxious-weed legislation.

Canada thistle was proscribed in Vermont in 1795 and the "New York Legislature took action against it" in 1813.[19] Connecticut enacted statutory measures against Canada thistle and wild carrot (*Daucus carota* L.) in 1821 and New York passed stricter legislation against the former in 1847.[20] Within a year, Canada thistle had also been outlawed in New Jersey.[21] Illinois passed a Canada Thistle Act in 1867 and most of the remaining northern states followed suit in the 1880s and early 1890s.[22]

By 1896, twenty-five states or territories had weed acts in place. Significantly, almost all were in the north and within the range of Canada thistle. Rarely found south of a line drawn west from Virginia, Canada thistle was outlawed or declared noxious in twenty-two of the twenty-five states with active legislation. In seven of these, it had the distinction of being the only weed specifically named; it was one of only two weeds identified by the laws of three more. The states in which several weeds were proscribed — Kansas, Michigan, Minnesota, New York, North Dakota, Ohio, Oregon, Pennsylvania, South Dakota, and Wisconsin — also had the most detailed and comprehensive regulations. Included among them are most of America's leading grain-producing states and all of the states bordering on Ontario and the prairie provinces.

A quick perusal of the laws of these ten states reveals a diversity of detail but a strong similarity in terms of intention and broad form. Simply put, they designated certain plant species as "noxious" or "public nuisances" and required land owners or occupiers to destroy them by a specified date or prior to the setting of seed. Failure to do so was punishable by fines ranging from five to one hundred dollars and in some cases a refusal to pay could result in a short prison sentence. Highway overseers, railways, and municipal corporations were also obligated to destroy weeds on lands under their jurisdiction and enforcement was the responsibility of county or township officials. This broad description applies equally well to the statutes in force by 1895 in Ontario, Manitoba, the North-West Territories, and even British Columbia.

Considerable variation exists in terms of specific plants listed as noxious by the different states and provinces but there is a decided correlation between the weed lists of Ontario and the eastern states and those of the Prairie provinces and immediate neighbours to the south. The common pasture weed ox-eye daisy (*Chrysanthemum leucanthemum* L.), for example, was classed as noxious only in Ontario, New York, Ohio, Wisconsin, and Minnesota.[23] Conversely, a weed that is generally associated with grain farming, wild mustard *(Sinapsis arvensis* L.), was listed in Manitoba and the North-West Territories but not in Ontario and it made the weed lists of only three westerly states: Wisconsin, Minnesota, and North Dakota.[24] Drought tolerant Russian thistle *(Salsola pestifer* Nels.) was even more of a westerner, being designated as noxious in Manitoba, Iowa, Minnesota, Nebraska, and the Dakotas.[25]

Professional agricultural scientists were some of the staunchest supporters of noxious-weed laws in the United States. These scientists primarily owed their existence to the passage of the Morrill Land-Grant College Act in 1862, and even more importantly, to the Hatch Act of 1887 which guaranteed federal funding for state agricultural research stations.[26] Between them, the Morrill and Hatch acts provided the institutional context for the professionalization of agricultural scientists in America. As this professionalization largely occurred "before there was an adequate basis of knowledge for them … Congress in a sense created scientific disciplines."[27] Mainly employed by the United States Department of Agriculture (USDA) and by numerous state agricultural colleges and research stations, by the 1890s, these scientists had become "fonts of agricultural wisdom" who were fast establishing themselves at "the apex of the agricultural pyramid."[28]

Like their state-funded counterparts to the north, American agricultural scientists also emerged as leaders of "the charge in the quest to extirpate weeds from fields and pastures."[29] Late-nineteenth-century botanists, agronomists, and field crop specialists such as William J. Beal of the University of Michigan, Lyster H. Dewey of the USDA, and H. L. Bolley of the North Dakota Agricultural Experiment Station gained widespread recognition as experts on the subject of weeds. To some extent their reputations were based on their pioneering work in weed control and biology. But, as research in these areas was still limited, they owed most of their fame as leading antiweed crusaders to a sound understanding of agricultural practices, to the authorship of a great deal of propaganda, and to the many patriotic speeches they delivered to both academic and practical agriculturists.

The findings, recommendations, and attitudes of American weed

experts were widely disseminated in Canada. The first federal weed publication — Lyster Dewey's 1893 bulletin on Russian thistle — formed the
basis of James Fletcher's 1894 pamphlet on the same subject. It also was
reprinted in full in an 1893 issue of the Winnipeg edition of the *Farmer's
Advocate*.[30] By the opening decade of the twentieth century, reports on
weed-related research underway at state agricultural experiment stations
in Minnesota, North Dakota, Wisconsin, and elsewhere had become
standard features in Prairie agricultural newspapers, and the editors of
these publications were just as familiar with American weed literature as
they were its Canadian equivalent. While reviewing George H. Clark's
and William Fletcher's *Farm Weeds of Canada* (1906), for example, the
editor of the *Farmer's Advocate* stated, "We have reviewed most of the
weed literature issued by our provincial and federal governments in
recent years, also most of the American publications bearing on the same
subject."[31]

Prairie agriculturists continued to pay close attention to American
developments in the field of weed control throughout the period 1906
to 1945. Many of the federal and provincial agricultural extension and
education programs discussed in the following section were inspired by
American precedents. So too were most of the major innovations in
tillage implements that are covered in the section that concludes this
chapter.[32] Some of the Prairie's leading sources of agricultural information and innovation such as the College of Agriculture at the University
of Saskatchewan were directly patterned upon American models and
relied heavily on American graduate schools for faculty training.[33] John
Bracken, to name but one, "was greatly influenced" by his graduate work
at the University of Illinois, which he attended after his 1909 appointment as professor of field husbandry at the University of Saskatchewan.[34]
Through his lectures, extension work, newspapers, and speaking engagements, Bracken soon emerged as one of the leading "ideologists of mixed
farming" and as a prominent campaigner in the antiweed crusade.[35]
Published shortly before his election as premier of Manitoba, his book,
Dry Farming in Western Canada (1921), became a standard text on farming techniques and weed control, and in the preface he readily acknowl-
edges his indebtedness to American research, to the USDA, and "to many
State Experiment Stations."[36]

American practices and beliefs also moved north with American set-tlers as did a number of combative weeds, most notably Russian thistle. The exchange of ideas, information, practices, implements, and plants, however, was far from one-way. Several states may have passed weed legislation well in advance of Ontario, but by the turn of the century, most of these laws were being described as "inoperative" or "ineffectual."[37] Western Canadian legislation fared much better and, by the First World War, American agriculturists were highly envious of "the very effective weed laws" being enforced in Alberta and Saskatchewan.[38] Canada led the way in the publication of government weed bulletins and has the dis-tinction of establishing in 1929, "the first organization especially set up to consider weeds, the Associate Committee on Weed Control."[39]

Formed under the auspices of the National Research Council (NRC) and drawing its membership from various levels of government, agri-cultural colleges, and the farm industry, the Associate Committee pro-vided Canada with a centralized command structure for coordinating and directing human resistance against the invasion of weeds. American weed fighters were inspired by the resolve shown by their northern allies. They banded together to form four regional weed science societies in the United States between 1938 and 1948 and loosely modelled the first pro-fessional association of weed researchers, the Weed Science Society of America (1954), on the earlier Canadian innovation.[40]

Early Canadian weed literature — notably Thomas Shaw's *Weeds and How to Eradicate Them* (1893) and the federal publication *Farm Weeds of Canada* (1906 with new editions in 1909 and 1923) by George Clark and James Fletcher — was highly esteemed and frequently cited by American weed specialists.[41] By the early 1930s, Canada was also home to some of the leading North American researchers working in the areas of weed biology, ecology, and crop competition. Thomas K. Pavlychenko, in par-ticular, is considered to have "provided the foundation for many of the principles of modern weed science" through his "research on biology and ecology at the University of Saskatchewan in the 1930s and 1940s."[42]

Canada also influenced agriculture in the northern United States through the southward migration of farmers, technology, and trouble-some plants. A 1945 Montana weed bulletin, for example, advocates the use of the Noble Blade, a tillage implement that was designed, patented, and popularized in southern Alberta by Charles Noble.[43] The direction of weed migration in both Canada and the United States has generally "followed latitudinal or east-west routes" in response to a similar orientation on the part of land transportation systems but a number of problem weeds have made their way south from Canada just as others have migrated north from the United States.[44] Russian pigweed (*Axyris amaranthoides* L.), one of the most abundant weeds in the Prairie provinces and a troublesome annual in grain fields, almost certainly spread to North Dakota from Manitoba where it was first reported in 1886.[45] Two more Eurasian imports that "seemingly" made their way to the United States via the Canadian Prairies are absinthe (*Artemisia absinthium* L.), an aromatic perennial that was previously used to flavour the alcoholic beverage of the same name, and the annual grass Persian darnel *(Lolium persicum* Boiss & Hoh.).[46]

Circumstantial evidence also suggests that tumble mustard (*Sisymbrium altissimum* L.) and perennial sow-thistle (*Sonchus arvensis* L.) spread south from an initial base of operation on the Canadian side of the line. As mentioned in the previous chapter, tumble mustard was first reported in the 1880s near Indian Head. By 1896, it was causing concern as far away as Michigan and had "been recently reported from nine different localities in the United States."[47] The smooth form (var. *glabrescens* Guenth., Grab. & Wimm.) of perennial sow-thistle had already become "a prominent weed" along the Canadian portion of the Red River Valley before it was first reported in 1900 in the northeast corner of North Dakota.[48] Just over a decade later, it was being described as "a very bad and aggressive weed in the Canadian Northwest and on the borders of North Dakota and Iowa" and it had become "one of the worst weeds" in Minnesota where it was "more or less confined to the northwestern part of the State."[49]

There is no need to belabour any further the point that western Canada had a significant impact on cultural developments in the northern tier states. It clearly did, although there can be little doubt that the American influence on Canada was relatively greater because of its larger population, earlier western settlement, and larger agricultural research establishment. The point that needs to be emphasized is that a common relationship between people and weeds evolved roughly simultaneously in western Canada and the northern United States in response to similar environmental and social conditions.

Despite different governmental structures, various states and provinces passed strikingly similar noxious-weed legislation. Farmers on both sides of the border practised much the same weed-friendly style of farming and both were engaged in increasingly heated combat with a common foe.[50] A recent comparison of weed survey data from Saskatchewan and North Dakota reveals the existence of "very similar weed problems" in both places and there is no reason to suspect that the situation was all that much different seventy-five years ago.[51]

Canadian and American agriculturists were very much aware of their mutual problem. For example, in 1928, the editor of the *Country Guide* (Winnipeg) explained that studies of "the weed situation in North Dakota" should be of interest to Canadian readers because "conditions there are quite similar to those in some of the badly infested areas of western Canada, and the results are just as applicable on the north as on the south side of the border."[52] Equally telling is the fact that the three most important American weed identification and control books published between 1911 and 1935 — L. H. Pammel's *Weeds of the Farm and Garden* (1911), Ada Georgia's *A Manual of Weeds* (1914), and Walter Muenscher's definitive work, *Weeds* (1935) — were expressly written for a combined Canadian and American readership, cite and draw heavily from both Canadian and American sources, and provide descriptions and control recommendations for the "more important weeds" of both countries. Muenscher was the most specific about the geographic boundaries of this shared culture: it was limited to "the northern United States and Canada."[53]

Farmers in both countries were also subject to intense government propaganda — propaganda that encouraged them to view weeds as foreign invaders through the use of similar rhetorical devices. The following poem from the front cover of an American weed bulletin, *Battling Weeds on Minnesota Farms* (1942), for example, expresses few sentiments that cannot be found in contemporary publications issued by the governments of Alberta, Saskatchewan, or Manitoba:

Poised like grim shadows o'er the land,
Weeds lurk to blight with evil hand
The tiller's harvest, waste his toil,
Mar his prospect, foul the soil.

Oh, you who plow and reap and sow,
Guard well your acres from this foe;
Nor vigil cease, nor labor spare,
Lest weeds become harsh tyrants there.[54]

The geographic boundaries of this shared culture correspond closely to the region where wheat is, or has historically been, king. With a few exceptions such as Quebec, this effectively means the provinces and states that had noxious-weed legislation in place by the last decade of the nineteenth century. According to an 1896 United States Department of Agriculture Report, none of the "southern States, where the nut sedge, giant ragweed, and wild onion are most serious pests, have passed any laws against weeds."[55] Weeds were clearly present in the southern United States but they were quite different from the weeds of the North because of vastly different climates, soils, labour conditions, and crops. Southern agriculturists also suffer proportionately greater crop losses from plant diseases and insect pests than their brethren in more temperate, northerly climes. The existence of more pressing issues, in other words, might explain why they were so slow to pass noxious-weed legislation.

Canada's eastern provinces were equally slow in passing significant weed legislation. Quebec had a weed statute in place by 1909 but the Maritime provinces were still without effective weed laws during the early 1920s. According to the Central Experimental Farm Botanist Herbert Groh, a lack of weed legislation in the East did not reflect a lack of weeds or the presence of more pressing concerns. Rather, "in most of the East a Weed Act would be only a dead letter for lack of a sufficiently compelling incentive for its enforcement, such as is found in the West."[56] Groh does not expand on this statement but presumably he was referring to the smaller scale and more diversified nature of eastern Canadian agriculture. Weeds cost eastern farmers money but they cannot be said to have threatened a farmer's very livelihood as they did in the West.

Noxious-weed legislation or more correctly, its absence, can just as easily be used to distinguish the relationship between people and weeds in western Canada and the northern states from its counterpart in Britain. Great Britain lacked a compelling reason to enact noxious-weed legislation until after the First World War. A severe labour shortage and greatly increased grain production had, by this time, disrupted traditional crop rotations and "led to the rapid fouling of land formerly clean."[57] As mentioned in chapter three, Parliament responded to these unusual circumstances by passing a weed regulation in 1920 as part of a major revision to the Corn Production Act of 1917. The Corn Production Act was repealed the following year. The Injurious Weeds Regulation, however, remained on the books because a great deal of "arable land was still out of its proper rotation in 1921 … and required expensive cultivation to conquer weeds before it could even be put down to grass."[58]

The passage of noxious-weed legislation in Britain suggests that the war had upset the traditional balance between farmers and weeds. Publications such as the *Journal of the Board of Agriculture* (which became the *Journal of the Ministry of Agriculture* in 1919/20) confirm this suspicion. Articles on troublesome vegetation increased substantially during and immediately after the First World War and the board used increasingly violent rhetoric to draw "the special attention of farmers to the great need for combating weeds."[59] Noxious-weed laws in foreign countries and the British Dominions also received considerable coverage and the "drastic" measures enforced in western Canada were singled out for particular praise and attention.[60]

With the cessation of hostilities and a gradual return to normalcy, however, the traditional British sense of restraint rapidly reasserted itself. Violent North American–style antiweed polemics, for example, are conspicuously absent in publications such as Winifred Brenchley's *Weeds of Farm Land* (1920) and H. C. Long's *Weeds of Arable Land* (1929).[61] The Injurious Weeds Regulation was enforced during the 1920s by County Agricultural Committees on behalf of the Ministry of Agriculture but convictions were few as were the number of weed notices served and most committees preferred making "suitable arrangements" with farmers to rigid enforcement.[62] Although noxious-weed legislation remained on the books for many decades, it quickly became a dead letter. In 1960, one

British weed scientist commented that the act "has never seemed really worthwhile amending" and he describes it as a relic of the time "when agriculture was in a bad way after the First World War."[63]

Weed laws were ultimately allowed to languish in Britain because they were not needed. Weeds were a constant problem but they were subject to a range of natural checks and balances. Just as importantly, unlike their North American counterparts, British farmers were "in possession of a vast amount of weed lore."[64] Through their knowledge of native plants, cultivation, and rotation, they had "developed and successfully applied" a system of weed control that remained in place "up to 1945" — a system that subsequently disappeared along with "the plentiful supply of cheap labor" upon which it "ultimately depended."[65] Because British farmers were quite capable of keeping weeds in check under normal circumstances, there was little need for the government to compel them to do so. There was also little need for agricultural authorities to dramatize the danger that farmers faced or to assume command of the war on weeds. As one British weed scientist explained in 1970,

> unlike the early pioneers of weed science in the United States and Canada during the thirties, the pre-war attitude in Great Britain was that weed control was part of the husbandman's art; it was not a subject to be studied in a scientific manner and there were few publications of scientific merit on weed control in British literature.[66]

War-time Regulation, Bureaucracy, and Troop Education

The western Canadian weed laws that evoked so much attention and praise in America and war-time Britain evolved into truly draconian measures between 1906 and 1945. As befits the earliest settled province and the first to be invaded, Manitoba led the way in the statutory assault on weeds. Between 1906 and 1941, Manitoba's Noxious Weeds Act underwent numerous revisions without altering the basic nature of the statute as it was established in the late nineteenth century. In general terms, these amendments greatly increased the power and control of provincial government weed officers over the activities of their municipal subordinates.

Lines of communication were strengthened as were methods of gathering intelligence — beginning in 1916, municipal inspectors were required to accurately map out weed infestations — and the province's list of enemy aliens was steadily increased as new weed species joined the fray.[67]

Towards the end of March 1942, the situation had deteriorated to such an extent that drastic new measures were implemented.[68] The first move was to divide the provincial noxious-weed list into four different classes with the gravest threat posed by the four perennial species placed in class one: leafy spurge (*Euphorbia esula* L.), field bindweed (*Convolvulus arvensis* L.), hoary cress (*Cardaria* spp.), and Russian knapweed (*Centaurea repens* L.). Drought tolerant and equipped with invasive, spreading root systems, these four relative newcomers to the province were so tough and tenacious that they threatened to overwhelm the farmers' defences if immediate action was not taken. With this in mind, the provincial government gave municipal authorities the right to pass emergency by-laws declaring farms heavily infested with class-one weeds as "weed infested areas." Municipal councils were then ordered to enter into a binding agreement with the landowner detailing the defensive actions that were to be taken. In the event the landowner refused to take up arms voluntarily, a further clause enabled the council to assume operation of the farm for a period of up to five years. Objecting farmers were permitted to remain in their homes but proceeds from the sale of crops were diverted to pay for the cost of the weed eradication effort.

The history of noxious-weed legislation in Saskatchewan and Alberta between 1906 and 1945 is very similar to that of Manitoba. Both provinces based their noxious-weed legislation on a 1903 ordinance inherited from the North-West Territories and both subjected their weed legislation to regular if often fairly minor revisions. Following the lead of Manitoba, Saskatchewan's Minister of Agriculture was given the right to usurp the power of municipal councils and appoint municipal weed inspectors in 1924.[69] Alberta followed suit in 1928.[70] That same year saw Alberta add a novel clause to its Noxious Weeds Act which required all settlers to clean their effects before moving to, or within, the province. They also had to provide the Minister of Agriculture with written testimony indicating their compliance. By the early 1930s, Alberta had the toughest regulations of all the Prairie provinces concerning the sale of weed-infested seed, feed, and screenings. It was also the first to pass legislation requiring operators of combine harvesters to clean their machines prior to moving to a new job.[71] Probably with less than spectacular results, in 1932, Alberta even attempted to force drivers of domestic trucks and automobiles to ensure that their vehicles were free of "any noxious weed seeds" before driving "upon any public highway, street or lane."[72]

More significant amendments were passed in the 1940s. In 1941, Alberta expanded its list of Class A weeds — the most serious category — to include field bindweed, hoary cress, leafy spurge, and Russian knapweed.[73] Four years later, municipal and improvement district authorities were given powers of expropriation similar to those of their counterparts in Manitoba. The Agricultural Service Board Act of Alberta (1945) gave local governments the right to take over the "supervision, rehabilitation or reclamation" of any land in the district that

> is debilitated or in the process of becoming debilitated through weed infestation, wind or water erosion, or for any other cause which has seriously affected or may seriously affect the productivity of the land or the welfare of the owner or occupant of the land, and that the land may become a menace to the community.[74]

Although the act was not solely aimed at battling the weed problem, weed infestations are clearly identified as the leading factor behind the need for farm rehabilitation. As the following section demonstrates, cultivation to control weeds was also a leading cause of soil erosion. Just as in Manitoba, proceeds from the sale of crops were earmarked to pay for rehabilitation work; unlike the situation in Manitoba, farmers could lose control of their land for an indefinite period. Possibly because of a stronger tradition of co-operation with farmers, Saskatchewan delayed passing similar legislation until later in the decade.[75]

Passage of these laws and their subsequent enforcement — by the end of 1945, nine Manitoba municipalities had taken control of 1,100 acres of leafy spurge-infested farm land — provides graphic evidence of the seriousness of the situation and the lengths that governments were prepared to go in an effort to stem the tide of weedy invasion.[76] The arbitrary powers they gave to the state also beg comparison with contemporary but much better known war-time acts and regulations. Alberta's Agricultural Service Board Act is doubly telling when one considers that property rights are probably more carefully guarded in Alberta than in any other province. Throughout the entire period that the bill was before the legislature and immediately after its passage — February through April 1945 — there is not a single article on the subject in the *Edmonton Bulletin,* the *Edmonton Journal,* or the *Calgary Herald.* Not one of the province's leading dailies mention the proposed legislation having aroused any serious debate nor did they see fit to criticize some of the act's more draconian measures.

Administering and enforcing these complex, compulsory bodies of legislation necessitated the creation of large, military-style bureaucracies and a veritable army of weed inspectors. Ultimate authority in all three provinces was vested in the Minister of Agriculture while the daily administration and supervision of the legislation was the responsibility of high-ranking ministry officials. In Manitoba, that official was the Provincial Weeds Inspector until the position was phased out in 1916 and replaced by a three-member Provincial Weeds Commission.[77] Saskatchewan and Alberta each employed a provincial weed inspector until the early 1920s, at which time supervision of noxious-weed legislation became a responsibility of the provinces' Field Crops Commissioners.[78] These officials became increasingly reliant on the services of a number of departmental field officers, or "field supervisors" as they were called in Alberta. By the 1930s, all three provinces also had a system of district agriculturists in place. Acting primarily as information officers, their duties included disseminating weed identification and control propaganda and interpreting increasingly complex weed regulations for the benefit of the troops.

Early in the twentieth century, agriculture departments in Alberta and Saskatchewan also employed a significant number of weed inspectors — the equivalent of noncommissioned officers in a military scheme of things. Alberta, for example, employed a total of eighty-five weed inspectors during the 1908 season. Beginning in late June, they worked between five and twenty-five days each and in total, they managed to inspect "about" 21,000 farms, issue 1,442 weed notices, and implement prosecutions against ten "very negligent" land owners.[79] Saskatchewan discontinued this policy in 1909, while the Alberta government continued to appoint and pay part of the salaries for weed inspectors in unorganized areas and improvement districts throughout the period covered by this chapter.[80]

Weed inspection in all three Prairie provinces was, however, primarily a municipal responsibility.[81] By the end of the First World War, the Prairie weed inspectorship had grown to an impressive size with over 800 inspectors being employed by rural and urban municipalities in Saskatchewan alone.[82] The cost of these programs was considerable. By 1920, the provincial government of Manitoba was annually spending $20,000 on weed inspection and related matters and municipal expenditures must have been at least as large.[83] A columnist for the *Country Guide* estimated that "this sort of weed control" was costing the provincial and municipal governments of Saskatchewan between $50,000 and $100,000 per year by 1930, and, in 1939, Alberta's Field Crops Commissioner presented figures which show that similar expenditures in Alberta were in the range of $40,000.[84]

Despite the clearly defined chain of command and impressive size of the weed control bureaucracy, the system was beset by a number of serious problems. Government officials regularly complained of a lack of responsiveness and enthusiasm for weed control on the part of municipal councils. Some, such as R. G. O'Malley, noxious-weeds inspector for Manitoba, even went as far as accusing councils of duplicity and outright hostility:

In my opinion the predominating factor which has brought about this unfortunate condition [the rapid spread of perennial weeds such as Canada thistle and sow-thistle] is the system of appointing municipal weed inspectors from among resident farmers of the municipality. To illustrate, the municipal councils are largely composed of farmers who, in general, are owners of farms which are badly infested with Canadian and perennial sow thistle as well as other noxious weeds; placing personal interest above that of the welfare of the municipality, they appoint as inspectors for the different wards resident farmers whose lands are even more polluted that their own. The result is natural; in some cases a small pretence is made to enforce "The Noxious Weeds Act," in many cases not even that. I could go even further and state that in some of these municipalities there exists a general feeling of hostility to the enforcement of the Act.[85]

O'Malley's counterpart in Saskatchewan, T. N. Willing, was confronted by a similar problem, and he suggested that perhaps it "is worth considering whether it would not be a good idea to have a special inspection made of the farms owned by councilors in districts where weed control is not actively enforced."[86]

Provincial government officials were not the only people to comment on the problem of municipal indifference. Feeling threatened by the rapid advance of perennial sow-thistle, John Turnbull of Cromer, Manitoba, wrote in 1911 that

> of all the municipal business, this duty of noxious weed inspection is the one which is handled in the most careless and indifferent manner. In some townships the inspection is so lax that the majority of farmers could not tell one the name of the man who is supposed to do the work, and I have a certain amount of sympathy with those who advocate the repeal of the act, having its place taken by an energetic and continuous campaign of education.[87]

Evidence presented by F. C. Nunnick, agriculturist for the Dominion Commission of Conservation, backs up Turnbull's claim. In 1914, he reported that in Manitoba, "Very few of the weed inspectors are doing their duty," adding that inspectors in Alberta were trying harder but the "areas allotted to each weed inspector are too large to be covered efficiently at the time when the inspecting should be done."[88]

Judging from a diminishing volume of complaints after the First World War, all three Prairie provinces seem to have largely solved the problem of municipal laxity by increasing provincial government control over municipal appointments and through closer supervision. Alberta ensured municipal compliance by hiring seventeen field supervisors to oversee the work of municipal inspectors and, by 1925, about ninety percent of the municipalities in the province were actively involved in weed control.[89]

Another problem that the provinces actively addressed was the ongoing difficulty of securing "real good live men who are familiar with the weeds and the methods to adopt to eradicate them."[90] Ignorance on the part of weed inspectors was excusable when they neglected their duties but when they insisted on adhering to the letter-of-the-law, their actions were guaranteed to raise the ire and ill-will of farmers. In 1909, for example, one municipal inspector in Manitoba received considerable publicity when he initiated proceedings against a farmer who "point blank refused" to cut down a patch of sow-thistle that had infiltrated his farm.[91] Imagine the inspector's chagrin and the damage done to the reputation of inspectors in general when at the trial, the weeds were shown to be nothing more than harmless dandelions (*Taraxacum officinale* Weber).

Incidents of this nature forced the three provincial governments to search for ways to improve the quality of municipal inspection. In 1911, Manitoba attempted to attract more qualified people to the position by forcing municipalities to extend the pay and period of employment for weed inspectors.[92] Preferring co-operation to coercion, Saskatchewan ran a successful campaign in 1912 to encourage municipal councils to hire fewer inspectors while at the same time, increasing their salaries and length of employment.[93] All three provinces created a regular system of weed officer training between 1911 and 1914 and, in 1929, Alberta instituted a mandatory certificate program at the University of Alberta.[94]

Tighter regulation, closer supervision, and better education probably reduced the number of embarrassing mistakes made by weed inspectors but, according to a number of authorities on the subject, by the era of the Great Depression the system still left much to be desired. As can be seen in a 1932 report sponsored by the National Research Council of Canada, many old problems persisted:

> Weed inspection in all three provinces is based upon the municipal system.... Most of the weak spots are traceable to municipal appointment. While many municipal inspectors are first-class men, they all lack prestige and often find it difficult to be impartial because of their being local residents. Their term of office is short, in some cases being limited to two weeks. They are frequently accused of being appointed for local political or economic reasons, or of working merely to obtain tax money. They are often no better equipped for the work than many other farmers in the district and are consequently merely law officers in the eyes of the farmer.[95]

Drought, crop failures, and financial hard times were also making it hard for weed inspectors to carry out their duties and for municipal councils and farmers to comply with weed control regulations. Alberta first encountered this problem in 1920. After three years of drought and facing the prospect of yet another poor crop, it had become

> practically impossible for the weed inspector to force the farmer to destroy his weeds.... It was often found when the local inspector approached a farmer he was simply told that he could not destroy the weeds on his land as he had neither feed nor money, besides the land was too hard and dry for summer-fallowing.[96]

Much the same situation existed throughout the next decade. In 1933, the Alberta government "discontinued all weed control work except that of a purely educational nature."[97] Four years later, the province's weed control program was again in trouble. Alberta's field crops commissioner reported that municipal councils and improvement districts lacked sufficient funds to "properly enforce the Act ... [the] result of this lack of inspection is a gradual spreading of noxious weeds over the Province."[98]

Probably the most serious weakness inherent in weed legislation was that its success primarily depended on the good-will and active co-operation of the farming community. Provincial and municipal governments lacked the resources to tackle the weed problem on their own and, while they could and frequently did make examples of the worst offenders, rigid enforcement of the law was simply not an option as few farms were completely free of proscribed weeds.[99] P. M. Abel, a correspondent for the *Country Guide*, summed up the situation in 1930 as follows:

> Weed inspectors? Yes, there are lots of them in all the prairie provinces, and among the ranks of these inspectors are men of judgment and ability. But in the very nature of things they have to enforce weed control as policemen enforce prohibition. Public opinion allows a little innocent indulgence in both cases. If the weed inspector plays his hand too strongly at the first appearance of noxious weeds, a farmer is likely to get riled. A farmer regards it as his inalienable right to have a little sprinkling of wild oats or Canada thistle. Public opinion won't back the law till the interests of the community are threatened.[100]

Although provincial governments were cognizant of the failure of legislation to halt the spread of weeds and the impossibility of universal enforcement, they were unwilling to concede the ineffectiveness of statutory measures. If nothing else, they provided a convenient device for calling the troops to attention, for dramatizing the danger they faced, and for disseminating propaganda. Municipal weed inspectors spent a great deal of time dispensing advice, distributing information, and handing out copies of the provincial weed act and all levels of the weed control bureaucracy increasingly placed education at the forefront of their duties.

Provincial officials were kept busy during the winter months speaking at farmers' institute meetings and running weed control short courses. All three Prairie governments began offering courses and lectures on weed identification and control during the late nineteenth and early twentieth centuries. By the late 1920s, the government of Saskatchewan was offering close to forty weed control courses per year at various locations throughout the province. Of all the extension courses offered by the Department of Agriculture, and they were many and varied, talks on weed control and livestock "proved to be the subjects most in demand" with the former, drawing average audiences of between forty and sixty people[101] Provincial weed specialists could also be heard at farming schools sponsored by wheat pools and implement manufactures such as International Harvester, J. I. Case, and the Oliver Plow Company.

Prairie governments also made attempts to reach immigrant communities. Interpreters were provided to municipal inspectors working in the areas of Doukhobor settlement in Saskatchewan and the province's first weed bulletin, *Weeds of the Farm and Ranch* (1908), was printed in English, German, and Icelandic.[102] Continuing a tradition begun in the 1890s, the federal and provincial governments freely issued weed bulletins by the thousands. Saskatchewan distributed 15,000 weed bulletins in 1914 alone; Alberta published its first bulletin in 1912 and, by 1915, the entire initial printing of 25,000 copies had been exhausted.[103] These publications were not merely pamphlets — the 1917 edition of Alberta's noxious-weed bulletin was 130 pages long — and the fact that most included photographs and even colour plates must have added considerably to their cost.[104]

State efforts to educate farmers received invaluable support from the regional farm press and many segments of the agriculture industry. Agricultural newspapers and journals, for example, regularly announced the release of the latest government bulletin and they printed a steady stream of articles dealing with the issue of weeds in general. During the 1930s and early 1940s, companies as diverse as Imperial Oil and the North-West Line Elevators Association also entered the fray. The former probably hoped to bolster its sale of fuel and lubricants by offering a free booklet on battling "WEEDS ... the Arch-enemy of Canadian Agriculture," whereas the latter seems to have provided a weed identification guide and service out of a more sincere commitment to cleaning up Prairie farms.[105]

Bulletins, newspaper articles, lectures, and chats with local inspectors were not the only means through which the danger of weeds was publicized. Borrowing an idea from the other war effort, provincial departments of agriculture conducted a number of massive poster campaigns. The 1917 Alberta campaign was particularly notable with 8,000 large colour posters of Canada thistle and perennial sow-thistle being posted in "conspicuous places" throughout the province.[106] In an effort to educate rural school children in Saskatchewan during the 1920s, the provincial government sponsored essay contests, sent district agriculturists to speak to the children, distributed mounted weed samples, and placed sets of colourful weed identification cards in over 1,700 classrooms.[107] Similar resources were made available to adult farmers at local seed fairs, grain-judging schools, and a wide range of public events. Alarmed over the potential threat from perennial sow-thistle, the Alberta government went as far as proclaiming a special "weed week" in July of 1929. The week's activities included a province-wide series of special weed meetings, the release of a new bulletin, a poster campaign, numerous press releases, and guest appearances on local radio talk shows.[108]

Following in the footsteps of both weeds and Dominion Botanist James Fletcher, government weed experts crisscrossed the Prairies in rail cars, spreading their antiweed message wherever they stopped. The three provincial governments regularly took advantage of the largess of the railways to provide their own travelling information services and, on

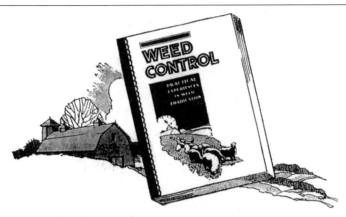

WEEDS....the arch-enemy
of Canadian Agriculture

"If my fields had been free of Wild Oats and Mustard last year," writes an Alberta farmer, "my extra crop profits would have enabled me to buy a car, two suits of clothes, redecorate my house and add a hundred dollars to my bank account. This year I'm going to clean up at least two fields."

The attitude of this Alberta farmer is commendable. If all farmers attack weeds vigorously, their efforts will be rewarded many times over in better crops, reduced costs and increased profits. To help them do this Imperial Oil Limited is publishing an interesting book which contains all the latest facts, figures and information pertaining to the weed problem.

This book—"Weed Control"—is full of constructive advice and suggestions. It explains in plain, simple language how to tackle the job of weed eradictaion most effectually. It has been compiled by The Honorable Duncan Marshall, former Minister of Agriculture for Alberta, and each chapter describes the experiences and processes adopted by weed authorities, experimental farms and farmers who have successfully fought weeds throughout the Dominion.

"Weed Control" is a companion volume to "Field and Farm Yard", which Imperial Oil distributed to more than 65,000 farmers in 1929. By filling in and mailing attached coupon, you will be assured of receiving your free copy as soon as the book is published.

Mail This Coupon Today

> IMPERIAL OIL LIMITED
> Toronto, Ontario or Regina, Sask.
>
> Please mail your *free* book "Weed Control" to me as soon as published.
>
> Name ....
>
> Address...............
>
> County and Province ....
>
> B-5

IMPERIAL OIL LIMITED
Serving Canada for 50 years

| 6 Refineries | 1900 Branches | Thousands of Dealers |

IMPERIAL OIL PRODUCTS FOR FARM USE

It is always good business to use the best gasoline, oils and greases. Poor petroleum products are wasteful. Imperial Oil Products cost less than unknown, inferior products because they render better service. Make sure of full value—buy "Imperial".

PREMIER GASOLINE	POLARINE MOTOR OILS	CAPITOL CYLINDER OIL	MICA AXLE GREASE
IMPERIAL ETHYL GASOLINE	POLARINE TRACTOR OILS	PRAIRIE HARVESTER OIL	IMPERIAL CREAM
ROYALITE COAL OIL	POLARINE TRANSMISSION	GRANITE HARVESTER OIL	SEPARATOR OIL
MARVELUBE MOTOR OILS	LUBRICANTS	CASTOR MACHINE OIL	EUREKA HARNESS OIL
MARVELUBE TRACTOR OILS	POLARINE CUP GREASE	THRESHER HARD OIL	IMPERIAL INCUBATOR OIL

Imperial Oil writes the book on fighting weeds (*Nor'-West Farmer*, 21 April 1930)

132

at least two occasions, representatives from the federal and provincial governments combined forces in a highly publicized verbal assault on weeds. The 1906 provincial-dominion "Special Seed Train" made numerous stops throughout the Prairies in an effort to publicize the danger of weeds and to advertise the federal government's newly passed Seed Act. Saskatchewan's representative, T. N. Willing, reported that it attracted close to 9,000 visitors and made seventy-one stops in his own province alone.[109] Willing was accompanied by such notable speakers as W. R. Motherwell and the veteran campaigner James Fletcher. Unfortunately, this tour proved to be Fletcher's last western sortie in his "constant warfare" against weeds, for he died in 1908 after a brief illness.[110] Equipped by the Canadian Pacific Railway and staffed by dominion and provincial specialists, the "Interprovincial Weed Train" made a similar journey in 1921. This train featured free motion pictures for children, "two lecture cars, a machinery car containing tillage implements and models of grain cleaning machinery," and "a demonstration car, containing, among other things, weed seeds and mounted specimens of weeds."[111]

Farmers mistrustful of all this free advice could see it translated into practice at their nearest Dominion Experimental Farm, Station, or Substation. Ten such stations had been established in the Prairies by 1918. Beginning in 1916, the Experimental Farms System also included a number of illustration farms. Devoted to practical demonstrations of "the suppression of weeds, the prevention of soil-drifting, the evasion of rust, and the securing of profitable yields," they were supervised by officials at Brandon, Indian Head, and Lethbridge and operated by farmers under contract to the federal government.[112] Manitoba boasted fourteen illustration farms by 1923, and nineteen by 1930; Saskatchewan had forty-one in place in 1946.[113]

Provincial governments also saw a need to provide practical weed control demonstrations. Saskatchewan created a thirty-acre weed research farm at Drinkwater in 1930, and the following year it established a 960-acre weed experiment station on a heavily infested farm in the Lockwood District.[114] In 1937, the government also inaugurated a system of weed control demonstration plots in southern Saskatchewan. Primarily designed to "illustrate the value of heavy seeding and fertilizer to control weeds," thirty-four plots were in place within a year.[115] Alberta instituted a similar service during the closing years of World War II.[116]

The increasing scale, scope, and complexity of government education programs provide mute testimony of an ongoing and increasingly severe weed problem. Confirmation can be found in the message these programs conveyed. Carrying on a late-nineteenth-century tradition, weeds were consistently portrayed as "one of the most persistent enemies that prairie farmers have to contend with" and farmers were taught to regard their activities as "a continual warfare against these intruders."[117] Government propaganda became increasingly florid as the situation worsened and ever more emphasis was placed on the link between weeds and declining profits. A 1941 *Country Guide* article by M. J. Tinline, superintendent of the Dominion Experimental Farm at Brandon, provides a colourful, if typical, example of how far both trends were carried. Under the headline "Weed Enemies are Vulnerable," Tinline explained that "farmers can win the war on weeds by combining the tactics of blitzkrieg and blockade, to the end that farming will be more profitable."[118] After informing his readers that "weeds are directly responsible for more financial failure on prairie farms than any other single cause," he urged them to plan their campaign with care:

> A frontal attack is not always the sanest. In war, the weaknesses of the enemy are studied and the attack is made on the weakest front. So in the war with weeds. Their weaknesses — and most weeds have weaknesses — have to be studied, and the attack planned accordingly.

Tinline's emphasis on the vulnerability of weeds strongly suggests that the troops were in need of encouragement. Farmers were not the only ones, however, to fall victim to despair. As early as 1916, W. R. Motherwell, model farmer and Minister of Agriculture for Saskatchewan, asked farmers to reject the appealing but misguided notion that weeds could be eliminated before they spread and caused serious problems. Instead, he urged farmers "to face the situation now and not only fight the further invasion of these enemies but control those that are here.... After all, we can only hope to control fields that get infested with such weeds as stink weed, as eradication seems to be impossible."[119] Motherwell blamed "exclusive grain growing" for causing the weed situation to become "gradually and in many cases rapidly worse," and he told his readers not to place too much hope in the efficacy of summer fallowing for it had become clear that weeds were "increasing in spite of fallowing every third year according to the best known methods."[120]

By the 1920s, Motherwell's skeptical assessment of the future of Prairie agriculture had become commonplace. Earlier optimism over the ability of farmers to battle weeds into submission had given way to the realization that "weeds will always be here, and will have to be dealt with as long as farming is followed."[121] Eradication had ceased to be a realistic goal and even the possibility of control seemed remote unless farmers fundamentally changed their methods of farming. As an editor for the *Nor'-West Farmer* observed in 1924, warnings over the potential danger of straight grain growing had become a "self-evident truth: if you want to beat the weeds change your methods; if you want them to beat you, keep right on growing grain year after year and the weeds will win out…. The straight grain growing farming system is the best ally weeds have."[122]

In the Trenches

Despite the increasingly obvious shortcomings of cereal monoculture, it remained the dominant production system on the Prairies through the end of World War II.[123] Government officials and members of the farm press often interpreted the slow rate of agricultural diversification as evidence of resistance to change and as a sign that their antiweed message was only reaching "a very small section of the farming community, frequently the section that least requires information."[124] While farmers seemed unwilling or unable to accept the bulk of government advice and tended to treat weed inspectors with scorn, they were not completely immune to appeals to their own self-interest. Virtually all of the farmers surveyed in Saskatchewan in 1914, and again in 1928, showed enough concern to use a "a seed cleaning machine of some kind," and government reports from the interwar period are liberally sprinkled with praise for the high quality of summer fallowing, improvements in tillage, the implementation of more systematic rotations, and a growing interest in the issue of weeds generally.[125] By 1950, it had even become clear that most of the important innovations in weed-fighting tillage implements made over the last thirty years were attributable to "the farmer" rather than to information disseminated by the government or to state-funded agricultural research.[126]

Just as it was in the late 1890s, regular summer fallowing remained the "the best means of cleaning up weeds and of ensuring a crop."[127] Regarded by experts as "a necessary evil" under "average western conditions," summer fallowing was considered "absolutely essential" in the drier parts of Alberta and Saskatchewan.[128] In Manitoba, where water conservation was "secondary to weed control," fallow as a percentage of total cultivated farm acreage rose steadily throughout the period in question.[129] Fallow occupied just over 13% of the cultivated land in the province between 1906 and 1910, rose to an average of 18.4% between 1920 and 1924, and stood at 21.3% in 1939.[130] Summer fallowing was at least as popular in Saskatchewan and Alberta and it continued to tie up many millions of acres of prairie soil well into the 1950s despite a gradual trend towards a more diversified form of agriculture.[131]

One reason that summer fallowing remained the primary defence against weeds throughout the Prairies was the persistence of certain traditional conditions and constraints. These include the ongoing dominance of continuous grain growing, short farming seasons, large farms, and an enduring labour shortage. Another is that it proved quite adaptable to local environmental conditions. As mentioned in the preceding paragraph, the technique was useful both for weed control and water conservation (or so people thought) and it could be tailored to meet either one or both of these requirements. Generally, the incidence of fallow decreased with an increase in precipitation. According to the Dominion Field Husbandman E. S. Hopkins, summer fallowing was "most frequently" employed every third year during the late 1920s but it ranged from every second year in parts of southern Saskatchewan and Alberta to once every fourth year in the more humid parts of the Prairies.[132]

Summer fallowing also remained popular because of its relative effectiveness. Although it did not provide a final solution to the weed problem, it was quite simply the best, and in many cases the only, economically viable solution available to farmers. Summer fallowing's effectiveness was considerably enhanced by the development and adoption of improved tillage implements. Prairie farmers traditionally used either moldboard or disc plows and conventional drag or disc harrows when cultivating their summer fallows.[133] These implements proved effective in combating annual and biennial weeds and they had the added advantage of working the soil into a fine tilth. A top layer of finely pulverized soil or a "dust mulch" as it was commonly called, was considered highly desirable because it was thought to reduce moisture loss by interrupting the capillary movement of water within the soil. Unfortunately, in drier regions and during periods of drought, fallowing with these implements was "chiefly an invitation to the surface soil to lift up with the wind and drift off in a generally easterly direction."[134] Both the disc and traditional drag harrow also proved ineffective when confronted with many perennial species:

> Western farmers have always been much addicted to the use of the disk harrow. Disking has long been a popular summer pastime. But aside from the exhilaration that comes from riding on the spring seat, nothing else particularly important results from using this implement in the cultivation of a summer fallow. As a matter of fact, disking just helps weeds with running root stalks to more generally establish themselves. For perennial sow and Canada thistle disking is a streak of luck. The disks cut up their roots, plant them again in a new place and substantially assist in spreading them over a field.[135]

A steadily mounting problem with perennial weeds and two serious droughts — one during the closing years of the First World War and one in the early 1920s — led to a search for new tillage implements and new ways of fallowing. Two of the earliest innovations to gain widespread acceptance were the "duckfoot" cultivator and the rod weeder. Capable of destroying perennial weeds without excessively pulverizing the soil, widetoothed cultivators had, by 1920, replaced both the harrow and the plow for working summer fallows in "many parts of Manitoba, and to a lesser extent in Saskatchewan."[136] Rod weeders were originally developed in the United States shortly before the First World War. Bearing the distinction of being "the first field implement to be designed exclusively, or even chiefly, for weed control" and causing only minimal disturbance to the soil's surface, they were well suited to use in western Canada where wind erosion was such a problem.[137] They began attracting considerable interest amongst Prairie farmers in the mid-1920s and over the following two decades they became a common tool for post-seeding weed control and for destroying newly germinated weeds on summer fallows.[138]

The search for new implements and fallowing techniques was given further impetus by the late-1920s discovery that dust mulches did little if anything to reduce soil water loss. As reported in a 1927 issue of the *Grain Growers' Guide* under the headline, "The Dust Mulch Theory is Exploded," S. Barnes of the Dominion Experimental Station at Swift Current had found that stirring the surface of the soil to produce a fine mulch was no "more effective in conserving soil moisture than where the surface has been untouched."[139] The further discovery that weeds were responsible for the "most serious loss of soil moisture" on summer fallows simply added to their importance and to their already long list of war crimes.[140] News of the debunking of the dust mulch theory spread rapidly. By 1928, Manley Champlin, professor of field husbandry at the University of Saskatchewan, reported that this "fact [was] now pretty generally known by the farmers throughout the prairie provinces and the north-western states."[141] A federal government bulletin officially confirmed the theory's demise the same year:

> It was formerly believed by many persons that a soil mulch would conserve soil moisture but experiments have shown that this is not the case on prairie soils. Weeds constitute the chief agency through which soil moisture is lost and, when these are kept down further cultivation is unnecessary. In fact, too fine pulverizing of the soil tends to make it blow, incurring serious injury.[142]

During the 1930s and 1940s, the finely tilled, "black fallow" gradually disappeared from much of the Prairie landscape. Stubble and dead weeds could increasingly be seen littering the surface of fallow fields as more and more farmers practised a technique variously known as "plowless tillage," "stubble mulching," or "trash farming."[143] The plant debris reduced wind erosion and moisture loss as did the use of a range of new implements which were designed to kill weeds without excessively pulverizing the soil and burying the trash. These included several types of disc machines, most notably the one-way disc and its successor, the discer, subsurface tillers such as the Noble Blade and heavy-duty cultivators that enabled

Massey-Harris line of weeders, ca. 1930 (*Nor'-West Farmer*, 5 January 1929)

farmers to work their fallows without having to resort to the plow.[144] By the late 1940s, earlier implements such as disc plows had effectively "disappeared" and use of even the ubiquitous moldboard plow was greatly restricted.[145]

As mentioned above, the search for new fallowing implements and techniques was sparked by the related problems of soil drifting and increasingly severe weed infestations. Efforts to solve the former served to highlight the importance of the latter and, by the end of World War II, summer fallowing had been identified as "the centre of the danger from a soil erosion standpoint."[146] Within a few years it had become equally clear the main function of tillage on the Prairies was "for the control of weeds."[147]

While fallow fields were the site of the most intensive tillage operations, mechanical weed control was also conducted in young stands of grain. "Weeders" or light harrows were "extensively introduced" for this purpose in the late 1890s and they soon became a common weapon in the Prairie farmer's arsenal.[148] The growing popularity of postemergence cultivation did not reduce the importance of summer fallowing but it certainly helped reduce crop losses through weed competition as well as the buildup of annual weed seeds in the soil.[149]

The same argument also applies to postharvest cultivation. Fall tillage of stubble to encourage weed germination and subsequent winter kill became popular in central Alberta around the time of the First World War. There it was often used as a substitute for summer fallowing as the latter was found to cause excessive lodging and delayed maturity in crops grown on the black loam soils of the region.[150] Discing or plowing immediately after binding, however, only became a widespread practice with the development of the gasoline tractor. Farmers in the vicinity of Portage la Prairie, Manitoba, were using this technique against perennial sow-thistle by the mid-1920s. A local development that was "gradually becoming known in other parts of the West," farmers had discovered that they could get fairly good results if they plowed their fields immediately after harvesting and "before the seeds start to blow."[151]

Tractors were considered "almost necessary" for the success of this operation because time was short and few farms had sufficient horses to operate binders and plows at the same time. The introduction of the one-way disc in the late 1920s further reinforced the importance of tractors.

This device tilled a much wider swath with less soil pulverization than plows and while it was credited with "enabling farmers to cultivate behind the binder with one implement" it was "of course heavy, and almost necessitates the use of the tractor."[152]

Gasoline tractors are widely considered to have had a revolutionary impact on prairie agriculture. Nonetheless, as Alberta's Department of Agriculture predicted in 1929: the "tendency towards power farming ... will not assist in weed control."[153] The relatively minor impact of tractors on weed control prior to the end of World War II reflects their slow rate of adoption — over sixty percent of Prairie farmers were still using horses in 1941 whereas a decade later, "almost all serious commercial farms were operating with tractors" — and more importantly, the way in which they were used.[154] Gasoline tractors did increase the speed of tillage operations and allow a few innovations such as fall cultivation but the main effects of power farming were huge increases in farm size, corresponding reductions in the number of farms, and a declining demand for farm labour.[155] Farmers, in other words, primarily used tractors to expand their cultivated acreage rather than to work existing farms more intensively. Power farming may have ushered in an era of "large scale weed destruction" but, as a *Country Guide* reporter commented in 1944, it also reinforced a system of large-scale weed production: "in areas such as western Canada, where land is comparatively cheap and where one man would like to take care of as much crop as he can see, many bad annual and perennial weeds are becoming established in spite of all our fine power equipment."[156]

Gasoline tractors were not the only innovation that failed to turn the tide of weedy invasion for Prairie weed populations appear to have increased dramatically between 1906 and 1945 despite marked improvements in seed cleaning, summer fallowing, tillage, and other control measures. Crop loss estimates and dockage statistics provide a good sense of the scale of the weedy counter-offensive. A "conservative estimate" in 1916 placed annual weed losses in Saskatchewan at $25,000,000.[157] John Bracken quoted the same figure a few years later and he suspected that "this item does not cost the average farmer in Saskatchewan more than it does the average one in either of the other Prairie Provinces."[158] Similar estimates from the 1930s place annual prairie crop losses from weed competition in the range of $40,000,000.[159]

These figures do not include the "high cost of additional cultivation done to keep weeds within bounds," nor do they reflect significantly increased costs for harvesting, threshing, handling and "shipping to Port Arthur and Fort William annually the equivalent of 96 train loads of 60 cars each of weed seeds."[160] Grain companies and farmers also had to bear the cost of seed cleaning and dockage — in 1933, dockage at Fort William, Port Arthur, Vancouver, Victoria, and Churchill amounted to 2.08% of the grain shipped, or 135,796 tons — and the depressing effect of weed seed contamination on the market price of grain.[161]

By the early 1940s, weeds were considered to be "the main factor in reducing crop yields" in the arid south-central portion of the Prairies where drought, soil drifting, and grasshopper attacks had long been serious problems.[162] In the more humid parts of the West, "crop losses due to weeds" were believed to amount to twenty-five percent.[163] Even in Alberta, the last province to be extensively settled by human and vegetative immigrants, the "expense incurred in weed control" was said to represent "the largest part of the cost required in producing crops."[164]

The most widespread and economically damaging weeds through to the end of World War II were the annual species that had invaded the Prairies during the earlier settlement period. Upon arriving on the eastern edge of the plains, these prodigious seed producers had embarked on a rapid march westward, leaving devastation and economic ruin in their wake. Tumble mustard and Russian thistle continued to battle farmers in the drier parts of the West and, by 1917, stinkweed was threatening Alberta after having overrun much of Saskatchewan.[165]

Within the ranks of these annual invaders one weed stood out amongst the rest — wild oats (*Avena fatua* L.). A nutritious grain in its own right, this species was an anathema to farmers because of its opportunistic nature and steadfast refusal to co-operate with their farming program. Wild oats spreads by seed that is difficult to clean from grain and impossible to separate from domesticated oats. It germinates early, is able to out-compete wheat and other cereals under all but optimum growing conditions, tolerates drought and frost, and, most importantly for farmers, sheds the bulk of its seed prior to harvest or upon the slightest touch from a harvester. To make matters worse, just enough seeds are retained on the stalk to contaminate harvested grain and straw. The seeds of wild oats have been known to lie dormant for decades and if a farmer neglects to cover them with soil they will bury themselves using a whip-like appendage that literally acts as a drill in response to changing moisture conditions.[166] They are more tolerant of poor soil conditions than domesticated cereals. They also are "highly self-fertile ... so an isolated plant can start an infestation."[167] Wild oats were commonly spread as a contaminant of straw used for packing material and either unintentionally or deliberately through animal feed. Seeds have been known to sprout in bird droppings and the manure of domesticated livestock and, to top everything off, there is even some suggestion that wild oats produce their own phytotoxins to ward off competitors.[168]

Quite possibly the most perfectly adapted of all the weedy associates of cereals, wild oats represents one of the most dangerous foes to invade the West during the pioneer era. A weed survey conducted by the Dominion Commission of Conservation in 1911 revealed that it had conquered all of the farms surveyed in Manitoba, seventy-one percent of the farms in Saskatchewan and, as of yet, only three percent in Alberta.[169] Results from the following year showed that the "invasion" was "widening and becoming faster."[170] By 1914, wild oats had marched "westward with a vengeance" to occupy over eighty percent of the Alberta farms surveyed.[171] Wild oats clung tenaciously to the territory it had won and during the 1930s and 1940s it remained the region's most widespread and prevalent weed except in the low rainfall districts of southern Saskatchewan and Alberta.[172]

Mere numbers, as impressive as they are, provide little indication of the devastation wrought by this single weed. Wild oats were so numerous on "many farms" around the time of the First World War that they were said to "leave little if any profit for the farmer."[173] There are even isolated reports of farms "being abandoned owing to wild oats and the stink weed."[174] These comments probably refer to the situation in Manitoba but, within a very short time, farmers in parts of Saskatchewan and Alberta were also being forced to retreat under the weed's onslaught. A correspondent to the *Country Guide*, for instance, reported in 1928 that there "are fields within ten miles of the city of Saskatoon where the wheat crop is reduced one-half or more by the presence of wild oats."[175] A more personal account of the ravages caused by this aggressive twin of domestic oats appeared in the same newspaper the following year:

Fifteen years ago this district had the reputation of the largest average yields per acre in the province of Saskatchewan.... Today we have the lowest average yield of any crop district in the province. Our farmers are nearly all bankrupt.... And the principal cause of our decline is weeds. Wild oats. This district is so completely in the grip of wild oats that it is practically impossible to grow a paying crop of wheat. Our farmers are dead beat in their efforts to control them. The man who finds a way of cleaning up land infested like this is, will have earned the lasting gratitude of this section of the province.[176]

If some farmers were left contemplating defeat because of the onslaught of wild oats alone, imagine their despair when confronted with an invasion comprising not one but many weedy species? Unfortunately for farmers, this was generally the case. The timing of tillage operations for annual species depends on when they germinate and how fast they mature and set seed and the entire issue of weed control is further complicated by the presence of perennials. Many procedures that are effective in suppressing annual weeds merely serve to propagate perennial species. Spring harrowing, for example, effectively controls early germinating annuals but if perennials are present, it often serves to spread their roots, rootstocks, or rhizomes throughout a field. By the end of World War I, farmers in all three Prairie provinces were faced with the situation outlined above. As the superintendent of Alberta's Seed and Weed Branch of the Department of Agriculture observed,

the condition of the Province with respect to weeds today is much different from what it was nine or ten years ago. In the early days such weeds as Stink Weed, Tumbling Mustard, Russian Thistle, Ball Mustard and Wild Oats, which are classified as either annuals or winter annuals, were the only weeds that appeared to trouble the farmers in their agricultural duties. Today these weeds are of secondary consideration, while such weeds as Canada Thistle, Perennial Sow Thistle, Couch Grass and Poverty Weed have come to the front. True they did not come as quickly as the first weeds but neither will they disappear as quickly because they are vicious perennial plants.[177]

Perennial sow-thistle was the first of these "vicious" perennials to launch a serious assault against western farmers. Introduced into Manitoba during the 1890s, *Sonchus arvensis* appears to have attracted little attention for over a decade either because it was not generally known or because it "was often mistaken for the dandelion."[178] The dandelion it most definitely was not! Within the space of little more than a decade it had gained a reputation "as one of the most serious menaces to farming in many parts of the West," and in districts of Manitoba it had "rendered whole fields unfit for grain production."[179] Manitoba farmers found that it was impossible to "get entirely rid of them by cultivation" and newspaper editors warned that the "spread of sow thistle through any district will, sooner or later, usher in the day of systematic 'mixed farming' or usher out the man who is determined to live on straight grain growing."[180]

Perennial sow-thistle had supplanted stinkweed and wild oats as the worst weed in Manitoba by the end of World War I. According to T. J. Harrison, professor of field husbandry at the Manitoba Agricultural College, the annual losses caused by this species were "enormous."[181] He estimated that yields of grain on land producing "a crop of sow thistle" were frequently reduced by one-half or even more, noted that "in some of the worst districts loan companies have refused to loan money on farm lands," and observed that the spread of the weed was "rapid and seemingly out of control." The threat of *S. arvensis* sparked a number of amendments to Prairie noxious-weed legislation and the country was liberally "plastered with warnings about the seriousness of this weed pest."[182]

Heedless of these human activities, perennial sow-thistle "marched steadily west."[183] By the late 1920s, it was "probably true that there isn't a wheat grower in the three prairie provinces who, if he hasn't some of this weed on his own place, lives within contamination's reach."[184] Official sources from Alberta indicate that perennial sow-thistle was "found in only a very few places" in 1910; by 1929, it could be found "in every part of the Province, where there has been cultivation for any period of time."[185] By 1932, Manitoba's Portage la Prairie district and the Red River Valley were also heavily infested as was the Quill Lake District of Saskatchewan and the extreme southeast portion of the province.[186]

Other perennial species that were contesting farmers for possession of Prairie homesteads include Canada thistle and couch or quack grass

(*Agropyron repens* (L.) Beauv.). Like perennial sow-thistle, both were present in the Prairies prior to the turn of the century and both had troubled farmers in Britain for centuries. Canada thistle and quack grass were "scattered all over the three provinces," with the worst infestations occurring in the more heavily watered portions of the West.[187] The quack-grass problem was so acute in some places that a writer for the *Country Guide* was led to seek solace in humour and a reinterpretation of a childhood song:

> As every one knows, the quickest way to get rid of a bad dose of quack grass is to plow the land deep in the fall and sell the farm before spring. But as this remedy is rather rough on the purchaser it is not widely recommended. Cases are not unknown, however, where the owner has been crowded off his land by quack grass without the opportunity of signing an agreement of sale. It is now generally believed that the reason Old Macdonald had a farm, and evidently hasn't got one now, is that the 'quack, quack here and a quack, quack there,' referred not to ducks, as the writer of the immortal song appears to have believed, but to patches of quack grass. Nor was he alone, for this persistent weed is licking more farmers than any other single weed in the older settled sections of this western country.[188]

The drought that attended the Great Depression seems to have slowed the spread of perennial weeds but, with the return of heavier precipitation in the late 1930s and 1940s, they resumed their slow but steady advance.[189] Their ranks were swelled by the conscription of several new perennial species, species that threatened to overwhelm farmers' remaining defences. Leafy spurge, Russian knapweed, hoary cress, and field bindweed began to attract serious attention during the early 1930s, by which time they had established isolated bridgeheads throughout the Prairies.[190] All were native to Europe or southern Russia and all found their new home and culture immensely favourable to a realization of their territorial ambitions. Leafy spurge is thought to have entered Minnesota around 1890 as a contaminant of seed oats imported from the Crimea and it was identified in Manitoba as early as 1911.[191] Russian knapweed and one or more species of hoary cress appeared in western Canada around the same time as a result of the importation of Turkestan alfalfa seed.[192]

Field bindweed probably immigrated at around roughly the same time and in a similar manner to the other three. By the early years of World War II, these four eastern European invaders were well established in the Prairie provinces and together they constituted one of the most serious threats to western agriculture.[193] Having arrived late on the scene and mainly spread by vegetative means, they had yet to form extensive infestations. Their threat, however, remained very real as "efficient" methods of controlling them had "not yet been demonstrated."[194] They could be eradicated by two or sometimes three years of continuous summer fallow, but as E. S. Hopkins of the Central Experimental Farm at Ottawa observed, this was not economical as the "cost of eradicating these weeds by cultivation is often more than the value of the land itself."[195]

Conclusion

By 1945, the weedy invasion of western Canada was nearing completion. The West had indeed lived up to its billing as a "land of opportunity," but more so for immigrant weeds than for their human compatriots. In accordance with the general rule that "the further the land is removed from breaking, the greater the weed menace," Manitoba was the first province to succumb.[196] Concerned observers such as R. D. Colquette, a columnist for the *Country Guide*, believed that farming in the province had reached a crossroads by the early 1930s. Past neglect and decades of continuous grain growing had left Manitoba farmers with "as foul a piece of land as the sun shines on in the course of 24 hours."[197] Weeds and, to a lesser extent, rust and declining soil fertility were simply "skimming enough of the cream of the agricultural income of the province to leave the milk a little too thin to sustain a prosperous agriculture."[198]

Farmers throughout the Prairies were soon facing a similar situation. Alberta's Field Crops commissioner commented in 1940 that,

in spite of extensive efforts by various agencies, governmental as well as private, weed infestation is growing in intensity. This may be due to neglect on the part of the farmer; his inability, or his present economic condition. That fact remains that an increasing proportion of land now in cultivation is losing its productivity due to the encroachment of noxious weeds…. Alberta is now entering upon or confronted with the third phase of weed control. It is the problem of dealing with a chronic situation, where the infestation of weeds has developed to such an extent that the farmer is unable to rehabilitate the land out of his own resources.[199]

O. S. Longman's assessment of the weed situation was even beginning to apply to the Peace River country, the last major frontier of Prairie settlement. One Alberta government official complained that Depression-era settlers were rapidly "fouling the new homestead with the weed filth of the old…. Thousands upon thousands of settlers driven out of Manitoba, Saskatchewan and Southern Alberta, by weeds, have blithely loaded up their second-hand machinery and other effects and headed north without cleaning the weeds out."[200] The effects of this dual migration were readily apparent by the end of World War II. Land in the Peace River district was already "polluted" by annual weeds "with the fecundity to occupy quickly the available space"; perennials such as Canada thistle, quack grass, perennial sow-thistle, and hoary cress were also present though "still in the process of invasion."[201]

The weedy invasion of the West is a testament to the futility of treating weeds as something separate from human culture, particularly in a country where most of the weeds are imported and relatively free of ecological constraints. The grain-fallow system of agriculture had reached its ultimate expression on the broad expanses of the Prairies but in the process had quite literally sown the seeds of its own destruction. Three generations of Canadian agricultural scientists had predicted this outcome; few had predicted just how serious a problem weeds would become. In the space of half a century or less, immigrant weeds had emerged as the leading cause of crop losses, the main reason for cultivation, and the largest single factor in the cost of crop production. They had been identified as the major source of soil moisture loss, were implicated in the Dust Bowl and, in extreme situations, were even credited with forcefully evicting farmers from their land.

The astonishing success of weeds in the West makes a mockery of noxious-weed laws and state educational programs. It also demonstrates that Canadian and American governments and state-funded agricultural scientists were singularly unsuccessful in bringing about a fundamental change in the way in which the land was farmed. At best, about all that they were able to accomplish was to increase awareness of the economic impact of weeds, to help farmers recognize some of the more dangerous species, and to suggest how to combat them within the limitations of the predominant grain-fallow system. At worst, governments, educators, and the farm press reinforced the idea that weeds were the farmer's worst enemy — the cause of declining profits rather than a symptom of environmentally unsound practices.

Farmers did not need to be taught to fear the enemy for they were the ones who felt the impact of weeds most keenly. Aggressive immigrant plants had forced them to adopt new tools and techniques and to labour longer and harder in order maintain their levels of income. Most authorities also believed that it was only a matter of time before weeds forced farmers to diversify and adopt a system of mixed farming. Expensive to convert to, unproven on the drier portion of the Prairies, impractical in areas where the cost of livestock production was high, and rendered less effective by a lack of suitable row crops, mixed farming held its own fears for farmers. Little wonder, therefore, that most struggled on in the hopes that through "some hocus pocus or action on the part of the government it will be possible to get rid of weeds and farming go on in the same old fashion."[202] The next chapter will show that, as unlikely as it sounds, this is precisely what happened.

6

The Bomb and Aftermath

1945 was a momentous year for two separate conflicts. Prairie farmers were embroiled in both and both witnessed the application of new technologies that changed the nature of warfare forever. Canadians were confident of victory in one of these conflicts, the outcome of which was all but decided before the first of the new technologies was even deployed. The second innovation, however, altered the entire course of a war. It injected new hope into troops that had been fighting a losing battle for decades and almost single-handedly averted an ignominious and near certain defeat. These two conflicts are, of course, World War II and the war on weeds in western Canada. The former was brought to a close through the dropping of the atomic bomb whereas the latter was indefinitely prolonged by the advent of 2,4-D and other selective herbicides.

The chapter begins with an account of the long but desultory search for a chemical solution to the weed menace in western Canada. This search was spearheaded by the government and driven by the increasingly desperate plight of farmers. Interest in the subject peaked on two separate

Wild oats, *Avena fatua*

occasions — once around the turn of the century and again in the late 1920s — only to wane in recognition of the serious limitations of the chemical weed killers that were then available. All this changed in 1945 with the commercial release of 2,4-D. Within the space of five years, 2,4-D "revolutionized" weed control on the western plains. It stiffened the resolve of embattled farmers and provided the impetus for the emergence of weed science as a distinct scientific discipline. As demonstrated in the final section, however, the arrival of powerful chemical weapons did not signal the end of the war on weeds as many had hoped. For, while modern herbicides can provide effective weed control when used on an ongoing basis, they have ironically become one of the mainstays of a cropping system that actively promotes the growth of unwanted vegetation.

Herbicide Development and Use in Western Canada to 1945

On the subject of chemical weed killers, H. T. Güssow, James Fletcher's successor as Dominion botanist, wrote in 1910: "There is something alluring in the thought of carrying on the fight in this way, instead of by the backbreaking use of the hoe, or by persistent attention to cultivation."[1] The allure of chemical weed killers, or "herbicides" as they came to be known, can be traced back to classical times but by the beginning of the nineteenth century, common salt was the only phytotoxic substance being used in Europe to any extent.[2] Salt's usefulness as a herbicide was limited by its indiscriminate nature — it kills most crops as well as weeds — and by the fact that when it is used at rates sufficient to suppress unwanted vegetation, it "leaves the soil almost indefinitely sterile."[3]

The first major breakthroughs in the development of "selective" herbicides occurred in the mid-1890s with the French discovery that weak solutions of copper or iron sulfate as well as dilute sulfuric acid were capable of destroying wild mustard (*Sinapis arvensis* L.) in fields of grain.[4] Professor H. L. Bolley of the North Dakota Agricultural Experiment Station began his own tests on these substances in 1896, and, in 1898, extensive trials were launched in Britain.[5] Canadian researchers were not far behind and, by the summer of 1899, copper sulfate tests were underway at the Central Experimental Farm in Ottawa and at the Ontario Agricultural College at Guelph.[6] Under pressure from the Winnipeg editor of the *Farmer's*

Advocate, the Manitoba government followed suit in 1905, and, in 1911, the Alberta Department of Agriculture began iron and copper sulfate spraying demonstrations at Olds College north of Calgary.[7]

The initial excitement died down once it became apparent that these chemicals were not about to revolutionize weed control in western Canada. There are isolated reports of farmers adopting this new technology with a fair degree of success.[8] Most, however, showed little interest because of the relatively high cost, the large size of Prairie farms, and the narrow range of weed species controlled.[9] The 1909 edition of *Farm Weeds of Canada* makes no mention of chemical weed control, and, while John Bracken did recommend iron and copper sulfate for eradicating wild mustard on Prairie farms in 1921, he observed: "In any case the practice of spraying for weed control is expensive and has not yet therefore come into general use."[10]

The American authors of the first book solely devoted to the subject of weed "control," *Weed Control: A Textbook and Manual* (1942), argued that following the "initial period (1896–1910)" of herbicide development,

> interest in the control of annual weeds lapsed in America. The lag in the production of adequate spray machinery, the frequent lack of success because of low humidity, and, above all, the immense scale upon which grain farms were operated, precluding the possibility of completing, within the short time during which both weeds and cereals were in the proper stages for treatment, a successful spray program, all contributed to this declining interest.[11]

Their observation also appears to hold true for Canada. Between 1910 and the late 1920s, there are almost no references to herbicide development or use in the leading Prairie agricultural periodicals and government testing was severely restricted.[12] There were a few commercial weed killers on the market but all were intended for use on noncrop areas and there is no evidence of aggressive marketing by chemical companies in the western Canadian farm press. Agricultural scientists began to hold out little hope for the discovery of a chemical "cure-all that [would] destroy all kinds of weeds."[13] The farm press, in turn, developed an abiding suspicion of the claims of various herbicide manufacturers:

The spread of thistles has aroused great interest in chemical weed killers. This solution of the weed problem has been with us from time immemorial. First it's one chemical, then another. Once in a while the old formulae are dressed up in new names and the product invites new confidence by becoming the invention of a Danish or a German or a Patagonian chemist.[14]

At about the time this passage was written in 1930, scorn was giving way to cautious optimism due to reports from the United States that indicated an effective chemical for combating deep-rooted perennials had been discovered.[15] The phytotoxic properties of calcium and sodium chlorate had been known since 1904 but, until the late 1920s, their use was restricted to vegetation control along railway lines.[16] The Field Crops Branch of the Alberta Department of Agriculture initiated preliminary trials with commercial chlorate formulations in 1927 and within a year the *Nor'-West Farmer* was reporting that,

there is considerable interest in the possibility of destroying weeds by applying certain chemicals. It has been brought to our attention that some firms are advertising the fact that the Government is using their chemical weed destroyers and on that account the effectiveness of the product is assured. So far as we know the only way in which Governments are using chemical weed destroyers at the present time is for experimental purposes. At any rate farmers will be well advised to investigate any such claims made by manufacturers and distributors before they invest much money in the product.[17]

By 1929, the "prominence being given recently to chlorates" encouraged extensive testing by the federal and all three Prairie departments of agriculture.[18] In the spring of that year, Chipman Chemicals, the manufacturer of the sodium chlorate herbicide "Atlacide," also launched a short-lived advertising campaign. Farmers were told to "Kill Those Weeds" and "make war on sow thistle with Chipman's Atlacide." Skeptics were reassured that it was "recommended by Saskatchewan and Alberta Departments of Agriculture."[19] Excitement over the potential of chlorate weed killers was so great that in the fall of 1929, the National Research

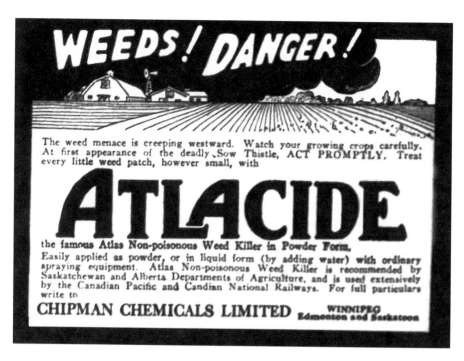

Halting the westward march of weeds with Chipman Chemical's Atlacide
(*Nor'-West Farmer*, 20 May 1929)

Council of Canada (NRC) held a conference in Edmonton to explore "the destruction of weeds by the means of chemicals."[20] Attended by delegates from various branches of the federal government, Prairie departments of agriculture, agricultural colleges and universities, and a number of commercial firms, the most significant outcome of the conference was the appointment of an Associate Committee on Weed Control that was charged with developing a coordinated weed control research program.

Composed of members drawn from all levels of government, the three Prairie universities, seed growers associations, the railways, and the chemical industry, the Associate Committee on Weed Control was soon responsible for sponsoring and coordinating a wide range of chemical trials as well as much overdue research into basic weed biology, ecology, and cultural control.[21] The NRC itself took responsibility for spearheading the experimental search for "new chemical herbicides" while the study of weed biology and ecology was assigned to researchers at the universities of Manitoba and Saskatchewan.[22] The Dominion Experimental Farms Branch had been indirectly studying weed control since 1911 through a Prairie-wide series of crop rotation experiments but, beginning in 1929, weed control became the subject of explicit research. Chemical and cultural control field trials were begun at Brandon that year and, by 1939, "special weed control experiments" were under way at Brandon, Indian Head, Regina, Melfort, Scott, Swift Current, and Lethbridge.[23] As mentioned above, herbicide trials were initiated in 1929 by all three Prairie departments of agriculture. These trials were continued in 1930 under a co-operative agreement with the NRC. Within a few years, however, most were cancelled or handed over to the federal government because of budgetary constraints and the need to address more pressing issues such as drought, serious grasshopper outbreaks, and farm relief.[24]

The arrival of the chlorate weed killers provided the impetus for extensive herbicide testing and, along with exploding weed populations, they helped raise the profile of weeds in general. As an author of one NRC report observed, because of the interest generated by these chemicals, weeds had finally begun "to occupy the serious attention of scientific investigators.... No such body of knowledge exists about weeds as about animal and plant diseases and insects, and until very recently no adequate investigations were under way to obtain such knowledge."[25]

Chlorate herbicides also provided farmers with an effective, if severely limited, weapon for attacking hard-to-control perennial species. Tests showed that sodium or calcium chlorate sprays were quite effective in killing weeds such as leafy spurge (*Euphorbia esula* L.), field bindweed (*Convolvulus arvensis* L.), hoary cress (*Cardaria* spp.), Russian knapweed *(Centaurea repens* L.), and some of the perennial thistles. It soon became apparent, however, that they were "too costly to be used on an acreage basis. The place of these chemicals [was] on small isolated patches and where tillage machinery cannot be used."[26] Because they were nonselective and quite persistent, chlorate weed killers also have the unfortunate effect of rendering the soil unsuitable for cropping for two or more years after application at the high rates necessary to provide effective control of perennial weeds. Not only were they a hazard to crops, but as J. E. Howitt of the Ontario Agricultural College warned: "when you are using sodium chlorate and it gets mixed with dry soil, underclothing or any other dry matter it is liable to burst into flames."[27]

In spite of their limitations, chlorates became the first chemical weed killers to gain a fair degree of acceptance on the Prairies. Their adoption cannot be credited to an aggressive marketing campaign by Chipman Chemicals and other manufacturers for there was none. Instead, provincial governments deserve most of the "credit" for their growing popularity. All three provincial departments of agriculture began recommending the use of chlorates in the early 1930s, and within five years they were supplying farmers with subsidized chemical and sprayers. Manitoba began supplying Atlacide to rural municipalities in 1934 in an attempt to halt the spread of leafy spurge. The Department of Agriculture paid approximately two-thirds the cost of the chemical and, by 1937, government officials were pleased to report that "considerable advantage has been taken of this offer."[28] Alberta and Saskatchewan implemented similar programs in 1936 and 1937 respectively.[29]

Herbicide use on the Prairies remained closely linked to government programs through to the end of the Second World War. By the late 1930s, selective sprays such as sulfuric acid and the recently introduced French discovery, Sinox (sodium dinitro-ortho-cresylate), were becoming increasingly popular for the control of wild mustard but, because they were expensive with treatment costs ranging from about $2.00 to $3.50 per acre, their use was strictly "limited to heavy weed infestations or to areas where intensive land use [was] practised."[30] They never, in consequence, seriously challenged sodium chlorate's position as the most commonly used chemical weed killer in western Canada.

The volume of government-subsidized sodium chlorate or Atlacide annually applied on the Prairies was initially quite modest. In 1938, for example, Alberta's Field Crop Branch distributed 5,264 pounds of sodium chlorate and 3,150 pounds of Atlacide to farmers for the treatment of small patches of hoary cress, leafy spurge, and Russian knapweed.[31] These numbers had risen substantially by the end of the war. The Saskatchewan government supplied seventy-four rural municipalities with 70,000 pounds of Atlacide "at cost" in 1945; Alberta distributed over 100,000 pounds of sodium chlorate the same year.[32] Manitoba did even better. According to Henry Wood of the Provincial Weeds Commission, 1,089,000 pounds of government-subsidized Atlacide was used in the province between 1940 and 1945.[33] Purchased in large quantities, governments were able to offer this chemical for sale to farmers at a reduced price and an added subsidy in Manitoba made it even more attractive.[34] In 1942, the Manitoba government further encouraged the use of Atlacide through changes to the provincial Noxious Weeds Act. Farmers whose land was declared a "weed infested area" under section seven of the act were compelled to enter into an agreement with the municipality detailing how patches of proscribed perennial weeds were to be controlled and the "application of chemicals" was clearly identified as a preferred method.[35]

2,4-D and the Dawning of the "Hormone Era," 1945–1950

The significance of the chlorate weed killers does not ultimately stem from the volume of chemical used or their revolutionary effect on Prairie agriculture. Wood's figure of 1,089,000 pounds of Atlacide, for example, sounds like a great deal. But, when one considers that it was used at the rate of about 1.5 pounds per 100 square feet, the total area treated by this chemical amounts to considerably less than 2,000 acres.[36] Chlorate weed killers are significant as a harbinger of the developments that followed, for generating sustained herbicide research, and for strengthening governments' commitment to chemical warfare.

The depth of their commitment was revealed in 1945 with the commercial release of 2,4-dichlorophenoxyacetic acid, commonly known as 2,4-D. Discovered independently in England and the United States in the early 1940s, 2,4-D was the product of plant hormone research rather than the agriculturists' somewhat random search for phytotoxic compounds and it proved to be far more potent than any herbicide previously developed.[37] One to two ounces per acre are all that is required to kill a wide range of broad-leaf species. More importantly, 2,4-D is also highly selective, for when it is applied at these rates, most grasses are unaffected. The potential use for such a chemical in a land dominated by cereal production and awash in broad-leaf weeds is obvious and before long it was being credited with signifying "the arrival of a new era in farming — the hormone era!"[38] For many agriculturists, the arrival of 2,4-D could not have been more timely: science had suddenly delivered the ultimate anti-weed weapon just as farmers were on the verge of admitting defeat in their war for economic survival.

Federal and provincial departments of agriculture began extensive testing of 2,4-D in the year of its release.[39] Reporting on this flurry of activity
in early 1947, Henry Wood of the Manitoba Weeds Commission speculated that it "may prove to be the most widespread and extensive series
of trials and demonstrations that has yet taken place on this continent
in testing a product in the field of agriculture."[40] Wood's comment can
be found in the first major article on 2,4-D to appear in *The Country
Guide*, western Canada's leading farm magazine, and in it he attributes the
intense interest generated by the new discovery to the chemical's selective
action, low toxicity, ease of handling, and low cost. Relatively inexpen-
sive to manufacture and not subject to patent restrictions because it was
developed at an American government institution, 2,4-D had, by then,
already become the "accepted treatment" for broad-leaf weed control on
lawns and golf courses, but Wood believed that its greatest potential lay
in selective control in cereal crops as well as the treatment of summer fallows where it promised to reduce labour costs and lessen "the hazard of
soil drifting."[41]

Agricultural scientists were attracted to 2,4-D for much the same reasons. On a less altruistic note, they also remarked that herbicide research
produced much faster results and was far easier to define and conduct
than experimentation on "other weed control measures such as tillage
or cropping practices."[42] By 1947, the volume of research under way
was so great that the successor to the Associate Committee on Weed
Control, the National Weed Committee, decided to convene a conference
in Regina to "bring together those engaged in, or closely associated with,
any of the many phases of weed work, and particularly the more recent
introduction of chemical weed control, so that we may pool our knowledge and better plan action in the immediate future."[43]

The first Western Canadian Weed Control Conference drew 142 delegates from across Canada. Canadian research was still primarily in the
hands of government investigators (most university research was government funded) but the conference was well attended by representatives
of the chemical and farm implement industries, many of whom hailed
from the United States.[44] The three-day event received extensive press
coverage, in part because of the promotional efforts of Henry Wood and

the other conference organizers. But, as the following account from the *Country Guide* implies, 2,4-D's obvious potential guaranteed that it would attract a great deal of attention in an era marked by a near absolute faith in science:

> The conference was avowedly limited to the discussion of 2,4-D,... The talking was left almost entirely to the technical investigators, a class of men who are generally cautious about predictions, but a layman checking the claims and counter-claims would be forced to conclude that chemical weed control has only made a beginning. It is not too much to expect that soon new chemicals will be forthcoming till farmers can obtain complete weed control in any crop. The picture is changing so fast that there is no guarantee that we shall be interested in 2,4-D ten years from now.[45]

Largely a World War II phenomenon, blind faith in science's ability to solve the world's problems was destined to grow even stronger in the 1950s and early 1960s. Right from the start, however, there were those who urged caution. More than one agricultural scientist felt that the "feverish activity" surrounding 2,4-D and other herbicides was beginning to obscure a pressing need for basic research on weed biology and ecology.[46] Others, including even the most ardent supporters of this new technology, were "not unmindful that any sound programme of weed control rests upon tried and tested farm practices, which can be summed up in a single phrase — good farming."[47]

Government scientists and officials continued to caution farmers throughout the remainder of the decade not to regard 2,4-D as a "cure-all" or as a "complete answer to the weed problem."[48] Unfortunately, this message was all too often overshadowed by their own unbridled enthusiasm for the new technology. The Manitoba Weeds Commission, for example, initially adopted a cautious approach but before long, chemical weed control was being "preached by the Commission Chairmen with missionary zeal; then adopted as common practice in the co-operative measures undertaken by provincial and municipal governments."[49]

Chemical companies were not under a similar obligation to stress caution and the value of conventional practices. Armed with official recommendations and glowing reports from federal and provincial author- ities, they launched a massive marketing campaign late in the 1946 season.[50] By 1948, the era of the "hard sell" had truly begun. Readers of the *Country Guide* were treated to full-page advertisements extolling the virtues of numerous brands of 2,4-D; ads for brands such as Green Cross's "Weed-No-More" that featured the picture of a starving child beside the caption "the whole world is crying for more food."[51] D. D. Fraser, a repre- sentative of the Winnipeg branch of Naugatuch Chemicals, estimated in 1950 that twenty-three companies were offering, through a multitude of dealers, one or more brands of 2,4-D on the Western Canadian market.[52] In the same year, the *Country Guide* reported that the number of herbi- cides registered under the federal Pest Control Products Act (1939) had risen from 91 in 1947 to 212 in 1950. One hundred and fifty-one of these represented various 2,4-D formulations and a further ten were combina- tions of 2,4-D and the related chemical 2,4,5-T (2,4,5-trichlorophenoxy- acetic acid).[53]

Both government and industry were clearly in the business of selling herbicides between 1945 and 1950 and, of the two, the state almost certainly played the leading role. Most of the numerous herbicide field demonstrations held during this period were staged by various govern- ment agencies. Herbicide manufacturers often supplied the chemical and application equipment while government provided the venue, publicity, organization, and stamp of authority.[54] As one Saskatchewan farmer observed in 1950, government scientists and officials also supplied a great deal of assurance:

> The last word has not been said on educating the farmers in the use of 2,4-D. Practical information must reach them down on the farm. More authoritative literature, in concise and precise form, must be placed in their hands. Gaudy literature by commercial companies, often worded extravagantly, is confusing to the farmer reader. He is inclined to heed the advice issued by Weed Councils, Experimental Farms and Departments of Agriculture.[55]

Even industry readily acknowledged its debt to the government. Federal officials, the Dominion Experimental Farms Branch, provincial

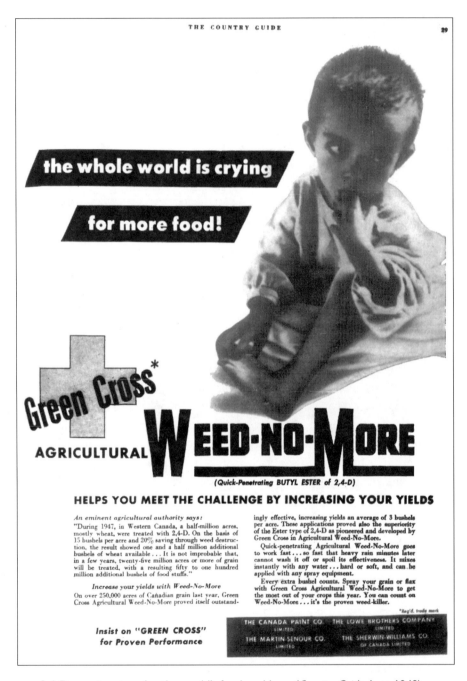

2,4-D promises to solve the world's food problems (*Country Guide*, June 1948)

universities, and various departments of agriculture were commended for being "most anxious to undertake extensive testing of the new herbicides where screening data warrants the study," for providing free publicity, and for helping sell chemicals through their "unbiased observations."[56]

Many of these arguments were repeated in Henry Wood's 1950 Western Canadian Weed Control Conference address. Presented under the revealing title, "'Selling' Chemical Weed Control," Wood, past chairman of both the Manitoba Weeds Commission and the National Weed Committee and currently an official with the Manitoba Department of Agriculture, told his listeners that in order to achieve "the universal use of selective chemical in weed control," the farmer must be taught to "use 2,4-D over most of, if not all, his crop each season."[57] He acknowledged that 2,4-D had its limitations — "if for no other reason than that a number of weeds, including some of the most common, are resistant or nearly so to the chemical" — but he felt that the chemical's value was sufficiently great that it was the responsibility of governments and industry alike to promote its use through expanded research, "intensified" extension work, the continuation of "an aggressive sales policy," and product standardization.[58]

Wood and his industry colleagues pointed to the dramatic increase in herbicide utilization in western Canada as evidence of the success of their selling job. The sheer rate at which this new technology was accepted, however, suggests that the idea of chemical warfare had already been sold. Hard-pressed western Canadian farmers were simply desperate for an economical solution to a weed problem that had reached crisis proportions — 2,4-D met their needs perfectly. Costing "under a dollar an acre for chemical and application combined," it was cheap enough to use on large acreages.[59] By virtue of its selective action, it also promised to provide safe and effective control of many of the most economically significant weeds plaguing the region's most important crops. Perhaps most importantly of all, farmers were able to incorporate the use of 2,4-D into existing production systems without fundamentally altering the way they farmed.

In 1947, 2,4-D was made available for commercial use on cereals and an estimated 500,000 acres of Prairie grain were treated that year.[60] Henry Wood reported that even "though very few operators of the several thousand machines used to apply this newest of chemicals were experienced, practically no complaints were lodged as to the job done." Moreover, he suggested that a larger acreage might have been treated if it were not for a "bottle-neck" created by a shortage of sprayers and dusters.[61] Implement manufacturers rushed to meet this demand and within two years, fourteen different makes of sprayers were available in Manitoba alone.[62] More sprayers, coupled with the development of low-volume nozzles, enabled farmers to treat upwards of 4,000,000 acres in 1948 and 8,200,000 acres in 1949, the latter figure prompting Wood to enthuse, "This marks a tremendous forward step in the control of what is now quite generally conceded to be responsible for the major crop loss over the whole of the cultivated area in western Canada."[63]

During the 1950 crop year, only five years after 2,4-D was introduced for field trials in Canada, it was applied to no less than 13,566,000 acres of Prairie crop land.[64] Saskatchewan farmers led the way as befits the leading grain-producing province — they treated an estimated 8,640,000 acres in 1950 — with Alberta farmers coming in second at 2,904,000 acres, and Manitoba third at 2,022,000 acres.[65] Henry Wood calculated that between 1947 and 1950, Prairie farmers had spent in excess of "$33,000,000 divided about equally between chemical and [application] equipment," and that this outlay had resulted in "an estimated increase in revenue of $130,000,000."[66]

Thirteen million acres still only represented about one-third of the crop acreage in the Prairie provinces and about three-quarters of the region's farmers still showed varying degrees of resistance to using the new technology.[67] The use of 2,4-D, however, had clearly passed the experimental stage and throughout the grain-producing regions of western North America it had already "lowered costs of weed control in cereal crops to a level that rules out many cultural and cropping procedures."[68] The psychological impact of 2,4-D was equally great. Farmers had been instilled with new hope and as T. K. Pavlychenko, Canada's leading weed researcher, remarked, "The year of 1944 will always remain as a turning point and a landmark in the long history of man's struggle against the most costly enemy to agriculture — weeds, as the first 2,4-D weed killer was commercially produced."[69]

Fallout

During the 1950s, government scientists and officials continued to warn farmers that, while the "elaboration in the use of chemicals has revolutionized weed control practices ... other methods of control should not be considered of secondary importance."[70] Good husbandry still had its advocates but, unfortunately for them, the first part of their message often conflicted with the second and the whole read as a tacit admission of the superiority of chemical control. The acreage treated with herbicides, primarily 2,4-D, remained relatively stable between 1950 and the middle of the decade, but even so, P. O. Ripley, head of the Field Husbandry Division of the Dominion Experimental Farms Service, was confident that "no other area in the world has a larger proportion of the cropped area sprayed than the Prairie Provinces of Western Canada."[71] To highlight this achievement, he provided statistics showing that only about eight to nine percent of the cropped area in the United States was annually treated with herbicides and that in no state did this figure exceed twenty-seven percent.[72] A few years earlier, Ripley had toured the United Kingdom and western Europe as part of a Canadian agricultural mission. There he was somewhat surprised to learn that chemical control "has not met with the enthusiasm which it has on this continent, following the introduction of growth regulating types of weed killers."[73] He attributed this difference to the cautious, conservative nature of European farmers and because

> the farmers of Britain, The Netherlands, Denmark, Sweden and France have farmed for centuries. They have practised good husbandry. They have had enough labor to do considerable hand work.... The crops in the main are magnificent, and clean.[74]

The development of a truly bewildering array of herbicides during the 1950s and 1960s broadened the appeal of a chemical solution to the weed problem. In 1950, for example, twenty five different chemicals were available for use in North America; by 1969, there were 120.[75] Between 1954 and 1968, the acreage treated with 2,4-D and other phenoxy herbicides tripled in Alberta, Saskatchewan, and Manitoba, and within a five-year span beginning in 1963, the use of other phytotoxic compounds "increased more than eleven-fold."[76]

By 1970, farmers had the ability to selectively control nearly all of the important weeds in all of the leading crops on the Prairies. The use of 2,4-D and closely related chemicals was being described as "almost universal" in cereals, and it had become "very difficult to visualize the production of crops in western Canada without the almost insistent use of herbicides."[77] Herbicide usage peaked in the United States during the early 1980s "when over 90% of the acreage of major crops was treated with herbicides."[78] It is safe to assume that equivalent figures for western Canada are just as high or even higher. The total volume of herbicides applied has probably declined slightly since then, largely because of the development of increasingly potent compounds, but chemicals easily remain the dominant method of weed control in the West and they promise to continue as such for the foreseeable future.

Soon after the release of 2,4-D, some Canadian agricultural scientists began to have premonitions that the allure of selective herbicides would prove too powerful to resist. They also foresaw that herbicides had the potential to transform the study of weeds into a bona fide science. The only question that remained was what kind of science was it going to be? Were herbicides going to dominate the research agenda of the new discipline so completely that it would become difficult to see the weeds for the sprays? The answers to these questions will become clear shortly. For now, it is important to note that "weed science" did become a recognized profession in North America by the early 1950s. According to T. K. Pavlychenko, late of the University of Saskatchewan and, since 1948, western Canadian director of research for the American Chemical Paint Company (one of the largest herbicide manufacturers in North America), great strides had already been made by 1950:

The extent of the psychological impression which the discovery and first performances of these chemicals had produced on public minds may be, at least partially, measured by the fact than in less than four years the entire North American continent was organized into regional weed control conferences where the best plant and chemical scientists and the most responsible agricultural authorities annually come together to appraise the available data concerning functions of the new herbicides.[79]

He added that all federal, state, and provincial departments of agriculture now had weed divisions and that "new scientific classes on weeds" had been initiated at practically every university in Canada and the United States.[80]

The four American regional weed control conferences referred to by Pavlychenko banded together in 1949 to form the Association of Regional Weed Control Conferences.[81] Canadian weed researchers from the Prairie provinces were well represented in at least one of these conferences — the north central — and they maintained their affiliation in 1954 when the Association of Regional Weed Control Conferences became the Weed Society of America (WSA).[82] Later called the Weed Science Society of America (WSSA), the WSA represents the first professional association of weed scientists in North America and a clear sign that the study of weeds had finally been elevated to the level of a distinct discipline — a distinction enjoyed by entomology and plant pathology for close to a century. Three years previously, the rapidly maturing discipline had acquired its own journal. Initially published by the Association of Weed Control Conferences, *Weeds* was the first scientific journal entirely devoted to "the science and art of weed control."[83] By the late 1980s, Canadian membership in the WSSA numbered about 172 out of a total North American membership of approximately 2,000, with the majority of Canadian members being employed by various government agencies.[84]

The American pesticide industry lent its wholehearted support to the formation of the WSA in 1954, and herbicides dominated the research agenda of the new discipline from the very start.[85] As early as 1951, over half of the weed control research in the United States was being conducted by chemical manufacturers who were quick to recognize the huge commercial potential of 2,4-D and the newer herbicides.[86] The number of American weed scientists employed by industry increased rapidly until it reached a peak in the early 1980s whereas the "numbers of public weed scientists dealing with research and education have shown meager increases since the early 1950s."[87] Although not wholly consumed with chemical investigations, American state-funded research has long been heavily weighted towards the study of herbicides. This partly reflects the fact that research "on competition and cropping methods is necessarily time-consuming and costly" and frequently yields questionable results because of the number of variables involved.[88] Other government weed scientists maintain that their fascination with herbicides simply reflects "necessity": chemicals provide "truly effective" weed control while numerous studies have shown that "cultivation, cropping, and all the other cultural and mechanical practices could, at best, only contain or slightly abate many of the weed problems."[89]

Canadian weed research has also focussed on herbicides since 1950, although a proportionately greater emphasis has been placed on the study of basic weed biology, ecology, and nonchemical means of control because of a reduced industry presence. As P. O. Ripley observed in 1953, the discovery and initial development of all the new selective weed killers took place outside of Canada, but Canadians "were fast to learn of the possibilities of these herbicides and have perhaps done as much as any country to learn how to apply them."[90] Of the 171 weed research projects underway in Canada that year, all but "a few" were being conducted by government agencies or university investigators and fully eighty percent were solely concerned with various aspects of herbicide chemistry, use, or modes of action.[91] Canada still lacked a dominant industry presence in 1970 but in the estimation of one weed scientist from the University of Guelph, this deficiency had done little to hinder the development of weed science into something more truly akin to a science of herbicides:

The basic chemistry in the discovery of the herbicides used in Canadian crop production is almost entirely imported. Indeed, a great deal of the formulated herbicide or technical material also is imported. Any discussion of the weed scientists' role in Canadian food production, therefore, is one of the development of the use of imported herbicidal compounds in our own crop production environment.... The general lack of a basic chemical industry has not hampered our progress simply because as soon as new compounds become known, we have the capacity to develop their use. The development of these compounds for use has been given top priority and the extension of this use has had equally top priority.[92]

Scientists and government officials of the late 1940s had accurately predicted the general direction, if not the extent, of the changes resulting from the introduction of selective herbicides to western Canada. They were also right in suggesting that while these chemicals presented farmers with an extremely potent weapon, they did not offer a final solution to the weed problem. The first difficulty to arise was a product of one of 2,4-D's greatest strengths — its highly selective nature. As early as 1948, government officials were afraid that the unbounded enthusiasm for 2,4-D was drawing attention away from "the seriousness of the Wild Oat problem."[93] Like most grasses, wild oats (*Avena fatua* L.) are resistant to 2,4-D and other phenoxy herbicides, and scientists feared that the widespread use of these chemicals would favour the "germination and development of wild oats" by removing competition from other weeds.[94]

These early fears proved to be well founded. Undeterred by the chemical weapons that were thinning the ranks of its fellow invaders, wilds oats had, by the mid-1950s, easily become "the most serious weed infesting cereal crops in Western Canada."[95] By then it is believed to have occupied "to some degree more than 75 percent of all the cultivated land in the Prairie Provinces."[96] Relatively effective chemicals for the control of wild oats in cereals and oilseed crops were developed in the 1960s and 1970s but, for a variety of reasons, they appear to have done little to check the damage done by this species. Late-1970s estimates of the annual losses due to wild oats on the Prairies range from a low of $120 million to upwards of $500 million, thus earning the species the distinction of being

> by far the most troublesome weed of almost the entire cultivated portion of the Northern Plains of the Great Plains Region of North America. This includes the prairie provinces of Canada, the northern half of South Dakota, the northwest fringe of Minnesota, North Dakota and Montana. The total area infested with wild oats in Canada and the United States is estimated at over 25 million ha.[97]

Avena fatua continues to extract millions of dollars annually from Prairie farmers, and it is not the only species to have benefited from the near universal use of 2,4-D and related compounds such as MCPA

(2-methyl-4-chlorophenoxyacetic acid). The results of an extensive late-1970s Saskatchewan weed survey suggest that the long-term popularity of phenoxy herbicides, most notably 2,4-D and MCPA, has had a profound influence on the province's weed flora — changes that would have come as quite a revelation to early proponents of chemical warfare![98] Green foxtail (*Setaria viridis* (L.) Beauv.), wild buckwheat (*Polygonum convolvulus* L.), and wild oats, for example, were found to be the three most abundant arable weeds in the province.[99] All three were present in a high proportion of the fields surveyed — up to eighty-three percent in the case of wild buckwheat — where they frequently occurred in dense stands.[100] All three, not coincidentally, also display resistance to the chemicals commonly used for broad-leaf weed control. Similar herbicide-induced changes in Prairie weed populations have also been reported by J. F. Alex of the Ontario Agricultural College:

> Several weeds have been increasing in importance in recent years. Notable among these are: *Asclepias speciosa* and *A. syriaca*, native perennials in the southern part of the prairies; *Setaria viridis* which has been sweeping westward across the prairies, seeming to invade new regions by becoming established first on the coarse-textured soils and then spreading out onto the medium and fine textures. *S. viridis* may also belong to the next group. *Saponaria vaccaria, Polygonum convolvulus, P. lapathifolium, P. scabrum, Silene noctiflora*, and other annual species which are tolerant of the widely used phenoxy herbicides have increased at the expense of the herbicide-susceptible annuals which previously had competed with and helped to suppress them.[101]

A second problem arising from the widespread use of herbicides is the development of resistance in previously susceptible species. As early as 1948, delegates to the Second Western Canadian Weed Control Conference were alerted to this possibility by Dr. L. M. Stahler of the United States Department of Agriculture: "it is conceivable that over a period of years of wide use of 2,4-D we will develop strains that are almost entirely immune to this herbicide."[102] Stahler's warning seems to have passed unnoticed and twenty years were to elapse before the first case of herbicide resistance was actually reported: triazine resistance in common groundsel (*Senecio vulgaris* L.).[103] Within a decade of this discovery, however, weed scientists were reporting that the "occurrence of herbicide resistant biotypes seems to be a general phenomenon in many weedy species."[104]

Initially, they found it "difficult to estimate" the significance of this new development.[105] Were farmers facing, or soon to be faced with, significantly increased competition from weeds? Did the ability of weeds to adapt to chemical warfare threaten the long-term viability of today's leading herbicides? Can science develop new weed killers faster than weeds can develop resistance? Today, most of these questions remain unanswered but few experts doubt that "evolved resistance" poses "a serious problem for chemical weed control."[106] Resistance to triazine herbicides has now been detected in fifty seven weedy species and, in addition,

at least 47 species have been reported to have biotypes resistant to one or more of 14 other herbicides or herbicide families … although herbicide resistance was later to appear than pesticide resistance in insects and fungi, resistance in weeds is rapidly increasing at a rate equivalent to that of insecticide and fungicide resistance.[107]

Increased use of herbicides has contributed to a number of other equally serious problems. These include escalating difficulties with volunteer cereals and the near absolute dependency of farmers on chemicals that are vulnerable to changes in price, regulation, and public opinion. In the final analysis, herbicides have been shown to create almost as many problems as they solve. They have done so in part because reliance on chemicals masks the underlying causes of weed problems and in part because chemical dependency perpetuates ecologically unsound farming practices:

Most of the traditional chemical herbicide industry is based on ignorance of the ecological niche concept. These chemical "silver bullets" kill undesirable plants all right, sometimes whole fields of them, but they do not destroy the niche. Unless other, more desirable plants are primed and ready to spring immediately into the empty niche, a new flush of weeds will simply occupy it again.[108]

Although continuing to harbour misgivings, North American weed scientists as a group remained firmly committed to chemical weed control for over thirty years after the introduction of 2,4-D. Throughout this period, the harshest criticism of chemical control came from outside the profession. In 1950, for example, the farmer, educator, and world traveller Joe Cocannouer prophesied that indiscriminate herbicide use could result in serious ecological problems. He added that "it is entirely possible that a very small amount of some poisons will create far more havoc than is at present suspected of them."[109] Agricultural "poisons" were, indeed, soon wreaking havoc but the antipesticide movement that arose in the wake of Rachel Carson's *Silent Spring* (1962) caused surprisingly little concern amongst weed science circles. Weed scientists comforted themselves with the knowledge that unlike insecticides and fungicides, herbicides rarely presented a direct toxicological threat to applicators, animals, or the food chain and what problems they did exhibit were within the realm of technology to solve "if given the chance."[110] As President Glenn Klingman told his listeners during the 1970 WSSA annual meeting in Montreal, there was simply no going back: "naturalists want 'natural foods' produced by 'nature's wisdom', in a 'balanced nature', and in an 'environment free from technology,'" yet they "have no interest, personally, in returning to a nature balanced by hunger, malnutrition, disease, insects, vermin, and a forbidding and often hostile environment."[111]

Within a decade or so of Klingman's denunciation of the naturalist movement, chemical weed control was again under attack. This time, however, criticism was far harder to deflect as much of it was being generated by weed scientists themselves. By the early 1980s, many of the problems associated with prolonged herbicide use had reached a level where they could no longer be ignored. Weed scientists, in other words, were being forced to admit that weeds "have persisted in spite of control."[112] Their response was to turn to the science of ecology for help and to emphasize the need to understand and manipulate weed populations rather than seeking to destroy them. They also began to advocate the use of a new term in place of the venerable phrase "weed control":

The weed control of tomorrow will not further insist on the 'ruthless fight until the last weed', as the hopes raised by the advent of herbicides proved to be exaggerated and today it seems that this fight will never come to an end. The farmers will have to work not against but with the weeds. By cunning use of modern knowledge of their biology the farmer will try to maintain and manipulate a certain weed population in his fields trying to avoid its negative effects but to preserve its positive ones: weed management instead of weed control. To make this "science fiction" vision possible a lot of research still has to be done.[113]

"Weed management" and the ecological concepts that it embraces has attracted a great deal of attention from weed scientists over the past fifteen to twenty years.[114] The influence of this new philosophy is readily apparent in a 1988 survey of the research priorities of WSSA members in Canada and the United States: the twenty-five Canadians who responded ranked the importance of developing "new ecological, biological, and non-chemical methods of weed control" a close second to developing "more efficient and less costly weed control technology for use in conservation tillage" in their list of most pressing research needs.[115] Herbicide dependency is now widely considered to be one of the leading impediments to the development of more effective production systems and public weed scientists are being urged to "redirect their activities after four decades of largely herbicide-focused research and undertake a major change in weed research objectives to develop basic information about weeds and integrated weed management systems."[116]

While the concept of weed management is being widely touted as something new, the product of recent developments in applied ecology and integrated pest management, in essence it is really quite old. J. D. Fryer, a British weed scientist, drew attention to this irony when the term weed management was first coming into vogue. He explained that weed management broadly combines

(a) procedures for destroying weeds already present or about to grow in a field and (b) cultural methods for suppressing or avoiding weeds. Examples of the former are hand-weeding, hoeing, ploughing, burning and herbicides. The latter consist of the many and varied ways by which farmers attempt to cheat weeds — or at least to live with them — by practising the art of what is often referred to as "good husbandry."[117]

Weed management is, in effect, little more than a modern variant of the traditional techniques that agricultural improvers in Canada, the United States, and Great Britain having been espousing for over a century.

Conclusion

Ten years after the introduction of 2,4-D for field trials, Henry Wood opened the Eighth Western Canadian Weed Control Conference with the announcement that after decades of retreat in the face of weedy aggression, "the inroads of this menace have been arrested to the point where it would seem safe to suggest that a turning point has been reached.... The day seems to be dawning when the farmer can truly say that he is mastering one of the most baffling of farm operations — weed control."[118] Wood attributed most of the farmers' change in fortune to the development of selective herbicides. With regard to the chemical that "has occupied the driver's seat for 10 years," he stated: "I think you will agree with me that the surprising thing about 2,4-D has been its success."[119] Speaking at the same conference, P. O. Ripley of the Dominion Experimental Farms Service was considerably less surprised by the ascendancy of this particular compound:

> Western Canada is a "natural" for herbicidal weed control. It really has not been such a tremendous sales effort to sell 12 million acres worth for spraying. Very little undersown grain is grown. Many of the weeds in grain crops have been fairly easy to control. Fields are large and there is little danger from drift. Large scale operations make spraying economical.[120]

Yet a third speaker at the 1955 Western Canadian Weed Control Conference, H. A. Friesen of the Lacombe Experimental Station in Alberta, pointed out that western Canada was a natural for chemical control because of the "basic method of farming" that had evolved in the region:

> Of our more than 40 million acres of seeded farm land, over one-half is seeded to wheat with the remainder divided more or less equally

between barley and oats. Very little of this vast acreage in cereal grains is under sown with grass and legumes. Due to our near-arid conditions virtually all of this area has been farmed in a short rotation consisting of one year of summer-fallow and one or two years of grain.... Cultural control by various tillage and cropping practices has been man's method of fighting weeds since the dawn of history. Although an estimated 30 million dollars has been spent annually on tillage for weed control, the farmers of Western Canada have felt that they were fighting a losing battle against weeds.[121]

Friesen added that the climate and soil of the region made the production of forage crops "a hazardous venture" and, in consequence,

the economy of the area is geared to grain production with little likelihood of a large-scale change to mixed-farming in the very near future, even in areas where sod crops do relatively well. Thus, both annual and perennial weeds have not only persisted but have tended to increase.[122]

The introduction of 2,4-D into western Canada was, therefore, seen to be timely and fortuitous and its subsequent success was entirely predictable. A chemical solution to the weed problem arrived at a time when society's faith in science was reaching new heights and farmers lacked viable alternatives. Past practices had created a weed problem which threatened their very livelihood and defied conventional means of control while a general retreat to the relative safety of mixed farming remained as elusive and unlikely as ever.

Government and the pesticide industry did not create the need or demand for herbicides in western Canada but they most certainly facilitated the new technology's rapid adoption. Industry's role in this process was relatively minor until 1945 after which chemical companies flooded the market with 2,4-D–based products and implement manufacturers worked furiously to meet the demand for improved application equipment. This flurry of commercial activity was actively supported by all levels of government. Federal and provincial agricultural authorities began exploring the potential of chemical control around the turn of the century and they, rather than industry, were the first to actively investigate and promote the use of herbicides on crop land in the Prairies. By the early 1930s, Canada had established a highly efficient, centrally coordinated, and well-publicized system for testing phytotoxic compounds. Directed by the National Weed Committee, this system was able to draw on the resources of the Dominion Experimental Farms Service, numerous agricultural colleges and schools, and the staff of provincial departments of agriculture. According to P. O. Ripley, it enabled Canada to realize the benefits of the new selective herbicides faster and more efficiently than any "other country."[123]

Through promoting the use of herbicides, governments unwittingly undermined decades of extensive crop rotation studies and inadvertently helped to preserve the weed-friendly style of farming that they had spent so long trying to change. Wheat remains the dominant crop on the Prairies, long rotations are rarely practised, and a large proportion of Prairie crop land is still being summer fallowed each year. In the late 1970s, for example, about 10,000,000 ha were being annually sown to field crops in Saskatchewan and an additional 7,000,000 ha were summer fallowed each year. Six crops — wheat, barley, rape, oats, flax and rye — accounted for ninety-seven percent of the total cropped acreage, and wheat alone accounted for over seventy percent.[124] Governments have played a less active role in selling herbicides in western Canada since the mid-1950s but they continue to advocate a chemical solution to weed problems through official recommendations, through the enforcement of noxious-weed laws, and through portraying weeds as dangerous enemies against which extreme measures are justified.

Pesticide companies are no longer in need of government assurances to allay the suspicions of farmers as the sheer "effectiveness" of the many herbicides available today speak for themselves. Because farmers remain committed to a form of agriculture as favourable to culturing weeds as it is to producing crops, there is also little need for aggressive marketing other than to sell specific herbicide brands or competing, patented compounds. The chemical industry is certainly "guilty of excesses in marketing" but, as has already been argued with regard to postwar insecticide use in America, chemical dependency is not the result of a commercial conspiracy.[125] Rather, it primarily reflects the way in which food production systems are organized, the social and economic situation of farmers, and the nature of public and private research. In the case of the evolution of herbicide dependency in western Canada, the environment must also be taken into account. By limiting the cropping options available to farmers while at the same time failing to constrain the growth and spread of immigrant weeds, the environment has ensured the development of an unprecedented weed problem and the ongoing popularity of chemical control.

Events such as the Dust Bowl suggest that the environment, in turn, has been affected by the activities of the two competing groups of immigrants who simultaneously laid claim to the arable lands of western Canada. The conflict that arose between them shaped the course of Prairie settlement and agricultural development and, as the current standoff on Prairie farms indicates, it is far from over. Herbicides were supposed to give farmers the initiative in this war for economic survival. They may have done so initially but, under severe pressure, weeds were able to adapt and mount a successful counterattack. Today, farmers and agricultural scientists are again on the defensive just as they were at the end of World War II. They are the ones being forced to adapt and it is they who are contemplating calling a truce. Proponents of the "new" doctrine of weed management firmly believe that farmers must learn to coexist with weeds, to treat weeds as unruly neighbours rather than as implacable enemies, and to better manage their own affairs rather than seeking to control the affairs of others.

This chapter brings the study to a close but it is by no means the last chapter in the steadily evolving relationship between people and weeds in western Canada. Some say that the future lies in the development of herbicide-resistant crops and increasing corporate control.[126] Others predict a shift towards weed management, good husbandry, and a greater spirit of coexistence. Whatever transpires, about all that is certain is that weeds will persist in one form or another as long as we persist in farming. Perhaps it is time for us to recognize this point and to cease fighting a war that can never truly be won.

Conclusion

The continuing success of weeds  in western Canada has forced weed scientists to recognize the shortcomings of herbicides and to embrace the "new" doctrine of weed management. These developments, in turn, provide but the latest example of the way in which weeds have shaped human culture in western Canada, in the northern United States, and in Great Britain over the past five centuries. Conversely, the evolution of herbicide-resistant weeds and recent chemical-induced changes to the Prairie weed flora, represent examples of the way in which culture shapes weeds.

Weeds are, in other words, both the products of and participants in culture. Changes in culture on either a physical or psychological level will always be accompanied by changes in the resident weed flora. The opposite is also true. For even if culture were to remain fixed, weeds are constantly evolving in order to make better use of available resources and opportunities. Sooner or later these changes will result in changes to culture and the whole cycle will begin anew.

Field bindweed,
Convolvuls arvensis

The curious relationship between weeds and culture represents a simplified version of the relationship between human society and "nature" in general. They can be, and frequently are, treated as separate entities or as separate spheres of existence. At the same time, few can deny that they are intimately and inextricably bound together. What we do and think shapes nature in both a physical and a psychological sense. Nature, in turn, profoundly influences our activities and perception. Continuing on in this vein runs the risk of falling into the false dichotomy mentioned above. It is important, therefore, to stress that linkages between the two are rarely direct and never simple. Their subtlety and extreme complexity, in fact, largely explains why people often tend to regard the human-nature relationship as a duality rather than as different aspects of a larger whole.

Our dynamic, reciprocal relationship with nature writ large is so complex that it defies a holistic approach. We can, however, gain insights into broader phenomena and processes through much narrower investigations. With this in mind, the reader is asked to mentally substitute the word "nature" for the term "weed" when reading the following summary of the study's main findings. On one level, it can be read as a warning against treating weeds as something separate from culture. On another, it represents a morality play about the consequences of anthropocentric thinking. On yet a third level, it serves to highlight the kinds of issues that environmental historians need to address if they wish to gain a deeper understanding of the ways in which human cultures interact with the environment. Can we, for example, make sense of the historical drama between weeds and farmers in western Canada without venturing across disciplinary boundaries and considering the issue of weed biology and ecology? Do we not need to understand what farmers were actually doing in order to appreciate what farming experts were saying? Was there any connection between how weeds were perceived and what was occurring, or between thoughts and deeds?

With regard to traditional British weed lore, the answer to this last set of questions seems to be yes. British agricultural improvers have traditionally been sensitive to the seemingly contradictory nature of weeds. Few doubted that these plants were a problem and that to ignore them spelled an end to profits and, quite possibly, the farmer's very livelihood. At the same time, they were strongly conscious of the link between weeds and human activities and the need to coexist with what they considered to be the less desirable members of the plant kingdom.

A rough "balance" was also established in terms of the physical relationship between people and weeds in Britain until after the Second World War. This term does not apply to the relationship between farmers and plants on individual farms where the situation was constantly in flux. Nor does it refer to short periods of time when exceptional circumstances such as war or poor growing conditions favoured one side or the other. Rather, it refers to the general situation after 1500 during which time weeds remained a constant nuisance and the species composition of Britain's arable weed flora changed very little. The slow evolution of more intensive farming techniques may have led to gradual reductions in weed populations and densities during the nineteenth century but there are no indications that these changes were particularly dramatic.

The physical and psychological balancing act in Britain can be attributed to the long coevolution of weeds and farming in a relatively stable social and environmental setting. This balance was not upset by large-scale weedy and human invasions nor was it altered by the advent of any revolutionary technology for suppressing the growth of unwanted vegetation. It was upset, however, when elements of traditional British culture were uprooted and transplanted to Ontario. Although British immigrants and their weedy compatriots were soon thriving in their new home, relatively stable coexistence was impossible to maintain because the culture that regulated their relationship simply did not make sense when isolated from the natural and social context that provided it with both substance and meaning.

The relationship between people and weeds in Britain had evolved in a country where weeds were native, labour was cheap and plentiful, land had been cultivated for centuries, and crop rotation was made possible by the existence of local markets for a wide range of agricultural products. This contrasts sharply with the situation in Ontario. There, most weeds were imported and free from the natural checks and balances that regulated their populations in Europe, labour was expensive and scarce, farm land had to be won from the forests, and a lack of markets and transportation facilities discouraged the establishment of mixed farming.

The first factor meant that Ontario was predisposed to the development of an unusually severe weed problem; implementation of an integrated system of weed management commonly referred to as "good husbandry" was effectively precluded by the other three factors. Settlers eschewed good husbandry because of its heavy labour requirements and because they were simply too busy clearing their land to attend to less pressing duties. The presence of stumps, roots, and stones in their fields discouraged all but the most cursory of tillage and their cropping options where severely limited by a pressing need to produce cash crops in the absence of markets for products other than wheat. Implementation of British-style agriculture was further discouraged by the sheer availability of land. A cheap, plentiful supply of land meant that Ontario farmers had the option of farming extensively. When the fertility of the soil began to decline or their land became choked with weeds, they simply had to clear new fields or sell out and start a new farm further west.

By the mid-nineteenth century, the profound discordance between immigrant culture and the New World context was slowly being resolved by the development of a new relationship between people and weeds. It was one shaped by an increasingly severe weed problem and marked by an overtly hostile attitude towards opportunistic immigrant plants. The unprecedented success of immigrant weeds led to them being portrayed as alien aggressors or as the "enemy." Ironically, this portrayal tended to divert attention away from the fact that much of their success was due to the establishment of a weed-friendly style of farming. The predominant grain-fallow system of agriculture that developed in Ontario made sense in a land where farms were being carved from the forest, labour was in short supply, and markets were severely restricted. Even in the British Isles, however, where weeds were native, summer fallowing in the absence of general good husbandry was known to be a recipe for disaster.

The emergence of a new relationship between agriculturists and their vegetative competitors is symbolized by the passage of the first noxious-weed legislation in Canada more than fifty years in advance of the enactment of similar legislation in Britain: the 1865 Canada Thistle Act of Upper Canada. It is also symbolized by the enhanced significance and new identity accorded to the plant singled out by this statute. *Cirsium arvense* (L.) Scop. is a ubiquitous weed throughout western Europe but, as its common name suggests, its prevalence in the Canadas led to the mistaken belief that it was native to its adopted home.

The relationship between people and weeds in Ontario continued to evolve away from its British antecedents as the nineteenth century drew to a close. Perhaps the most significant development during this period was the rise of local weed experts who soon supplanted British authorities as the main source of information on weeds and their eradication. Employed by the state through institutions such as the Ontario Agricultural College and the Dominion Experimental Farms Service, these early agricultural scientists attempted to provide guidance and encouragement to a relatively inexperienced farming community faced with an alarming and rapidly escalating weed problem. Backed by centuries of tradition and informed by a wealth of weed lore, British farmers had little need of similar assistance until the advent of selective herbicides and rapidly rising labour costs fundamentally altered the nature of British weed control after the Second World War.

Late-nineteenth-century government experts were conscious of the subjective nature of weeds — "a plant out of place" became their standard definition — but in an effort to enlist the active co-operation of farmers, they chose to downplay the link between weeds and human cultural activities and to focus instead on the aggressive, adversarial side to their vegetative foes. Their official publications are littered with military metaphors, further entrenching the idea of weeds as the enemy and, before long, their views were being widely promoted in the Prairies.

The story of post-Confederation western settlement subtly parallels the earlier British settlement of Ontario. As we well know, immigrants from Ontario arrived with a great deal of cultural baggage; what we have failed to notice is that stowed in this baggage were most of the immigrant plants that were proving so troublesome in Ontario and an accompanying set of ideas about weeds and farming. Some aspects of immigrant culture made sense in the new surroundings. The grain-fallow system, for example, was well suited to the Prairies for many of the same reasons that it had been widely adopted in Ontario. In many ways it made even more sense in the West where the harsh climate greatly restricted the number of crops that could be grown and essentially ruled out all but the crudest of rotation schemes.

Other immigrant beliefs and practices, however, were at odds with the new environmental and social setting and significant changes soon resulted. Most of these changes were ones of emphasis rather than of kind. Regarding weeds as alien invaders, as foreign aggressors bent on territorial expansion, made as much sense in the West as it did in the East because most of the worst weeds in both places were immigrants. The weed problem in the Prairies, however, rapidly eclipsed even that of Ontario. Weeds were able to conquer the Prairies in an amazingly short time because of the relative ease and speed with which land could be brought into production, because of the early establishment of a rapid mode of transportation in the form of the railways, and because the open, windswept terrain favoured the spread of wind-borne plants and seeds. When combined with the inability of farmers to practice good husbandry, the arrival of human and weedy immigrants from climates roughly similar to the Prairies, and the scale on which farming was soon being practised, the result was the rapid establishment of diverse weed colonies that made even those of Ontario look insignificant by comparison. These developments provided further justification for regarding weeds as the enemy and they lent an added sense of urgency and fear to an already strongly adversarial view of opportunistic immigrant plants.

The relationship between people and weeds that had emerged on the Prairies by 1905 was marked by a weed flora comprising many species familiar to farmers of British descent and many, such as Russian thistle (*Salsola pestifer* Nels.) and a number of indigenous species, that were not. Most of these weeds continue to trouble Prairie farmers to this day, especially farmers who remain committed to the dominant grain-fallow production system that was well established by the first decade of the twentieth century. By the turn of the century, weeds were being depicted in an even more blindly oppositional way than they were in Ontario and the noxious-weed laws of the three Prairie provinces had become far harsher and more comprehensive than the eastern statutes that had initially served as their model and inspiration. Eastern experts such as James Fletcher were being supplanted by local authorities and the Prairie governments had begun to provide far more active leadership in the war on weeds than governments elsewhere in the country.

Physical conflict was the only basic element of the modern relationship between people and weeds in western Canada that was conspicuously absent at the turn of the century. Weeds had not yet had time to consolidate their hold on the more recently settled portions of the Prairies and, in Saskatchewan and Alberta in particular, farmers were still able to avoid the issue through the simple expedience of breaking more land when older fields became infested. Their ability to practise avoidance, however, was rapidly declining with the expansion of Prairie settlement, and about the time of the First World War an era of relatively peaceful, parallel territorial expansion had come to an end.

It was during the period bounded by the two world wars that farmers, journalists, and government officials came to universally describe the relationship between people and weeds in the West in terms of a war. Rhetoric, for once, provided an accurate depiction of reality. Hostilities raged on both sides of the international border as American and Canadian agriculturists sallied forth to do battle with a common enemy. The presence of similar weed problems, noxious-weed legislation, antiweed sentiments, and weed-friendly styles of farming in countries with a shared environment but with disparate political systems and settlement histories provides graphic evidence of the way in which human cultures are shaped by their natural surroundings. An analysis of the cultural ties between western Canada and the northern-tier states also suggests that cultural exchange between the two countries was reciprocal rather than one way.

Americans, for example, regarded western Canadian noxious-weed legislation as being far in advance of their own and Canada's Associate Committee on Weed Control (1929) was used as a model for the later development of similar organizations in the United States. Upon its creation, the federally organized Associate Committee acted as a command centre for the war on weeds in the West. It coordinated the research activities of weed workers employed by various federal and provincial agencies, promoted general awareness of the weed menace, and provided a forum for the discussion of strategy through its annual meetings. Provincial departments of agriculture comprised the next level of command in this military-style organization. Ministry officials helped formulate amendments to provincial noxious-weed statutes — statutes that rivaled war-measures acts by the mid-1940s in terms of the powers of expropriation they accorded to the state — and they were responsible for issuing a barrage of antiweed propaganda. They also directed the activities of municipal governments and ensured their compliance with provincial weed laws. Enforcement of these statutes was primarily the responsibility of municipal councils and other rural district representatives. They and the veritable army of noxious-weed inspectors they employed can be seen as the lowest and most numerous ranking. Equivalent to noncommissioned field officers, they were charged with shoring up the farmers' defences and, if possible, turning the tide of weedy invasion.

Despite the development of an impressive, military-style chain of command, the passage of increasingly draconian legislation, a massive effort to educate the troops, and significant improvements in weed-fighting tools and techniques, farmers fared poorly in the escalating conflict with weeds. By 1945, the situation had become desperate and weeds were poised on the brink of victory. First annuals and then perennials had successively overrun each new frontier of Prairie settlement and, by the end of World War II, weeds were causing greater average annual crop losses in the Prairie region than any other factor. Weed control had become the largest single cost in crop production, the main reason for tillage and, apart from drought, the leading contributor to the Dust Bowl and an ongoing problem with soil drifting. In extreme cases, weeds were being credited with forcing farmers from their land; in all cases, they were seriously eroding the profitability of Prairie agriculture.

The extraordinary success of immigrant weeds in the West in such a comparatively short time stands as a testament to the innate adaptability and impressive fecundity of these plants, particularly when they are released from natural constraints. It also serves to condemn the style of farming that had developed on the Prairies. By the close of the Second World War, the weed problem alone had cast doubt on the future of an entire culture and many observers believed that it was only a matter of time before they witnessed a general shift away from grain monoculture towards a system of mixed farming and careful crop rotations. Prairie farmers had resisted this change for decades and, for the majority, mixed farming still remained untested and uneconomic. Imagine, therefore, their response when science came to the rescue in 1945 and "'out of the blue' descended 2,4-D."[1]

Within five years of its initial release in western Canada, 2,4-D was well on its way to becoming the main weapon in the Prairie farmer's anti-weed arsenal. By then, the Prairie West boasted a higher proportion of herbicide-treated farm land than anywhere else in the world and industry and government officials were congratulating themselves on their success in selling the idea of chemical control. Herbicide and implement manufacturers contributed to this process by improving their products and meeting a rapidly escalating demand. Governments did even more to promote the use of chemicals through their position of trust in the farming community, by their alarmist portrayal of weeds, through successful provincial Atlacide spraying programs and, most importantly, by providing the infrastructure necessary to rapidly test, register, release, and advertise phytotoxic compounds such as 2,4-D. The true selling job, however, was done by 2,4-D itself. Cheap, highly effective, and suitable for use on the vast cereal acreage of the West with minimal labour inputs, 2,4-D perfectly fit the urgent needs of Prairie farmers. In the final analysis, 2,4-D's rapid and widespread acceptance is a far better measure of the desperation of farmers or the proliferation of weeds than it is of the success of governmental and industry marketing schemes.

Chemicals subsequently became the farmer's main defence against unwanted plants in western Canada. The new discipline of weed science owes its very existence to the development of selective herbicides and these compounds have proven so effective that western farmers have been able to carry on farming in much the same way as they have for the past four or five generations. Herbicides have clearly not revolutionized western Canadian agriculture nor have they spelled an end to the war on weeds. Rather, they have become a critical mainstay of a production system that actively produces weeds and whose very survival is now predicated on constant chemical warfare.

Widespread and incessant use of herbicides have wrought significant changes to the weed flora of western Canada over the last five decades. Weeds as a group, however, remain as successful as ever. Their success can be attributed to their impressive ability to adapt to changes in human culture and to the allure of chemicals drawing attention away from the need for fundamental changes in farming practices. The persistence of a serious weed problem in the West has already forced many Canadian weed scientists to reconsider their faith in technology. If their predictions are correct, it will also force Prairie farmers to adopt a new system of farm management: "good husbandry" in all but name.

With the rediscovery of "good husbandry" in western Canada, this summary has come full circle. All that remains is to draw a number of firm conclusions for the benefit of three different audiences. Weed scientists are reminded of the folly of treating weeds as something separate from culture; as something that can be objectively identified, isolated, and controlled. They are also reminded that noxious-weed laws have been singularly unsuccessful in halting the establishment and spread of immigrant plants. These statutes are unwieldy and difficult, if not impossible, to enforce strictly and they merely treat the symptoms of an underlying malady.[2] On a more positive note, this study lends credence to the recent trend towards weed management and away from weed control. It confirms the long-held suspicion of weed scientists that their subject has not received the attention it deserves and suggests that they are justified in regarding the weed issue as central rather than "incidental" to arable production systems.[3]

Devotees of the increasingly esoteric field of environmental history may also want to take note of some of the implications of this study. Environmental history essentially is an interdisciplinary activity and, as such, specialist jargon is probably best avoided. Jargon provides a poor substitute for explanation and it is almost guaranteed to alienate a large proportion of a study's potential readership. Theories culled from the humanities or social sciences should also be used with caution. Most are anthropocentric in nature and few are derived from sound historical research. In effect, they take the place of historical research and, in doing so, transform environmental history into something more akin to environmental philosophy.

Frieda Knobloch's 1996 study, *The Culture of Wilderness*, provides a good example of the pitfalls of this approach. Steeped in the field of cultural analysis and based on a relatively cursory reading of weed-related literature, her analysis suggests that the development of an unprecedented problem with imported weeds on the American portion of the Great Plains simply "mirrors" the aggressive, westward expansion of industrial capitalism.[4] While there is a great deal of truth in her argument, it does tend to state the obvious. Moreover, it pays little heed to the agency of weeds or to their nonhuman dimension. Rather than portraying weeds as "a horrifying doppelgänger, bearing an uncanny resemblance to the colonists who exclude them," this study suggests that weeds must also be seen as agents of nature bent on colonizing an ecological niche created by the activities of another weedy species, *Homo sapiens*. Nature's "goal" is to fill all available niches and it does not matter whether they are filled by domesticated crops, by plants people regard as weeds, or by native species that inhabited a region prior to large-scale human disturbance. All that matters is that the niche is filled, and in the case of arable land, the plants most suited to fill this niche are the comparatively small number of readily identifiable species that grace the pages of historic farming manuals and modern weed science literature. Weeds are more than just figments of the imagination or vegetative shadows of the capitalist farmer. They are, instead, products of and participants in a larger evolutionary drama within which the development of human society and culture is merely a subplot.

There are also a number of lessons in this study for Canadian historians. First, it illustrates the potential of an environmental history approach for illuminating neglected, but far from insignificant, aspects of our past. Canadian historians have only just begun to explore the possibilities opened up by this American-dominated field and, in consequence, they remain unaware of many important issues that can and need to be addressed. These range from relatively simple analyses of the relationship between individuals and discrete elements of local ecosystems to complex assessments of the coevolution of culture and the environment.

Secondly, an investigation of weeds and weed control in western Canada indicates that historians have consistently overlooked practical if seemingly mundane topics such as this. Western Canadian historiography contains scant reference to the existence of a massive weed problem on the Prairies which leads one to suspect that other issues of equal or greater significance have also been ignored. Historians must remember that practical concerns dominate the lives of most farmers and that you cannot understand farmers without understanding farming. We must, in other words, question our traditional preoccupation with the political and social activities of past generations of farmers and our corresponding neglect of the practical issues that governed their daily lives. Practical considerations played a significant role in shaping Prairie settlement, they guide the leading economic activity in the Prairie region today, and farming continues to dominate the Prairie landscape even though farmers now represent a small minority of the population.

Apart from suggesting that western Canadian historiography is seriously incomplete, this study leads to the conclusion that much of what has been written may well be deeply flawed. The conventional tale of western settlement places man and nature in opposition and when the two interact, the consequences are direct and simple. When coupled with a profound humanistic tendency amongst historians, the result is a story of human hopes, aspirations, and actions being played out before a periodically changing but essentially passive and static environmental backdrop. It is a progressive tale of the slow but successful development of capitalist agriculture under harsh Prairie conditions; a "cycle of prairie agricultural history" that ends around 1930 by which time the "grain economy rested on sure foundations."[5]

An investigation of a single aspect of the settlement process, the relationship between farmers and weeds, makes a mockery of this claim. Western Canadian agriculture was not resting on a firm foundation by 1930 but was, instead, on the verge of collapse. The process of adapting agriculture to the environment was not drawing to a close for it has really just begun and it promises to continue for the foreseeable future. Using weeds as a symbol of nature writ large, it becomes clear that historians, like weed experts, have made the mistake of regarding nature and culture as a duality. Treating weeds as something independent of culture has resulted in the persistence of a massive weed problem that costs farmers hundreds of millions of dollars annually in terms of crop losses and expenditures on herbicides. Treating culture as something separate from nature has caused historians to lose sight of the fact that modern society continues to be shaped by its natural surroundings.

Appendix 1

The 1865 Canada Thistle Act of Upper Canada

Source: Canada, *Statutes*, 1865, 29 Vict., c.40.

CAP. XL.

An Act to prevent the spreading of Canada Thistles in Upper Canada.

[Assented to 18*th September,* 1865.]

HER Majesty, by and with the advice and consent of the Legislative Council and Assembly of Canada, enacts as follows:

1. It shall be the duty of every occupant of land in Upper Canada, to cut, or to cause to be cut down all the Canada thistles growing thereon, so often in each and every year as shall be sufficient to prevent them going to seed; and if any owner, possessor, or occupier of land shall knowingly suffer any Canada thistles to grow thereon and the seed to ripen so as to cause or endanger the spread thereof, he shall upon conviction be liable to a fine of not less than two nor more than ten dollars for every such offence.

2. It shall be the duty of the Overseers of Highways in any Municipality to see that the provisions of this Act are carried out

within their respective highway divisions, by cutting or causing to be cut all the Canada thistles growing on the highways or road allowances within their respective divisions, and every such overseer shall give notice in writing to the owner, possessor, or occupier of any land within the said division whereon Canada thistles shall be growing and in danger of going to seed, requiring him to cause the same to be cut down within five days from the service of such notice; And in case such owner, possessor or occupier, shall refuse or neglect to cut down the said Canada thistles, with the period aforesaid, the said Overseer of Highways shall enter upon the land and cause such Canada thistles to be cut down with as little damage to growing crops as may be, and he shall not be liable to be sued in action of trespass therefor; Provided that no such Overseer of Highways shall have power to enter upon or cut thistles on any land sown with grain; provided also, that where such Canada thistles are growing upon non-resident lands, it shall not be necessary to give any notice before proceeding to cut down the same.

3. It shall be the duty of the Clerk of any Municipality in which Railway property is situated, to give notice in writing to the Station Master of said Railway resident in or nearest to the said Municipality requiring him to cause all the Canada thistles growing upon the property of the said Railway Company within the limits of the said Municipality to be cut down as provided for in the first section of this Act, and in case such Station Master shall refuse or neglect to have the said Canada thistles cut down within ten days from the time of service of the said notice, then the Overseers of Highways of the said Municipality shall enter upon the property of the said Railway Company and cause such Canada thistles to be cut down, and the expense incurred in carrying out the provisions of this section shall be provided for in the same manner as in the next following section of this Act.

4. Each Overseer of Highways shall keep an accurate account of the expense incurred by him in carrying out the provisions of the preceding sections of this Act, with respect to each parcel of land entered upon therefor, and shall deliver a statement of such expenses, describing by its legal description the land entered upon, and verified by oath, to the owner, possessor, or occupier of such resident lands, requiring him

to pay the amount; in case such owner, possessor, or occupier of such resident lands shall refuse or neglect to pay the same within thirty days after such application, the said claim shall be presented to the Municipal Council of the Corporation in which such expense was incurred, and the said Council is hereby authorized and required to credit and allow such claim, and order the same to be paid from the funds for general purposes of the said Municipality; the said Overseer of Highways shall also present to the said Council a similar statement of the expenses incurred by him in carrying out the provisions of the said section upon any non-resident lands; and the said Council is hereby authorized and empowered to audit and allow the same in like manner; Provided always that if any owner, occupant, or possessor, amenable under the provisions of this Act, shall deem such expense excessive, an appeal may be had to the said Council (if made within thirty days after delivery of such statement) and the said Council shall determine the matter in dispute.

5. The Municipal Council of the Corporation shall cause all such sums as have been so paid under the provisions of this Act, to be severally levied on the lands described in the statement of the Overseers of Highways, and to be collected in the same manner as other taxes; and the same when collected shall be paid into the Treasury of the said Corporation to reimburse the outlay therefrom aforesaid.

6. Any person who shall knowingly vend any grass or other seed among which there is any seed of the Canada thistle, shall for every such offence, upon conviction, be liable to a fine of not less than two nor more than ten dollars.

7. Every Overseer of Highways or other officer who shall refuse or neglect to discharge the duties imposed on him by this Act, shall be liable to a fine of not less than ten nor more than twenty dollars.

8. Every offence against the provisions of this Act shall be punished, and the penalty hereby enforced for each offence shall be recovered and levied, upon conviction, before any Justice of the Peace; and all fines imposed shall be paid into the Treasury of the Municipality in which such conviction takes place.

Appendix 2

Line drawings of the leading cast of weeds

Reprinted from Clarence Frankton and Gerald A. Mulligan,
Weeds of Canada (Ottawa: Minister of Supply and Services, 1974)

Quack grass, *Agropyron repens*; A, plant; B, spikelet; C, seed from front and side;
D, junction between leaf and sheath showing auricles.

Wild oats, *Avena fatua*: A, plant; B, spikelet; C, seed; D, seed after threshing.

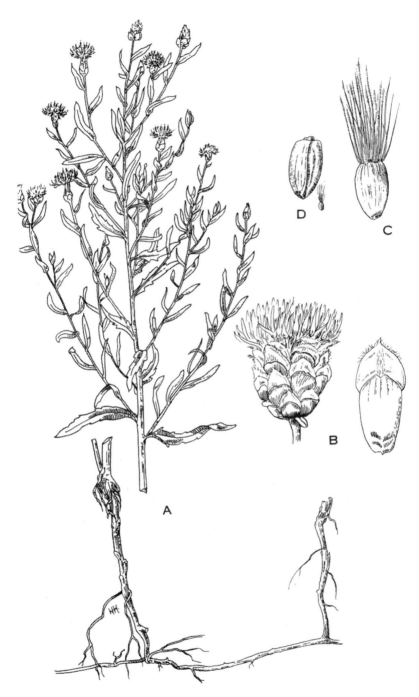

Russian knapweed, *Centaurea repens*: A, plant; B, head of flowers and to the right
a bract of the head; C, seed with pappus; D, seed with pappus removed.

197

Canada thistle, *Cirsium arvense:* A, plant; B, seed with pappus;
C, seed with pappus removed.

Field bindweed, *Convolvuls arvensis*: A, plant; B, seed.

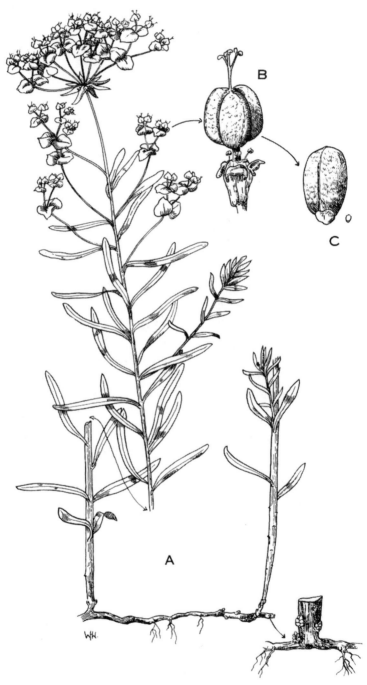

Leafy spurge, *Euphorbia esula*: A, plant; B, a single female flower with several male flowers at its base; C, seed.

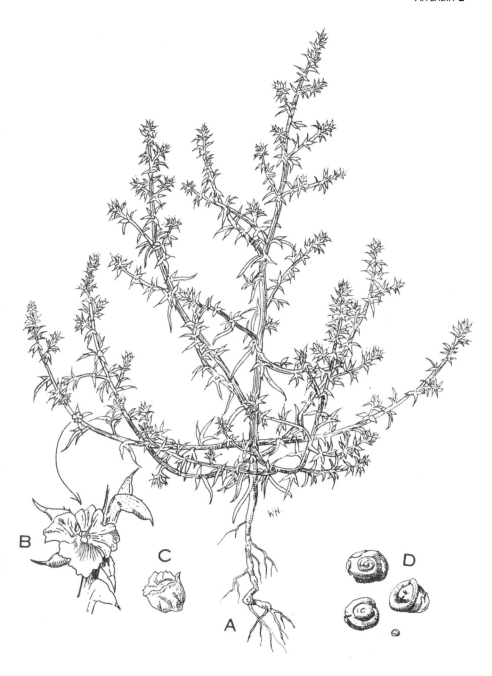

Russian thistle, *Salsola pestifer*: A, plant: B, flower; C, seed covered by sepal bases; D, seeds.

Wild mustard, *Sinapis arvensis*: A, plant; B, pod; C, seed.

Tumble mustard, *Sisymbrium altissimum*: A, plant; B, mature pods; C, seeds.

Perennial sow-thistle, *Sonchus arvensis*: A, plant; B, seed

Stinkweed, *Thlaspi arvense*: A, plant; B, upper part of plant with maturing pods;
C, mature pods; D, opening pod and seed.

Appendix 3

Colour Plates

Reprinted from George H. Clark and James Fletcher, *Farm Weeds of Canada,*
2nd. ed. (Ottawa: Department of Agriculture, 1909)

Couch, quack or scutch grass, *Agropyrum repens,* L.

Wild oats, *Avena fatua*, L. var. glabrata, petermann.

208

Wild mustard or charlock, *Brassica sinapistrum*, Boiss.

Canada Thistle, *Cirsium arvensis* L.

Field bindweed, *Convolvulus arvensis*, L.

Tumbling mustard, *Sisymbrium altissimum*, L.

Perennial sow-thistle, *Sonchus arvensis*, L.

Stinkweed or pennycress, *Thlaspi arvense*, L.

Notes

Notes to Introduction

1. J. Stan Rowe and Robert T. Coupland, "Vegetation of the Canadian Plains," *Prairie Forum* 9 (1984): 245.
2. Clarence Frankton, *Weeds of Canada* (Ottawa: Department of Agriculture, 1955), 1.
3. LeRoy Holm, "The Role of Weeds in Human Affairs," *Weed Science* 19 (1971): 485.
4. Most of the small number of histories on weeds and their control have been written by agricultural scientists. A good and frequently cited example of their work is: F. L. Timmons, "A History of Weed Control in the United States and Canada," *Weed Science* 18 (1970): 294–300. The prominent American environmental historian, Alfred Crosby, is only one of two historians to have addressed the issue of weeds in a substantive manner. His most notable treatment of the subject can be found in *Ecological Imperialism: The Biological Expansion of Europe, 900–1900* (Cambridge: Cambridge University Press, 1986), 145–170. For a more recent study that portrays weeds as a social rather than biological phenomenon, see historian Frieda Knobloch's *The Culture of Wilderness: Agriculture as Colonization in the American West* (Chapel Hill: University of North Carolina Press, 1996), 113–145. George Ordish has written several popular books on the history of crop pests in which he consistently ignores weeds. For example, in *The*

Constant Pest: A Short History of Pests and Their Control (New York: Charles Scribner's Sons, 1976), he observes on page 75 that weeds in eighteenth-century England were "the great pest of agricultural crops in those days—in fact, in these too," yet, he devotes all of two paragraphs to a discussion of weeds in his 240-page study. There are a number of recent academic studies on the history of insect pests and their control including: Thomas R. Dunlap, "Farmers, Scientists and Insects," *Agricultural History* 54 (1980): 93–107; Dunlap, *DDT: Scientists, Citizens and Public Policy* (Princeton: Princeton University Press, 1981); Paul W. Riegert, *From Arsenic to DDT: A History of Entomology in Western Canada* (Toronto: University of Toronto Press, 1980) and Conner Sorenson, "The Rise of Government Sponsored Applied Entomology, 1840–1870" *Agricultural History* 62, 2 (1988): 98–115. Plant pathology has received less attention but even it has been the subject of a book-length study: G. C. Ainsworth, *Introduction to the History of Plant Pathology* (Cambridge: Cambridge University Press, 1981).

5. Frankton, 1.
6. "Round Table on Environmental History," *Journal of American History* 76 (1990): 1087–1147. The 1990 Journal of American History round table discussion on environmental history brings together papers from many of the field's leading American practitioners—Donald Worster, Alfred Crosby, Carolyn Merchant, Richard White, William Cronon, and Stephen Pyne—who, despite advancing their own specific research agendas, are united on a number of key issues. These include a determination to advance the common goal of locating human history within the larger realm of nature by studying interactions between people and the environment over time, and the notion that natural phenomena can, and frequently do, act as independent historical agents.
7. Analyzing human-nature relationships using a trilevel conceptual scheme has somewhat pretentiously been coined "an interactive theory of nature and culture" by Arthur McEvoy in his essay, "Toward an Interactive Theory of Nature and Culture: Ecology, Production and Cognition in the California Fishing Industry," in *The Ends of the Earth: Perspectives on Modern Environmental History*, ed. Donald Worster (Cambridge: Cambridge University Press, 1988), 211–228. Carolyn Merchant and other "ecofeminists" would prefer to add "reproduction" as a fourth level but

they probably would concede the validity of the simpler scheme. For a good summary of Merchant's conceptual scheme, see her article, "The Theoretical Structure of Ecological Revolutions," *Environmental Review* 11 (1987): 265–274.

8. Knobloch, 2.

9. See, for example: Donald Worster, *Dust Bowl: The Southern Plains in the 1930s* (New York: Oxford University Press, 1979); John McCallum, *Unequal Beginnings: Agriculture and Economic Development in Quebec and Ontario until 1870* (Toronto: University of Toronto Press, 1980); Vernon C. Fowke, *Canadian Agricultural Policy: The Historical Pattern* (Toronto: University of Toronto Press, 1947) and Fowke, *The National Policy and the Wheat Economy* (Toronto: University of Toronto Press, 1957).

Notes to Chapter 1

1. For an introduction to the etymology of the term "weed" and its western European language equivalents, see: Lawrence J. King, "Some Early Forms of the Weed Concept," *Nature* 179 (1957): 1366; and King, *Weeds of the World: Biology and Control* (New York: Interscience Publishers, 1966), 1–6.

2. W. Holzner, "Concepts, Categories and Characteristics of Weeds," in *Biology and Ecology of Weeds*, eds. W. Holzner and M. Numata (The Hague: Dr. W. Junk Publishers, 1982), 3.

3. Edgar Anderson, *Plants, Man, and Life* (Boston: Little, Brown and Company, 1952), 32.

4. Richard Bradley, *The Country Gentleman and Farmer's Monthly Director*, 6th ed. (London: Printed for D. Browne and T. Woodman, 1732), 83.

5. William Ellis, *Chiltern and Vale Farming Explained* (London: Printed for Weaver Bickerton, 1733), 296.

6. John Mortimer, *The Whole Art of Husbandry; Or The Way of Managing and Improving Land*, 2nd ed. (London: Printed by J. H. for H. Mortlock and J. Robinson, 1708), 453, 470.

7. Edwin R. Spencer, *Just Weeds* (New York: Charles Scribner's Sons, 1940), 119; Claire S. Haughton, *Green Immigrants: The Plants that Transformed America* (New York: Harcourt Brace Jovanovich, 1978), 104–105; Richard N. Mack, "The Commercial Seed Trade: An Early Disperser of Weeds in the United States," *Economic Botany* 45 (1991): 263–264.

217

8. Winifred E. Brenchley, "Useful Farm Weeds," *Journal of the Board of Agriculture* 25 (1918/19): 949–958.

9. Alberta, Department of Agriculture, *Annual Report*, 1924, 30.

10. Thomas A. Hill, *The Biology of Weeds* (London: Edward Arnold, 1977), 2.

11. A. M. Mortimer, "The Biology of Weeds," in *Weed Control Handbook: Principles*, 8th ed., eds. R. J. Hance and K. Holly (Oxford: Blackwell Scientific Publications, 1990), 2.

12. Clyde E. Leighty, "Crop Rotation," in *Yearbook of Agriculture, 1938: Soils and Men* (Washington, D.C.: GPO, 1938), 417.

13. Clarence Frankton and Gerald A. Mulligan, *Weeds of Canada* (Ottawa: Agriculture Canada, 1993), 2.

14. Holzner, "Concepts, Categories and Characteristics," 18.

15. Jack R. Harlan and J. M. J. De Wet, "Some Thoughts About Weeds," *Economic Botany* 19 (1965): 21; Jack R. Harlan, *Crops and Man* (Madison, Wisc.: American Society of Agronomy and the Crop Science Society of America, 1975), 97–98 and Holzner, 17–18.

16. Wood P. Anderson, *Weed Science: Principles* (St. Paul, Minn.: West Publishing Co., 1977), 14.

17. John L. Harper, *Population Biology of Plants* (New York: Academic Press, 1977), 70–71.

18. Richard N. Mack, "Invasion of *Bromus tectorum* L. into Western North America: An Ecological Chronicle," *Agro-Ecosystems* 7 (1981): 145–155.

19. Ada Hayden, "The Story of Weed Seed Dissemination," in *The Weed Flora of Iowa*, ed. L. H. Pammel and Charlotte M. King (Des Moines, Iowa: Iowa Geological Survey, 1926), 567–568.

20. Canada, Dominion Experimental Farms, *Annual Report*, 1893, 192.

21. Lyster H. Dewey, "Migration of Weeds," *Yearbook of the United States Department of Agriculture, 1896* (Washington, D.C.: GPO, 1897), 273.

22. Robert L. Jones, *History of Agriculture in Ontario, 1613-1880* (Toronto: University of Toronto Press, 1946), 92.

23. R. J. Moore, "The Biology of Canadian Weeds. 13. *Cirsium arvense* (L.) Scop." *Canadian Journal of Plant Science* 55 (1975): 1038.

24. L. B. Nadeau and W. H. Vanden Born, "The Root System of Canada Thistle," *Canadian Journal of Plant Science* 69 (1989): 1205.

25. Jethro Tull, *The Horse-Hoing Husbandry: or, an Essay on the Principles of Tillage and Vegetation* (London: Printed for the author, 1733), 37.

26. Francis Home, *The Principles of Agriculture and Vegetation* (Edinburgh: Printed for G. Hamilton and J. Balfour, 1757), 157; Adam Dickson, *A Treatise of Agriculture*, vol. 1, 2d ed. (Edinburgh: Printed for A. Kincaid and J. Bell, 1765), 85.

27. In one his very popular agricultural encyclopedias, Morton effectively paraphrased Tull when he defined weeds as "every plant different from the crop, and growing with the crop to its hindrance." Morton was seconded by Buckman, a professor at the Royal Agricultural College, Cirencester, who suggested in an influential 1855 essay "that every plant growing with the crop to its hindrance is a weed." Writing nearly forty years after Buckman, James Fletcher began one of the first of a long line of federal government bulletins on weeds with the statement: "There are many definitions of the word weed, but perhaps from a farmer's standpoint the best one is: 'any troublesome or unsightly plant that is at the same time useless or comparatively so.'" John C. Morton, ed., *A Cyclopedia of Agriculture* (London: Blackie and Son, 1855), 2:1110; James Buckman, "On Agricultural Weeds," *Journal of the Royal Agricultural Society of England* 16 (1855): 359; and James Fletcher, *Weeds*, Canada, Department of Agriculture, Central Experimental Farm, Bulletin 28, 1897, 6.

28. J. C. Loudon, *An Encyclopedia of Agriculture* (London: Printed for Longman, Hurst, Rees, Orme, Brown, and Green, 1825), 877; Henry Stephens, *The Book of the Farm*, vol.1 (Edinburgh: William Blackwood and Sons, 1844), 939.

29. For example, in John Percival's book *Agricultural Botany: Theoretical and Practical*, which was first published in London in 1900 and remained a standard text for over thirty years, weeds are defined as: "any plant whose growth interferes with that of the crop to which the soil for the time being is devoted. The idea of uselessness is always present in the mind when weeds are being spoken of." Winifred Brenchley, a long-time employee at the Rothamstead Agricultural Research Station, and perhaps Britain's leading authority on weeds in the early twentieth century, similarly defined weeds of arable land as "any plant other than the crop sown." John Percival, *Agricultural Botany: Theoretical and Practical*, 4th ed. (New York: Henry Holt and Company, 1915), 571 and Winifred Brenchley, *Weeds of Farm Land* (London: Longmans, Green and Co., 1920), 2.

30. A. J. Pieters, "What is a Weed?" *Journal of the American Society of Agronomy* 27 (1935): 781; King, *Weeds of the World*, 6.

31. Benjamin Holdich, "The Weeds of Agriculture," in *Hortus Gramineus Woburnensis*, 4th ed., by George Sinclair (London: Ridgways, n.d.), 299.

32. William Darlington, *American Weeds and Useful Plants*, 2nd ed. (New York: Orange Judd and Company, 1859 [1847]), xiii.

33. Two of the earliest government weed bulletins which define weeds as plants out of place are J. Hoyes Panton, *Weeds*, Ontario Agricultural College, Bulletin 10, 1887, 3 and E. S. Goff, *The Russian Thistle: A New and Dangerous Weed to Wisconsin*, Wisconsin Agricultural Experiment Station, Bulletin 37, 1893, 6.

34. Charles C. James, *Agriculture* (Toronto: George N. Morang and Co., 1899), 71. James's school book was distributed to schools in Ontario, western Canada, and even the American Mid-West.

35. Floyd M. Ashton and Thomas J. Monaco, *Weed Science: Principles and Practices*, 3rd ed. (New York: John Wiley and Sons, 1991), 5.

36. Weed Society of America, Terminology Committee, "Terminology Committee Report," *Weeds* 4 (1956): 283.

37. F. A. Waugh, "Some Phases of Weed Evolution," *Science*, New Series, 5 (May 21, 1897): 789.

38. Pieters, 781–783. Equally subjective definitions were offered contemporaries of Pieters including Purdue University agronomist Elmer G. Campbell. In 1923, Campbell proposed that a "workable" definition for the term weed "is an independent plant whose species is persistently obnoxious on cultivation areas." A year later, noted weed expert O. A. Stevens expressed reservations about ever being able to develop a "scientific" definition for the term. But, because the "word seems to serve a purpose in common use," he suggested that it "might be said to refer to a plant which is detrimental to man's interest, displeasing to the eye or of no evident value." Elmer G. Campbell, "What is a Weed?" *Science* 58 (July-December, 1923): 50; and O. A. Stevens, "What is a Weed?" *Science* 59 (April 18, 1924): 361.

39. Pieters, 781.

40. Several weed scientists and plant ecologists have surveyed twentieth-century definitions for "weed" in an effort to establish a viable, working definition. Overviews of twentieth-century definitions can be found in: King, *Weeds of the World*, 1-6; Harlan, *Crops and Man*, 85–88; Holzner,

"Concepts, Categories and Characteristics," 4–5; and M. L. Navas, "Using Plant Population Biology in Weed Research: A Strategy to Improve Weed Management," *Weed Research* 31 (1991): 172–174.

41. E. W. Claypole, "On the Migration of Plants from Europe to America, with an Attempt to Explain Certain Phenomena Connected Therewith," *Report of the Montreal Horticultural Society and Fruit Growers' Association of the Province of Quebec* 3 (1877): 82.

42. Asa Gray, "The Pertinacity and Predominance of Weeds," *The American Journal of Science and Arts*, Third Series, 18 (1879): 161.

43. A. H. Bunting, "Some Reflections on the Ecology of Weeds," in *The Biology of Weeds*, ed. John L. Harper (Oxford: Blackwell Scientific Publications, 1960), 12.

44. Harlan and De Wet, 19.

45. The prominent weed specialist and plant ecologist, Herbert Baker, for example, sounds a similar note when he writes that "a plant is 'weed' if, in any specified geographical area, its populations grow entirely or predominantly in situations markedly disturbed by man." Thomas Muzik, an agronomy professor at Washington State University, proposed in 1970 that a weed, "in the broadest sense, may be considered as an organism that diverts energy from a direction desired by man." Eight years later, W. Holzner submitted that weeds "are plants adapted to manmade habitats and interfering there with human activities." R. J. Aldrich entered the fray in 1984 with his important book on weed-crop ecology. In it, he defines weed as "a plant that originated under a natural environment and, in response to imposed and natural environments, evolved, and continues to do so, as an interfering associate with our crops and activities." Finally, in 1991, M. L. Navas, a French weed specialist, concluded his survey of weed definitions with yet another: "A plant that forms populations that are able to enter habitats cultivated, markedly disturbed or occupied by man and potentially depress or displace the resident plant populations which are deliberately cultivated or are of ecological and/or aesthetic interest." Herbert G. Baker, "The Continuing Evolution of Weeds," *Economic Botany* 45 (1991): 445; Thomas J. Muzik, *Weed Biology and Control* (New York: McGraw-Hill, 1970), 2; Holzner, 5; R. J. Aldrich, *Weed-Crop Ecology: Principles in Weed Management* (North Scituate, Mass.: Breton Publishers, 1984), 6; and Navas, 174.

46. Navas, 173.

47. Brenchley, *Weeds of Farm Land*, 1.

48. Herbert G. Baker, "Human Influences on Plant Evolution," *Economic Botany* 26 (1972): 32.

49. J. C. Chacón and S. R. Gliessman, "Use of the 'Non-weed' Concept in Traditional Tropical Agroecosystems of South-Eastern Mexico," *Agroecosystems* 8 (1982): 1–11.

50. William Cronon, *Changes in the Land: Indians, Colonists, and the Ecology of New England* (New York: Hill and Wang, 1983), 42–45, 127; R. Douglas Hurt, *Indian Agriculture in America: Prehistory to the Present* (Lawrence, Kansas: University Press of Kansas, 1987), 1, 11, 31–34, 45, 55–59; Carolyn Merchant, *Ecological Revolutions: Nature, Gender, and Science in New England* (Chapel Hill: University of North Carolina Press, 1989), 74–80, 108.

51. For a detailed discussion of crop mimicry in weeds, see: Spencer C. H. Barrett, "Crop Mimicry in Weeds," *Economic Botany* 37 (1983): 255–282.

52. J. M. J. De Wet and J. R. Harlan, "Weeds and Domesticates: Evolution in the Man-Made Habitat," *Economic Botany* 29 (1975): 100.

53. Charles Darwin, *The Variation of Animals and Plants Under Domestication*, American Edition (New York: Orange Judd and Co., 1868), 1: 383.

54. Anderson, *Plants, Man, and Life*, 9, 15.

55. Alfred W. Crosby, *Ecological Imperialism*, 145–170. For a readable book that abounds with many intriguing examples of the links between weeds and culture, consult Sir Edward Salisbury's *Weeds and Aliens* (London: Collins, 1961). Salisbury was a botanist who, for many years, served as the director of the Royal Botanic Gardens at Kew.

Notes to Chapter 2

1. J. D. Chambers and G. E. Mingay, *The Agricultural Revolution, 1750–1880* (London: B. T. Batsford Ltd., 1966), 2–4.

2. Eric Kerridge, *The Agricultural Revolution* (London: George Allen and Unwin Ltd., 1967), 40, 328.

3. Salisbury, 24.

4. H. Godwin, "The History of Weeds in Britain," in *The Biology of Weeds*, ed. John L. Harper (Oxford: Blackwell Scientific Publications, 1960), 2–4.

5. Hill, 5.

6. Brenchley, *Weeds of Farm Land*, 1.

7. A. M. Mortimer, 10. For a similar argument and further examples of weedy plant introductions since the seventeenth century, see Salisbury, 50–80.

8. The 1960s studies by Kerridge and Chambers and Mingay are still considered standard references on the history of British agriculture from the sixteenth through the nineteenth centuries. P. R. Finberg and Joan Thirsk, eds., *The Agrarian History of England and Wales*, 8 vols. (Cambridge: Cambridge University Press, 1967-) represents the richest single source on Britain's agrarian history.

9. Lord Ernle, *English Farming Past and Present* (London: Longmans, Green and Co., 1961 [1912]).

10. Studies that cast agricultural writers as publicists rather than innovators include: Chambers and Mingay, 73-75; Kerridge, 15; G. E. Fussell, "Science and Practice in Eighteenth-Century Agriculture," *Agricultural History* 43 (1969): 18; Joan Thirsk, "Agricultural Innovations and their Diffusion," in *The Agrarian History of England and Wales*, vol. 5.2, *1640–1750: Agrarian Change*, ed. Joan Thirsk (Cambridge: Cambridge University Press, 1985), 537; and Stewart Richards, "Agricultural Science in Higher Education: Problems of Identity in Britain's First Chair of Agriculture, Edinburgh 1790–c1831," *Agricultural History Review* 33 (1985): 59.

11. Stuart MacDonald, "The Diffusion of Knowledge among Northumberland Farmers, 1780–1815," *Agricultural History Review* 27 (1979): 30–39; Stuart MacDonald, "Agricultural Improvement and the Neglected Labourer," *Agricultural History Review* 31 (1983): 81–90; and Nicholas Goddard, "The Development and Influence of Agricultural Periodicals and Newspapers, 1780–1880," *Agricultural History Review* 31 (1983): 116–131.

12. A recent article by Andrew McRae suggests that a number of the more popular sixteenth- and seventeenth-century husbandry manuals must have been read by members of "the lower socio-economic orders" rather than just by the gentry and their social superiors (Andrew McRae, "Husbandry Manuals and the Language of Agrarian Improvement," in *Culture and Cultivation in Early Modern England: Writing and the Land*, eds. Michael Leslie and Timothy Raylor [Leicester: Leicester University Press, 1992], 44–45).

13. Joan Thirsk, "Making a Fresh Start: Sixteenth-Century Agriculture and

the Classical Inspiration," in *Culture and Cultivation in Early Modern England: Writing and the Land*, eds. Michael Leslie and Timothy Raylor (Leicester: Leicester University Press, 1992), 15–16.

14. For a discussion of the use of the term "profit" in early farming manuals and for "the gradual emergence of the modern usage of the word" in sixteenth-century improvement literature, see McRae, 36–37, 48–49.

15. John Worlidge, *Systema Agriculturae; the Mystery of Husbandry Discovered*, 3rd ed. (London: Printed for Thomas Dring, 1681), in unpaginated dedication.

16. Christabel S. Orwin and Edith H. Whetham, *History of British Agriculture, 1846–1914* (London: Longmans, Green and Co., 1964), 28; Sir John Russell, *A History of Agricultural Science in Great Britain, 1620–1954* (London: George Allen and Unwin Ltd., 1966), 10; Fussell, "Science and Practice," 7–18; Fussell, "Agricultural Science and Experiment in the Eighteenth Century: An Attempt at a Definition," *Agricultural History Review* 24 (1976): 44–47; Mingay, 4, 65; and Richards, 59.

17. The earliest British weed experiments that include enough controls and replications to be described as truly "scientific" were conducted in 1898 by J. A. Voelcker. They consisted of a series of simple spraying trials using iron and copper sulphate to eradicate charlock (J. Augustus Voelcker, "The Destruction of Charlock," *Journal of the Royal Agricultural Society of England*, 3rd Series, 10 [1899]: 766–775). One of Britain's leading agricultural scientists during the first half of the twentieth century, Sir John Russell, argues that the first scientific research into weed biology and ecology in Britain was begun in 1905 at the Rothamstead Research Station under the direction of Winifred Brenchley (Sir John Russell, 439).

18. Sir Anthony Fitzherbert, *The Boke of Husbandry* (London: T. Berthelet, 1534), 16. Fitzherbert's treatise was first published in 1523.

19. Frequent references to weeds and lists of the most widespread weed problems are common features of British farming manuals published from the sixteenth century onwards. Unfortunately, until the late eighteenth century, most writers identified weeds by their common or provincial names. Common names provide insights into how plants are perceived by different people but they often make it difficult to determine the exact species under consideration. A single species can have many local identities and, not infrequently, two quite different plants can share the same common name. While I have endeavored to provide scientific

names wherever possible, in light of this difficulty, they often represent educated guesses rather than positive identifications. In determining scientific names, I have relied heavily on the following sources for their fairly detailed lists of both the current and historic names associated with common British weeds: Brenchley, *Weeds of Farm Land*, 206–226 and Plant Protection Limited, *Common Farm Weeds Illustrated* (London: Butterworth's Scientific Publications, 1952).

20. Chambers and Mingay, 73.

21. William Marshall, *The Rural Economy of Yorkshire* (London: Printed for T. Caddell, 1788), 1:355; Marshall, *The Rural Economy of Gloucestershire* (Gloucester: Printed by R. Raikes for G. Nicol, 1789), 1:92; and Marshall, *The Rural Economy of the Midland Counties* (London: Printed for G. Nicol, 1790), 1:211.

22. Brenchley, *Weeds of Farm Land*, 209.

23. William Marshall, *Minutes of Agriculture* (London: Printed for J. Dodsley, 1778), entries for April 20, 27, and 29, 1775.

24. Marshall, *Rural Economy of Gloucestershire*, 1:91.

25. A modern study which illustrates the tendency of specific weed problems to vary quite markedly between counties in England is R. J. Chancellor and R. J. Froud-Williams, "A Second Survey of Cereal Weeds in Central Southern England," *Weed Research* 24 (1984): 29–36.

26. For a detailed discussion of the relationship between crops and weeds in Britain, see Brenchley, *Weeds of Farm Land*, 158–174.

27. Fitzherbert, 16–18.

28. William Ellis, *The Modern Husbandman, or, the Practice of Farming* (London: Printed for T. Osborne and M. Cooper, 1744), 2, Month of May: 42.

29. Gervase Markham, *Markham's Farewell to Husbandry* (London: Published by M. F. for Roger Jackson, 1625), 13.

30. John Mortimer, 57, 64.

31. Edward Lisle, *Observations in Husbandry*, ed. Thomas Lisle (London: Printed by J. Hughs for C. Hitch, L. Hawes, J. Rivington, J. Fletcher, W. Sandby and R.& J. Dodsley, 1757), 389, 398. Lisle appears to have had some notion of publishing his observations but he died in 1722 before he realized his ambition. His writings were subsequently collected and published by his son Thomas.

32. W. Harwood Long, "The Low Yields of Corn in Medieval England," *Economic History Review* 32 (1979): 469. Long's argument has been recently challenged by David Postles. After a careful analysis of contemporary sources, Postles concludes that "although weediness may have been a contributory cause of low yields of grain," low yields were the "consequence of a failure to adopt" a number of intensive farming practices. Weediness in short, "was a contributory factor, but not a sole determinant." David Postles, "Cleaning the Medieval Arable," *Agricultural History Review* 37 (1989): 130, 142.

33. Thomas Hale, *A Compleat Body of Husbandry* (London: Printed for T. Osborne, J. Shipton, J. Hodges, T. Trye, S. Crowder and H. Woodgate, 1756), 365.

34. Jethro Tull, *The Horse-Hoing Husbandry: or, an Essay on the Principles of Tillage and Vegetation* (London: Printed for the author, 1733), 38.

35. Robert Maxwell, *The Practical Husbandman* (Edinburgh: Printed by C. Wright and Company, for the author, 1757), 307.

36. Marshall, *Rural Economy of Gloucestershire*, 1:72.

37. Buckman, 374.

38. Timmons, 295.

39. William Marshall, *The Rural Economy of the West of England* (London: Printed for G. Nicol, G. G. and J. Robinson, and J. Debrett, 1796), 1:188.

40. Walter of Henley, "Husbandry (ca 1286)," in *Walter of Henley and Other Treatises on Estate Management and Accounting*, ed. and trans. Dorothea Oschinsky (Oxford: Clarendon Press, 1971), 323; Fitzherbert, 17; Thomas Tusser, *Five Hundreth Points of Good Husbandry* (London: Richard Tottell, 1574), 48; Postles, 137.

41. Tull, *The Horse-Hoing Husbandry*, 39

42. Ellis, *The Modern Husbandman*, 2, Month of May: 36.

43. William Marshall, *The Rural Economy of Norfolk* (London: Printed for T. Caddell, 1787), 1: 226.

44. William Marshall, *The Rural Economy of Gloucestershire*, 1: 98–99.

45. Loudon, 363–364; Stephens, 941–942; James Caird, *English Agriculture in 1850–51*, 2d. ed. (London: Frank Cass and Co., 1967; reprint of 1852 edition with a new introduction by G. E. Mingay), 138; John Percival, "Weeds and Their Suppression," *The Journal of the Board of Agriculture* 10 (1903/1904): 465; Orwin and Whetham, 10.

46. Peter J. Bowden, "Agricultural Prices, Farm Profits, and Rents," in *The Agrarian History of England and Wales*, Vol. 4, *1500–1640*, ed. Joan Thirsk (Cambridge: Cambridge University Press, 1967), 662; Bowden, "Agricultural Prices, Wages, Farm Profits and Rents," in *The Agrarian History of England and Wales*, Vol. 5.2, *1640–1750: Agrarian Change*, ed. Joan Thirsk (Cambridge: Cambridge University Press, 1985), 92.

47. Marshall, *Rural Economy of Gloucestershire*, 1:99–100.

48. Arthur Young, *A Six Months Tour Through the North of England* (Dublin: Printed for P. Wilson, J. Exshaw, H. Saunders, W. Sleater, D. Chamberlaine, J. Potts, J. Hoey Jr., J. Williams, W. Colles, J. Porter, C. Ingham, and T. Walker, 1770), 3:82.

49. Sir John Sinclair, *The Code of Agriculture* (London: B. McMillan, 1817), 235.

50. John Mortimer, 45.

51. Tusser, 39; Walter Blith, *The English Improver Improved* (n.p., 1652), 109; Worlidge, 35; John Mortimer, 45; and Dickson, 84.

52. Marshall, *Rural Economy of the West of England*, 1:138.

53. Marshall, *Rural Economy of Yorkshire*, 1:361–362.

54. Ibid.

55. Joan Thirsk, "Farming Techniques," in *The Agrarian History of England and Wales*, vol.4, *1500–1640*, ed. Joan Thirsk (Cambridge: Cambridge University Press, 1967), 179. For more on the early importance of summer fallowing see: Walter of Henley, 321; Tusser, 53; Fitzherbert, 15–16, 18; Long, 463–465; and Postles, 142–143.

56. Thirsk, "Farming Techniques," 179.

57. Tull, *The Horse-Hoing Husbandry*, 38-39; Hale, 712; Marshall, *Minutes of Agriculture*, Nov.5, 1774 and May 21, 1776; and Marshall, *Rural Economy of Gloucestershire*, 1:69–70.

58. Caird, 137.

59. Prominent nineteenth-century agriculturists that strongly advocated summer fallowing include: Sinclair, *The Code of Agriculture*, 228; Holdich, "317; and Buckman, 375. For recent studies on the nineteenth-century decline of summer fallowing, see Jonathan Brown and H. A. Beecham, "Farming Practices," in *The Agrarian History of England and Wales*, Vol. 6, *1750–1850*, ed. G. E. Mingay (Cambridge: Cambridge University Press, 1989), 282–283; and David Grigg, *English Agriculture: An Historical Perspective* (Oxford: Basil Blackwell, 1989), 48.

60. Sinclair, *The Code of Agriculture*, 227.

61. Caird, 299, 320.

62. Colin A. M. Duncan, "Legal Protection for the Soil of England: The Spurious Context of Nineteenth Century 'Progress,'" *Agricultural History* 66, no. 2 (1992): 83, 89.

63. Ibid., 89.

64. For the most recent biography of Tull, see: Norman Hidden, "Jethro Tull I, II, and III," *Agricultural History Review* 37 (1989): 26–35.

65. Ernle, 169.

66. Tull, *The Horse-Hoing Husbandry*, 25.

67. Ibid., 25–37.

68. Ibid., 39.

69. For a concise summary of Tull's changing reputation in the eyes of historians since Ernle and a balanced assessment of his contributions to British husbandry, see E. R. Wicker, "A Note on Jethro Tull: Innovator or Crank?" *Agricultural History* 31 (1957): 46–48.

70. Chambers and Mingay, 70.

71. Roger Wilkes, "The Diffusion of Drill Husbandry, 1731–1850," in *Agricultural Improvement: Medieval and Modern*, ed. Walter Minchinton (Exeter: University of Exeter, 1981): 65–94. For contemporary explanations of the slow adoption of Tull's horse-hoeing husbandry, see Arthur Young, *Rural Oeconomy* (London: Printed for T. Becket, 1770), 316 and Patrick Brodie, "On the Destruction of Weeds," *Communications to the Board of Agriculture* 7 (1811): 67.

72. Ellis, *The Modern Husbandman*, 1, Month of March: 17, and Marshall, *Rural Economy of Norfolk*, 1:226.

73. Arthur Young, *Six Months Tour*, 1:49, 25.

74. Brodie, 69.

75. Marshall, *Minutes of Agriculture*, July 1, 1775; Dickson, 1: 105; and Stephens, 3: 944–947.

76. Ellis, 304; Sinclair, *Code of Agriculture*, 247; and Buckman, 376–377.

77. Tusser, 23.

78. J. A. R. Lockhart, A. Samuel and M. P. Greaves, "The Evolution of Weed Control in British Agriculture," in *Weed Control Handbook: Principles*, 8th ed., eds. R. J. Hance and K. Holly (Oxford: Blackwell Scientific Publications, 1990), 53–54.

79. Ellis, *Chiltern and Vale Farming*, 329. Adjusting seeding rates to discourage the growth of weeds was advocated by many agricultural improvers beginning with Thomas Tusser in the sixteenth century (Tusser, 17).

80. Marshall, *Rural Economy of Norfolk*, 1:254. For other early references to the use of smother crops, see William Ellis, *Agriculture Improv'd: or, the Practice of Husbandry Display'd* (London: Printed for T. Osborne, 1746), 1:12–13 and Home, 159.

81. Thirsk, "Farming Techniques," 177; Tusser, 17.

82. Thirsk, "Farming Techniques," 177.

83. Ibid., 178.

84. Orwin and Whetham, 5; Chambers and Mingay, 58–59; and Grigg, 49.

85. Caird, 503.

86. William Pitt, "On the Subject of Weeding; or the Improvements to be Effected in Agriculture by the Extirpation of Weeds," *Communications to the Board of Agriculture* 5 (1806): 255.

87. Lockhart, Samuel and Greaves, 44–45.

88. Some improvers such as Sir John Sinclair argued that the adoption of turnips in rotations had significantly reduced the incidence of weeds on arable land by the early 1800s (Sinclair, *The Code of Agriculture*, 235).

89. Chambers and Mingay, 61.

90. Marshall, *Rural Economy of Norfolk*, 1:267–268.

91. Arthur Young, *Rural Oeconomy*, 82–84.

92. Pitt, 233; Brodie, 64; and Lockhart, Samuel, and Greaves, 44.

93. Marshall, *Minutes of Agriculture*, July 29, 1775.

94. Keith Thomas, *Man and the Natural World: Changing Attitudes in England*, 1500-1800 (London: Penguin Books, 1983), 270.

95. Ibid.

96. Fitzherbert, 17; Tusser, 37; Conrad Heresbach, *Four Books of Husbandry*, ed. and trans. by Barnabe Googe (London: Printed for Richard Watkins, 1577), 18; Thomas Hill, *The Profitable Art of Gardening* (London: Henry Bynneman, 1579), 18; Blith, 120; Worlidge, 214.

97. Tull, *The Horse-Hoing Husbandry*, 25, 37-38.

98. Ellis, *Chiltern and Vale Farming*, 293; Ellis, *The Modern Husbandman*, 4, Month of March: 17.

99. Young, *Rural Oeconomy*, 83–84; Sir John Sinclair, *An Account of the Systems of Husbandry Adopted in the More Improved Districts of Scotland*, 2nd ed. (Edinburgh: Printed by James Bellantyne and Company, 1813), 1:364.

100. For evidence of this change of style, consult any of the nineteenth-century references cited in this chapter.

101. Brodie, 64.

102. Ellis, *Chiltern and Vale Farming*, 304.

103. Maxwell, 234.

104. Ordish, 75.

105. The first British publication solely devoted to the issue of weeds and weeding appears to be William Pitt's essay "On the Subject of Weeding." For early attempts to estimate the cost of weeds and the profits of weeding, see Arthur Young, *A Six Months Tour Through the North of England*, 3: 74–86 and John Wright, "Experiments on Weeding Broad-cast Crops," *Communications to the Board of Agriculture*, 6, Part 2 (1810): 387–388.

106. Marshall, *Rural Economy of the Midland Counties*, 2:152; Pitt, 257; George Rennie, "On Weeding or Cleaning Land," *Communications to the Board of Agriculture* 7, part 2 (1813): 297; and Sinclair, *The Code of Agriculture*, 248. Sinclair mentions that a "clause enforcing the extirpation of weeds in hedges, along the sides of roads, passed the House of Commons; but was thrown out by the Lords."

107. G. C. Ainsworth, *Introduction to the History of Plant Pathology* (Cambridge: Cambridge University Press, 1981), 8, 34–35. Sir Joseph Banks, for example, was probably the first British writer to alert British agriculturists to the true nature of blight or rust in wheat. Sir Joseph Banks, "A Short Account of the Cause of the Disease in Corn, called by Farmers the Blight, the Mildew, and the Rust," *Communications to the Board of Agriculture* 4 (1805): 399.

108. Markham, 22; Francis Bacon, *Sylva Sylvarum, or a Natural History in Ten Centuries* (London: Printed for W. Lee, 1628), 120, 131–134, 139-140; Bradley, 133–135.

109. Lisle, 44–45.

110. Tull, *The New Horse-Houghing Husbandry*, 32; Hale, 273.

111. Dickson, 85–86.

112. Ellis, *Chiltern and Vale Farming*, 292.

113. Marshall, *Rural Economy of Gloucestershire*, 1:70.

114. Rennie, 297.

115. Sinclair, *Code of Agriculture*, 235.

116. Caird, 136.

117. Orwin and Whetham, 114–116; Brown and Beecham, 288.

118. Duncan, 93.

119. Ellis, *The Modern Husbandman*, 4, Month of December: 29.

120. Pitt, 234.

121. Blith, 109; Mortimer, 56–66; Buckman, 359; and Morton, 2:1118.

122. Tull, *The New Horse-Houghing Husbandry*, 43–44.

123. Ellis, *Chiltern and Vale Farming*, 327–328.

124. Hale, 711–712.

125. Rennie, 296; Buckman, 374.

126. Rennie, 296.

127. For a detailed discussion of the theological emphasis on man's dominion over creation in Tudor and early Stuart England and a subsequent shift in emphasis during the seventeenth and early eighteenth century towards stressing the benevolence of God's design, see Keith Thomas, 17–21.

128. Markham, 3–4.

129. Keith Thomas, 24.

130. Blith, 3.

131. Ellis, *The Modern Husbandman*, 2, Month of May: 47.

132. Pitt, 233–234.

133. Ellis, *Chiltern and Vale Farming*, 292.

134. Keith Thomas, 20.

135. Pitt, 234, and Brodie, 65.

136. For a brief biography of Holdich and the publication history of his essay "On the Weeds of Agriculture," consult G. E. Fussell, *The Old English Farming Books*, vol.3, *1793–1839* (London: The Pindar Press, 1983), 111–112.

137. Stephens, 3:950.

138. Harold C. Long, "The Identification and Eradication of Some Common Weeds, I," *Journal of the Board of Agriculture,* 18 (1911/12): 290; Long, "The Identification and Eradication of Some Common Weeds, IV," *Journal of the Board of Agriculture,* 19 (1912/13): 276, and Brenchley, *Weeds of Farm Land,* passim.

139. Holdich, 323–324.

140. Great Britain, Board of Agriculture and Fisheries, *Weeds and their Suppression*, Leaflet No. 112, 1904, 2–4.

141. G. E. Blackman, "Recent Developments in the Control of Weeds," *Journal*

of the Royal Horticultural Society 73 (1948): 134. Blackman first delivered his paper in 1947.

142. Three British weed specialists suggest that "from the 18th century onwards there was an increasing awareness that efficient weed control was essential to successful crop production, and the husbandry of those days increasingly incorporated control measures into all systems of land and crop management" (Lockhart, Samuel, and Greaves, 44).

143. For a similar argument and more detailed treatments of these issues, see Brown and Beecham, 282–283, 288; Grigg, 70, 156–158; and Lockhart, Samuel, and Greaves, 43–53.

Notes to Chapter 3

1. For nineteenth-century commentary on the European origins of most of Ontario's weeds, see Panton, 3, and Thomas Shaw, *Weeds and How to Eradicate Them* (Toronto: J. E. Bryant and Co., 1893), 2–4. Foreign plants continue to dominate Canada's weed flora to this day. For example, in the most recent edition of the standard federal government weed identification guide, *Weeds of Canada*, of the 114 weeds discussed in detail, 54 are described as native to Europe, 31 hail from Eurasia and only 24 are listed as native to North America. In terms of percentages, this translates into 47% from Europe, 27% from Europe and/or Asia and 21% from North America. The remaining 5% have arrived from Asia, South America, and parts unknown (Frankton and Mulligan, 1993).

2. A number of European weed species are known to have been well established in New England by the late seventeenth century. J. F. Alex, "Canada," in *Biology and Ecology of Weeds*, eds. W. Holzner and M. Numata (The Hague: Dr. W. Junk Publishers, 1982), 3; Cronon, 142–144; and Crosby, 155–156.

3. Alex, "Canada," 309; J. E. Burton, *Essay on Comparative Agriculture, or a Brief Examination into the State of Agriculture as it now Exists in Great Britain and Canada* (Montreal: Printed at the Montreal Gazette Office, 1828), 58.

4. Charles F. Grece, *Essays on Practical Husbandry, Addressed to the Canadian Farmers* (Montreal: Printed by William Gray, 1817), 89, and C. F. Cresinus, "On the Agriculture of Canada, No.10," *Canadian Magazine and Literary Repository* 4 (1825): 408.

5. Burton, 61.

6. Ibid., 57–58.

7. Adam Fergusson, *On the Agricultural State of Canada and Part of the United States of America* (Leith, Scotland: Printed by William Reid and Son, 1832), 5.

8. Cresinus, 218.

9. Patrick Shirreff, *A Tour Through North America; Together with a Comprehensive View of the Canadas and the United States as Adapted for Agricultural Emigration* (Edinburgh: Oliver and Boyd, 1835), 140.

10. Ibid., 127.

11. *British American Cultivator*, June 1847, 161–163.

12. Ibid., November 1847, 344.

13. *The Canadian Agricultural Reader* (Niagara: John Simpson, 1845), 43.

14. Ibid., 16, 20; *The Canadian Agriculturist*, June 1, 1849, 161–162.

15. James F. W. Johnston, *Notes on North America: Agricultural, Economical, and Social* (Edinburgh: William Blackwood and Sons, 1851), 1: 272, 305, 368.

16. *The Canadian Agricultural Reader*, 14–20.

17. *The British American Cultivator*, June 1847, 162.

18. Kenneth Kelly, "Wheat Farming in Simcoe County in the Mid-Nineteenth Century," *Canadian Geographer* 15 (1971): 102; Robert L. Jones, 61; and *The Canadian Agricultural Reader*, 3–4.

19. William Evans, *A Treatise on the Theory and Practice of Agriculture* (Montreal: Fabre, Perrault and Co., 1835), and *The Canadian Agricultural Reader* (Niagara: John Simpson, 1845).

20. Sir John W. Dawson, *First Lessons in Scientific Agriculture* (Montreal: John Lovell, 1864), and Egerton Ryerson, *First Lessons on Agriculture; For Canadian Farmers and their Families* (Toronto: Copp, Clark and Co., 1870).

21. There has been considerable debate over the relative importance of wheat and its role as a staple in the nineteenth-century economy of Ontario. For the two sides to this issue, see McCallum, and R. M. McInnis, "Perspectives on Ontario Agriculture, 1815–1930," *Canadian Papers in Rural History* 8 (1992): 17–48.

22. Jones, 91.

23. James O'Mara, "The Seasonal Rounds of Gentry Farmers in Early Ontario: A Preliminary Analysis," *Canadian Papers in Rural History* 2 (1980): 109.

24. Joan Thirsk, "Farming Techniques," 179, and Jones, 92.

25. William Marshall, *The Rural Economy of Gloucestershire*, 1: 69–70.

26. *The Canadian Agriculturist*, November 1855, 326.

27. Robert L. Jones, 196.

28. *The Canadian Agriculturist*, December 1850, 269.

29. Ibid., November 1855, 327.

30. Ibid., July 1858, 146.

31. James Croil, "Lecture on Practical Agriculture, Delivered before the Dundas County Agricultural Society," *Transactions of the Board of Agriculture and of the Agricultural Association of Upper Canada* 3 (1859): 79.

32. Rennie, 296.

33. *The Canadian Agriculturist*, December 16, 1860, 643 and February 16, 1861, 98.

34. Ibid., February 16, 1861, 97.

35. Ibid., January 1863, 2.

36. Ibid., March 1863, 81.

37. Ibid., September 1863, 334 and October 1863, 369.

38. Canada, *Statutes of Upper Canada*, 1793, 33 Geo.3, c.4, sect.9.

39. Canada, *Statutes of Canada*, 1849, 12 Vict., c.81, sect.30(21).

40. Ibid., 1853, 16 Vict., c.190, sect.60 and c.169, sect.7.

41. *The Canadian Agriculturist*, January 1863, 7.

42. Ibid., September 1, 1861, 517.

43. Ibid., March 1863, 82.

44. Canada, *Statutes of Canada*, 1865, 29 Vict., c.40.

45. British agricultural improvers who pushed for the enactment of weed laws include: Marshall, *The Rural Economy of the Midland Counties*, 2:152; Pitt, 257; Rennie, 297; and Sinclair, *The Code of Agriculture*, 248. The Isle of Man and Northern Ireland had noxious-weed legislation in force by 1900 and 1909 respectively, but it was not until 1920 that Great Britain passed its first official weed law in the form of a brief amending clause to the Corn Production Act of 1917. Great Britain, "Weeds Act in the Isle of Man," *The Journal of the Board of Agriculture* 7 (1900/01): 245; Great Britain, *Statutes of Northern Ireland*, 1909, 9 Edw.7, c.31; and Great Britain, *Statutes*, 1920, 10 and 11 Geo.5, c.76, s.10.

46. Moore, 1038.

47. John Nicholson, *The Farmers' Assistant* (Albany, N. Y.: Printed by H. C. Southwick, 1814), 263.

48. A footnote in Robert Jones's *History of Agriculture in Ontario* suggests that Canada thistle was introduced into what is now Ontario during the era of the fur trade as a stowaway in the straw mattresses of the men who crewed the bateaux (Jones, 92).

49. Thomas Shaw, *Weeds, and How to Eradicate Them* (Toronto: J. E. Bryant and Company, 1893), 4.

50. Charles E. Whitcombe, *The Canadian Farmer's Manual of Agriculture* (Toronto: James Adams and Company, 1874), 278.

51. J. C. Rykert, "Annual Address," *Transactions of the Board of Agriculture and of the Agricultural Association of Upper Canada, 1864 to 1868* 6 (1872): 144.

52. Marshall, *The Rural Economy of Yorkshire*, 1:363.

53. Aldrich, 374.

54. For one of the earliest discussions of this phenomenon, see C. S. Rafinesque Schmaltz, "An Essay on the Exotic Plants, Mostly European, Which have been Naturalized and Now Grow Spontaneously in the Middle States of America," *Medical Repository* 2 (1811): 330–345.

55. This argument has been offered in Claypole, 80; Asa Gray, 163; Dewey, "Migration of Weeds," 284; John M. Fogg, *Weeds of Lawn and Garden: A Handbook for Eastern Temperate North America* (Philadelphia: University of Pennsylvania Press, 1945), 10; and Holzner, 9.

56. Claypole, 87.

57. Asa Gray, 162.

58. J. McNeil, "The Taxonomy and Evolution of Weeds," *Weed Research* 16 (1976): 407–408.

59. Crosby, *Ecological Imperialism,* 287–290, 309–310. Crosby does cite Asa Gray on page 166 of *Ecological Imperialism* but he incorrectly implies that the main thrust of Gray's article was to suggest that European flora had the advantage over American flora because it was either older or younger. Gray does mention these ideas but simply in order to dismiss them!

60. Tom Pritchard, "Race Formation in Weedy Species with Special Reference to *Euphorbia cyparissias* L. and *Hypericum perforatum* L.," in *The Biology of Weeds*, ed. John L. Harper (Oxford: Blackwell Scientific Publications, 1960), 62.

61. For recent explanations for the unusual success of immigrant weeds in North America, see Thomas A. Hill, 43; Aldrich, 375; and Baker, "The Continuing Evolution of Weeds," 445.

62. Kelly, "Wheat Farming in Simcoe County in the Mid-Nineteenth Century," 102.

63. Fergusson, 29.

64. James Johnson, "Annual Address," *Transactions of the Board of Agriculture and of the Agricultural Association of Upper Canada* 6 (1872): 23.

65. Robert Barclay Allardice, *Agricultural Tour in the United States and Upper Canada, with Miscellaneous Notices* (Edinburgh: William Blackwood and Sons, 1842), 64.

66. Robert L. Jones, 73; Kenneth Kelly, "The Impact of Nineteenth Century Agricultural Settlement on the Land," in *Perspectives on Landscape and Settlement in Nineteenth Century Ontario*, ed. J. David Wood (Toronto: McClelland and Stewart, 1975), 66.

67. Estimates of forest clearance rates for the 1820s to 1840s are generally accepted to be in the range of five to seven acres per year. Peter Russell has recently challenged these figures as being far too high, and he suggests that for the period 1822–1839, the "average" rate of clearing was more likely in the range of "around one and one-half acres per year" (Peter A. Russell, "Forest into Farmland: Upper Canada Clearing Rates, 1822–1839," *Agricultural History* 57 [1983]: 328).

68. Kelly, "Wheat Farming in Simcoe County," 104.

69. *The Canadian Agriculturist*, October 1858, 236-237.

70. Robert L. Jones, 53, and McCallum, 21. For more on the reasons why relatively few farmers engaged in mixed farming, see Kenneth Kelly, "Notes on a Type of Mixed Farming Practiced in Ontario During the Early Nineteenth Century," *Canadian Geographer* 17 (1973): 205, and O'Mara, 105.

71. Croil, 77.

72. Ibid., 80–81.

73. McCallum, 21.

74. Kelly, "Wheat Farming in Simcoe County," 98.

75. Ibid., 100, 106.

76. John Wade, "Annual Address," *Transactions of the Board of Agriculture and of the Agricultural Association of Upper Canada, 1860 to 1863* 5 (1864): 40.

77. *The British American Cultivator*, November 1847, 325; Kelly, "Wheat farming in Simcoe County," 107; and McCallum, 13.

78. Croil, 78; Rykert, 143; Ontario, Agricultural Commission, "Testimony

of George Buckland," *Report of the Commissioners and Appendices*, Vol. 4 (Toronto: C. Blackett Robinson, 1881), 156; and Robert L. Jones, 323.

79. J. G. Elliot, "The Contribution of Weed Science to Food Production in Great Britain," *Weed Science* 18 (1970): 682.

80. Whitcombe, 278.

Notes to Chapter 4

1. James Fletcher, *The Russian Thistle or Russian Tumble-Weed* (Ottawa: Government Printing Bureau, 1894), 4.

2. For detailed summaries of late-nineteenth-century agricultural change in Ontario, see: Robert L. Jones, 244–249, 304–327, and G. Elmore Reaman, *A History of Agriculture in Ontario* (Toronto: Saunders, 1970), 1:124–151.

3. Robert L. Jones, 324; James Fletcher, *Weeds*, Dominion Department of Agriculture, Central Experimental Farm, Bulletin 28, 1897, 9.

4. The colonial and provincial governments of Ontario did little to support agricultural improvement directly until the 1880s (Robert L. Jones, 332–333 and Reaman, 104).

5. Ontario Agricultural Commission, *Report of the Commissioners and Appendices*, and Ontario Agricultural Commission, *Canadian Farming: An Encyclopedia of Agriculture* (Toronto: Williamson and Co., 1889).

6. For a concise summary of the agitation leading up to the establishment of the OAC, see Jones, 331–335, and Alexander M. Ross, *The College on the Hill: A History of the Ontario Agricultural College* (Toronto: Copp Clarke, 1974), 1–28.

7. Ralph H. Estey, "Publicly Sponsored Agricultural Research in Canada since 1887," *Agricultural History* 62 (Spring 1988): 51. T. H. Anstey's *One Hundred Harvests: Research Branch, Agriculture Canada, 1886–1986* (Ottawa: Supply and Services Canada, 1986) provides a detailed history of the Dominion Experimental Farms Service.

8. Ontario Agricultural Commission, *Report of the Commissioners*, 5:18; Great Britain, Board of Agriculture, "Agricultural Education in the United States and Canada," *Journal of the Board of Agriculture* 17 (1910/1911): 915; and Sir John Russell, 268–288.

9. Ontario, Ontario Agricultural and Experimental Union, *Annual Report*, 1904, 81–83; Henry Morgan, ed., *The Canadian Men and Women of the*

Time: A Hand-book of Canadian Biography of Living Characters, 2nd ed. (Toronto: William Briggs, 1912), 1014.

10. *The Canadian Who's Who* (Toronto: The Musson Book Company Ltd., 1910), 243; Alexander M. Ross, 36, 47.

11. Herbert Groh, "A Survey of Weed Control and Investigation in Canada," *Scientific Agriculture* 3 (1922/23): 415.

12. Paul W. Riegert, "James Fletcher," in *Dictionary of Canadian Biography*, vol. 13, ed. Ramsay Cook (Toronto: University of Toronto Press, 1994), 347–348.

13. John Macoun, *Catalogue of Canadian Plants*, Part II, *Gamopetalae* (Montreal: Dawson Brothers, 1884), 271.

14. Ibid., 47.

15. Thomas Shaw, 5–6.

16. Panton, *Weeds*, 3, and Thomas Shaw and C. A. Zavitz, *Weeds and Modes of Destroying Them*, Ontario Agricultural College, Bulletin 85, 1892, 3.

17. F. C. Harrison and William Lockhead, *Some Common Ontario Weeds*, Ontario Agricultural College and Experimental Farm, Bulletin 128, 1903, 17.

18. Canada thistle, wild mustard, wild oats, quack grass, and several other long-established species continued to top lists of Ontario's worst weeds during the closing decades of the nineteenth century. Ontario Agricultural Commission, 1:384–386; James Mills and Thomas Shaw, *The First Principles of Agriculture* (Toronto: J. E. Bryant Co., 1890), 98; J. Hoyes Panton, *Weeds of Ontario*, Ontario Agricultural College and Experimental Farm, Bulletin 91, 1893, 2; Ontario, Ontario Agricultural College and Experimental Farm, *Annual Report*, 1894, 25; and F. C. Harrison, *Some Common Ontario Weeds* (Toronto: Ontario Department of Agriculture, 1900), 80.

19. Panton, *Weeds*, 5; Panton, *Weeds of Ontario*, 2; OAC, *Annual Report*, 1896, 10–11; Harrison, 10–11.

20. J. Eaton Howitt, *The Perennial Sow Thistle and Some Other Weed Pests of 1908*, Ontario Agricultural College and Experimental Farm, Bulletin 168, 1908, 5

21. Ontario Agricultural Commission, 1:382. The 1865 Canada Thistle Act underwent minor amendments in the late 1860s and 1870s and it was substantially revised in 1884. Significant revisions include outlining the

duties of municipal inspectors in greater detail, new fines for selling contaminated seed and an expansion of the noxious-weed list to include
ox-eye daisy, wild oats, ragweed, and burdock. Ontario, *Statutes of Ontario*,
1884, 47 Vict., c.37. Ontario's 1884 noxious-weed legislation was amended
a number of times over the following decades but it was not seriously
overhauled until 1935: Ontario, *Revised Statutes of Ontario*, 1897, c.279;
Statutes, 1912, 2 Geo.5, c.68; *Statutes*, 1927, 17 Geo.5, c.81 and *Statutes*,
1935, 25 Geo.5, c.49.

22. Whitcombe, 278, and Ontario Agricultural Commission, 1:384 and 4:100.
23. Harrison and Lockhead, 17.
24. Ibid.
25. OAC, Annual Report, 1889, 63–74.
26. Ibid., 1896, 6–7.
27. J. F. Alex, *Ontario Weeds* (Toronto: Ontario Ministry of Agriculture and
Food, 1992) and Panton, *Weeds.*
28. The first official British weed bulletin is represented by a four-page leaflet
outlining the use of chemical weed killers against charlock: Great Britain,
Board of Agriculture and Fisheries, *Destruction of Charlock*, Leaflet 63,
1900. In 1904, the British Board of Agriculture and Fisheries published an
equally short but more general pamphlet titled *Weeds and Their Suppression*,
Leaflet 112, 1904.
29. Harrison, 1.
30. Fletcher, *The Russian Thistle*; Fletcher, *Weeds*; and George H. Clark
and James Fletcher, *Farm Weeds of Canada* (Ottawa: Department of
Agriculture, 1905). The second edition of *Farm Weeds of Canada* (1909) ran
to the impressive length of 192 pages.
31. Canada, Dominion Experimental Farms, *Annual Reports*, 1892, 147; 1894,
223; 1895, 177; 1896, 275.
32. James, *Agriculture* (1899).
33. The first British book-length publication solely devoted to the issue of
weeds is Winifred E. Brenchley's *Weeds of Farm Land* (1920).
34. For a more detailed discussion of this issue, see chapter one. Late-
nineteenth-century Ontario publications that define weeds as "plants out of
place" include: Panton, *Weeds*, 3; James, *Agriculture*, 71; and Harrison, 2.
35. Shaw, *Weeds and How to Eradicate Them*, 3.
36. Harrison, 7.

37. OAC, *Annual Reports*, 1891, 49–52; 1895, 15; 1896, 7 and 1899, 3; and Canada, Dominion Experimental Farms, *Annual Report*, 1899, 194–196.

38. Shaw, *Weeds and How to Eradicate Them*, 1, 6.

39. Ibid., 6, 11.

40. Panton, *Weeds of Ontario*, 1, and Fletcher, *Weeds*, 5.

41. Panton, *Weeds of Ontario*, 1.

42. Fletcher, *Weeds*, 5, 11.

43. Mills and Shaw, 97, and James, *Agriculture*, 72.

44. For a standard summary of this process, see Gerald Friesen's *The Canadian Prairies: A History* (Toronto: University of Toronto Press, 1987), 195–241.

45. Stanley N. Murray, "A History of Agriculture in the Valley of the Red River of the North, 1812 to 1920," (Ph.D. diss., University of Wisconsin, 1963), 153.

46. John Macoun, *Manitoba and the Great North-West* (Guelph, Ontario: The World Publishing Co., 1882), 197.

47. Henry Tanner, *Report Upon Canada* (London: The Freemason Printing Works, 1883), 22.

48. *Nor'-West Farmer* (Winnipeg), June 1886, 501; Allan R. Turner, "Pioneer Farming Experiences," *Saskatchewan History* 8 (Spring 1955): 46.

49. William Fream, *Canadian Agriculture, Part 1, The Prairie* (London: William Clowes and Son, 1885), 91. For similar discussions of the nature of late-nineteenth-century Prairie agriculture, see virtually any issue of the *Nor'-West Farmer* or the *Farmer's Advocate-Western Edition* (Winnipeg). Murray, 205–270, probably provides the most detailed modern account of early Prairie farming practices.

50. Manitoba, Department of Agriculture and Immigration, *Annual Report*, 1900, in unpaginated introduction.

51. Alexander Ross, *The Red River Settlement: Its Rise, Progress, and Present State* (London: Smith, Elder and Co., 1856), 112, and John Bracken, *Dry Farming in Western Canada* (Winnipeg: The Grain Growers' Guide Ltd., 1921), 6–7.

52. Angus Mackay, as quoted in Fletcher, *Weeds*, 9, and Thomas D. Isern, "The Discer: Tillage for the Canadian Plains," *Agricultural History* 62, no. 2 (1988): 80.

53. Joseph H. Ellis, *The Ministry of Agriculture in Manitoba, 1870–1970* (Winnipeg: Manitoba Department of Agriculture, 1970), 142.

54. Bracken, 6, and Isern, "The Discer," 80.

55. *Farmer's Advocate*, June 5, 1893, 209.

56. *Nor'-West Farmer*, September 1888, 237; G. A. Mulligan and L. G. Bailey, "The Biology of Canadian Weeds. 8. *Sinapsis arvensis* L.," *Canadian Journal of Plant Science* 55 (1975): 177. For a concise summary of early farming activities around fur-trading posts, see Lewis H. Thomas, "A History of Agriculture on the Prairies to 1914," *Prairie Forum* 1 (1976): 31–35.

57. Murray, 262, and Fream, 45.

58. *Farmer's Advocate*, July 5, 1894, 261.

59. Ibid., May 1892, 177.

60. Canada, Dominion Experimental Farms, *Annual Report*, 1894, 333.

61. *Nor'-West Farmer*, July 1890, 548.

62. Canada, Dominion Experimental Farms, *Annual Report*, 1899, 185. James Fletcher's 1899 report includes a complete copy of his four page 1898 bulletin, *The Worst Weeds of the North-West*.

63. Manitoba, *Statutes,* 1871, 34 Vict., c.24.

64. Ibid., 1882, 45 Vict., c.12.

65. North-West Territories, *Revised Ordinances of the North-West Territories*, 1888, c.21.

66. Manitoba, *Statutes*, 1890, 53 Vict., c.34.

67. Fream, 38.

68. *Nor'-West Farmer*, July 1887, 895.

69. Ibid., August 1890, 576.

70. *Farmer's Advocate*, September 5, 1894, 345.

71. Groh, "A Survey of Weed Control", 419; Canada, Dominion Experimental Farms, *Annual Report*, 1898, 184.

72. Manitoba, Department of Agriculture and Immigration, *Noxious Weeds and How to Destroy Them* (Winnipeg: Department of Agriculture and Immigration, 1897), 2.

73. Ibid., 2–3.

74. Ontario, Ontario Agricultural and Experimental Union, *Annual Report*, 1904, 80. A survey of turn-of-the-century reading habits in pioneer Saskatchewan indicates that the *Farmer's Advocate* was one of the "most favoured" newspapers (Catherine Tulloch, "Pioneer Reading," *Saskatchewan History* 12, no. 3 [1959]: 97).

75. During June and July of 1899, for example, the Regina *Leader* published long, often repetitive accounts of all seventeen of Fletcher's North-West Territory speaking engagements.

76. For Fletcher's own accounts of his first four tours, see Canada, Dominion Experimental Farms, *Annual Reports*, 1896, 224; 1898, 169; 1899, 197–198.

77. Ibid., 1896, 275; 1899, 199; *Leader* (Regina), July 13, 1899, 1.

78. *Farmer's Advocate*, July 5, 1894, 261; September 5, 1899, 455; September 5, 1900, 483.

79. *Leader* (Regina), June 29, 1899, 4.

80. *Farmer's Advocate*, October 1, 1903, 895.

81. The first botanist to comment on the greater weedy ability of western native species was Asa Gray (162-163).

82. Fream, 66.

83. Manitoba, *Noxious Weeds and How to Destroy Them*, 4.

84. Canada, Dominion Experimental Farms, *Annual Report*, 1899, 189–190.

85. Ibid., 190.

86. *Farmer's Advocate*, March 6, 1893, 88.

87. Canada, Dominion Experimental Farms, *Annual Report*, 1899, 185, 187, and Thomas Shaw, 177.

88. *Farmer's Advocate*, March 6, 1893, 88; Manitoba, Advisory Board, *Our Canadian Prairies* (Toronto: C. Blackett Robinson, 1895), 88; Herbert Groh, *Canadian Weed Survey: Second Annual Report* (Ottawa: Department of Agriculture, 1943), 21.

89. K. F. Best and G. I. McIntyre, "The Biology of Canadian Weeds. 9. *Thlaspi arvense* L.," *Canadian Journal of Plant Science* 55 (1975): 283; John Macoun, *Catalogue of Canadian Plants, Part I, Polypetalae* (Montreal: Dawson Brothers, 1883), 56.

90. Frankton and Mulligan, 76.

91. *Farmer's Advocate*, March 6, 1893, 88.

92. Best and McIntyre, 280, 283.

93. *Nor'-West Farmer*, August 1890, 576.

94. *Farmer's Advocate*, September 5, 1893, 329.

95. Dominion Experimental Farms, *Annual Report*, 1895, 181.

96. *Leader* (Regina), July 13, 1899, 1.

97. Canada, Dominion Experimental Farms, *Annual Report*, 1892, 256–257.

98. Thomas Shaw, 186.

99. Ibid.

100. Ibid., 187.

101. Canada, Dominion Experimental Farms, *Annual Report*, 1894, 225.

102. James A. Young, "The Public Response to the Catastrophic Spread of Russian Thistle (1880) and Halogeton (1945)," *Agricultural History* 62, no. 2 (1988): 124.

103. Fletcher, *Russian Thistle*, 4; United States Secretary of Agriculture, *Report of the Secretary of Agriculture, 1893/94* (Washington, D.C.: GPO, 1895), 163.

104. Canada, Dominion Experimental Farms, *Annual Report*, 1893, 192.

105. *Farmer's Advocate*, September 20, 1893, 353, and February 5, 1894, 43.

106. *Leader* (Regina), June 21, 1894, 3.

107. National Archives of Canada, Records of the Royal Canadian Mounted Police, RG 18, Vol. 1319, file 229-1894, H. H. Smith of the Department of the Interior to L. W. Herchmer, Commissioner of the North-West Mounted Police, 3 August 1894.

108. Canada, Dominion Experimental Farms, *Annual Report*, 1893, 193.

109. Ibid., 1894, 224.

110. Ibid., 1894, 224–225.

111. *Farmer's Advocate*, August 20, 1894, 318, and October 5, 1894, 383.

112. Canada, Dominion Experimental Farms, *Annual Report*, 1894, 225; *Farmer's Advocate*, October 5, 1894, 383.

113. Young, 124.

114. *Leader* (Regina), June 29, 1899, 1.

115. Fletcher, *Weeds*, 21–22.

116. Manitoba, Department of Agriculture and Immigration, *Annual Report*, 1901, 316.

117. *Nor'-West Farmer*, August 1898, 370.

118. Clark and Fletcher, 54; Groh, *Canadian Weed Survey: Second Annual Report*, 19.

119. *Leader* (Regina), June 29, 1899, 1.

120. Manitoba, Advisory Board, *Prairie Agriculture* (Winnipeg: The Advisory Board of Manitoba, circa 1890), 83.

121. *Farmer's Advocate*, July 5, 1899, 347.

122. Ibid., 346.

123. Fletcher, *Weeds*, 9.

124. *Farmer's Advocate*, May 20, 1899, 260.

125. Fletcher, *Weeds*, 9; *Leader* (Regina), July 13, 1899, 51; *Farmer's Advocate*, July 5, 1899, 345–347.

126. *Farmer's Advocate*, October 5, 1894, 383.

127. For a discussion of the origins and early history of the position of noxious-weed inspector in Manitoba, see Joseph H. Ellis, 131–133.

128. The Ontario government did not make provisions for provincial government weed inspectors until 1935 (Ontario, *Statutes*, 1935, 25 Geo.5, c.49, s.22).

129. *Farmer's Advocate*, March 20, 1894, 102.

130. Manitoba, *Statutes*, 1894, 57 Vict., c.24. Ontario weed inspectors did not receive similar powers until 1935 (Ontario, *Statutes*, 1935, 25 Geo.5, c.49).

131. North-West Territories, *Ordinances*, 1897, No.25.

132. Ibid., 1899, c.22; 1900, c.31; 1903, c.24.

133. Saskatchewan, *Statutes*, 1906, 6 Edw.7, c.46; Alberta, *Statutes*, 1907, c.15.

134. *Leader* (Regina), June 29, 1899, 1.

135. Ibid., June 29, 1899, 1, and Manitoba, Department of Agriculture and Immigration, *Annual Report*, 1900, 25.

136. Manitoba, Department of Agriculture and Immigration, *Annual Report*, 1903, 18.

137. Manitoba, *Our Canadian Prairies*, 84.

138. Ibid., 89.

139. *Nor'-West Farmer*, June 1898, 262.

140. Manitoba, Department of Agriculture and Immigration, *Annual Report*, 1900, 26.

141. Canada, Dominion Experimental Farms, *Annual Report*, 1898, 169, and *Nor'-West Farmer*, August 1898, 363.

142. Manitoba, Department of Agriculture and Immigration, *Annual Report*, 1900, 25–26.

143. As early as January 1893, the *Farmer's Advocate* called for high-school students to make weed collections (*Farmer's Advocate*, January 1, 1893, 4).

144. *Leader* (Regina), August 23, 1894, 8.

145. Manitoba, *Our Canadian Prairies*, 17.

146. *Nor'-West Farmer*, May 1897, 156.

147. *Farmer's Advocate*, October 1, 1903, 895.

148. *Nor'-West Farmer*, February 1898, 56.

149. Canada, *Statutes*, 1905, 4–5 Edw.7, c.41.

150. *Nor'-West Farmer*, April 1898, 169; *Farmer's Advocate*, March 8, 1905, 329.

151. Turner, "Pioneer Farming Experiences," 53.

152. Alberta, Department of Agriculture, *Annual Report*, 1905/06, 24.

153. *Farmer's Advocate*, May 25, 1904, 756.

154. Ibid.

155. *Nor'-West Farmer*, February 1898, 56.

Notes to Chapter 5

1. Hamilton County Agricultural Society, *The Western Agriculturist and Practical Farmer's Guide* (Cincinnati: Robinson and Fairbank, 1830), 27–28.

2. Paul W. Gates, *The Farmer's Age: Agriculture 1815–1860* (New York: Holt, Rinehart and Winston, 1960), 356; Clarence H. Danhof, *Change in Agriculture: The Northern United States, 1820–1870* (Cambridge, Mass.: Harvard University Press, 1969), 49; and John T. Schlebecker, *Whereby We Thrive: A History of American Farming, 1607–1972* (Ames: Iowa State University Press, 1975), 25.

3. Gates, 399.

4. Danhof, 277.

5. Henry F. French, "Observations on English Husbandry," *Report of the Commissioner of Patents for the Year 1860* (Washington, D.C.: GPO, 1860), 155.

6. Nicholson, 263.

7. John Torrey and Asa Gray, *A Flora of North America* (New York: Hafner Publishing Co., 1969; reprint, New York: Wiley and Putnam, 1838–1843), 2:461.

8. Darlington, 197, and F. Lamson Scribner, *Weeds of Maine* (Augusta, Maine: Printed at the Kennebec Journal Office, 1869), 27.

9. Lewis D. De Schweinitz, "Remarks on the Plants of Europe Which Have Become Naturalized in a More or Less Degree, in the United States," *Annals of the Lyceum of Natural History of New York* 3 (1832): 155.

10. Ibid.

11. Darlington, xiii.

12. Ibid.

13. Ibid., xv.

14. Daniel W. Gade, "Weeds in Vermont as Tokens of Socioeconomic Change," *Geographical Review* 81 (1991): 157.

15. Ibid.

16. E. S. Goff, *Noxious Weeds*, Wisconsin Agricultural Experiment Station, Bulletin 39, 1894, 3.

17. Wheeler McMillen, "Father's War Against Weeds," *Agricultural History* 63, no. 4 (1989): 79.

18. Ibid., 72.

19. Albert A. Hansen, *Canada Thistle and Methods of Eradication*, United States Department of Agriculture, Farmers' Bulletin 1002, 1918, 4.

20. Lyster H. Dewey, *Legislation Against Weeds*, United States Department of Agriculture, Division of Botany, Bulletin 17, 1896, 17, 39.

21. Ibid., 39.

22. Ibid., 16–60.

23. Ontario, *Statutes*, 1884, 47 Vict., c.37; Dewey, *Legislation*, 8.

24. Manitoba, *Statutes*, 1882, 45 Vict., c.12; North-West Territories, *Revised Ordinances of the North-West Territories*, 1888, c.21; and Dewey, *Legislation*, 8.

25. Manitoba, *Statutes*, 1894, 57 Vict., c.24, and Dewey, *Legislation*, 8.

26. Margaret W. Rossiter, "The Organization of Agricultural Improvement in the United States, 1785–1865," in *The Pursuit of Knowledge in the Early American Republic*, eds. A. Oleson and S. Brown (Baltimore: Johns Hopkins University Press, 1976), 292. For a more detailed discussion of early agricultural science in America, see Rossiter's book *The Emergence of Agricultural Science: Justus Liebig and the Americans, 1840–1880* (New Haven, Conn.: Yale University Press, 1975).

27. David B. Danbom, "The Agricultural Experiment Station and Professionalization: Scientists' Goals for Agriculture," *Agricultural History* 60, no. 2 (1986): 247–248.

28. Alan I. Marcus, *Agricultural Science and the Quest for Legitimacy: Farmers, Agricultural Colleges, and Experiment Stations, 1870-1890* (Ames: Iowa State University Press, 1985), 217.

29. Gade, 159.

30. Lyster H. Dewey, *The Russian Thistle*, USDA, *Farmers' Bulletin* 10, 1893; James Fletcher, *The Russian Thistle* (1894); and *The Farmer's Advocate-Western Edition* (Winnipeg), September 20, 1893, 353–354.

31. *Farmer's Advocate*, October 2, 1907, 1500.
32. For an excellent summary of the pronounced American influence on tillage in western Canada, see Thomas Isern's article "The Discer: Tillage for the Canadian Plains," 81–89.
33. R. Bruce Shepard, "Walter Murray, Evan Hardy, and the American Presence at the University of Saskatchewan," *Agricultural History* 62, no. 2 (1988): 65.
34. Shepard, 72; John Kendle, *John Bracken: A Political Biography* (Toronto: University of Toronto Press, 1979), 20.
35. Ian MacPherson and John Herd Thompson, "An Orderly Reconstruction: Prairie Agriculture in World War Two," *Canadian Papers in Rural History* 4 (1984): 12.
36. Bracken, v-viii.
37. United States, "Weeds," *Yearbook of the United States Department of Agriculture, 1897* (Washington, D.C.: GPO, 1898), 96, and Lyster H. Dewey, *Weeds and How to Kill Them*, United States Department of Agriculture, Farmers' Bulletin 28, second revision, 1905, 8.
38. H. R. Cates, "The Weed Problem in American Agriculture," in *Yearbook of the United States Department of Agriculture, 1917* (Washington, D.C.: GPO, 1918), 214.
39. Timmons, 301, and King, 351. J. Hoyes Panton's *Weeds* (1887) appears to be the first government weed bulletin published in North America. For a succinct account of the formation of the National Research Council's Associate Committee on Weed Control, see G. P. McRostie, L. E. Kirk, G. Godel, W. G. Smith and J. M. Manson, *Weeds and their Control*, National Research Council of Canada, Report 27, 1932, 4–6.
40. Larry W. Mitich, "Looking Back to See," *Weed Technology*, 5 (1991): 240–242.
41. American publications that identify Thomas Shaw's *Weeds and How to Eradicate Them* (1893) and George H. Clark and James Fletcher's *Farm Weeds of Canada* (1906, 1909, 1923) as standard texts on the subject include: L. H. Pammel, *Weeds of the Farm and Garden* (New York: Orange Judd and Co., 1911), v; L.H. Pammel and Charlotte M. King, eds., *The Weed Flora of Iowa* (Des Moines: Iowa Geological Survey, 1926), 661–662; and Walter C. Muenscher, *Weeds* (New York: The Macmillan Co., 1952 [1935]), x. Pammel and King's book is heavily indebted to Clark and Fletcher for weed descriptions and control recommendations.

42. Carol J. Bubar and Ian N. Morrison, "Thomas K. Pavlychenko: Pioneer Weed Experimentalist," *Weed Science* 30 (1982): 434. For similar comments, see A. S. Crafts and W. A. Harvey, "Weed Control," *Advances in Agronomy* 1 (1949): 291, and Virgil Freed, "Weed Science: The Emergence of a Vital Technology," *Weed Science* 28 (1980): 621; Mitich, 242.

43. S. C. Litzenberger, A. H. Post and H. E. Morris, Important *Perennial Weeds in Montana: Their Identification and Control*, Montana State College Agricultural Experiment Station, Bulletin 426, 1945, 6–7.

44. Frank Forcella and Stephen J. Harvey, "Patterns of Weed Migration in Northwestern U.S.A.," *Weed Science* 36 (1988): 199. Similar observations have been made by Lyster H. Dewey, "Migration of Weeds," *1896 Yearbook of the United States Department of Agriculture* (Washington, D.C.: GPO, 1897), 280–283, and Alex, "Canada," 309–312.

45. W. H. Blackwell, "The History of Russian Pigweed, *Axyris amaranthoides* (Chenopodiaceae, Atripliceae), in North America," *Weed Science* 26 (1978): 83.

46. Forcella and Harvey, 199.

47. Michigan, Secretary of the State Board of Agriculture, *Annual Report*, 1895/96, 134.

48. O. A. Stevens, *North Dakota Weeds*, North Dakota Agricultural Experiment Station, Bulletin 162, 1922, 17; O. A. Stevens, *Perennial Sow Thistle: Growth and Reproduction*, North Dakota Agricultural Experiment Station, Bulletin 181, 1924, 5–7 and Groh, *Canadian Weed Survey: Second Annual Report*, 55.

49. Pammel, 65; W. L. Oswald and Andrew Boss, *Minnesota Weeds: Series II*, Minnesota Agricultural Experiment Station, Bulletin 139, 1914, 45.

50. For a similar argument in the context of shared tillage practices and technology, see Isern, "The Discer," 89.

51. A. Gordon Thomas, "Weed Survey System Used in Saskatchewan for Cereal and Oilseed Crops," *Weed Science* 33 (1985): 42.

52. *Country Guide* (Winnipeg), March 1, 1929, 14.

53. Pammel, v.; Ada E. Georgia, *A Manual of Weeds* (New York: Macmillan, 1914), quote taken from subtitle; Muenscher, ix. Macmillan and Company also published Georgia's book in Toronto.

54. H. K. Wilson, L. M. Stahler, A. C. Arny, R. B. Harvey, A. H. Larson and R. H. Landon, *Battling Weeds on Minnesota Farms*, Minnesota Agricultural Experiment Station, Bulletin 363, 1942.

55. Dewey, *Legislation*, 8.

56. Groh, "A Survey of Weed Control," 419–420.

57. Great Britain, *Journal of the Ministry of Agriculture* 28 (1921/22): 275.

58. Edith H. Whetham, "The Agriculture Act, 1920 and its Repeal—the 'Great Betrayal'," *Agricultural History Review* 22 (1974): 49, and Canada, *Statutes*, 1921, 11-12 Geo.5, c.48.

59. Great Britain, *Journal of the Board of Agriculture* 22 (1915/16): 1061.

60. Great Britain, "State Action for the Eradication of Weeds and the Provision of Pure Seeds," *Journal of the Board of Agriculture* 24 (1917/18): 711, and "Weed Control in Canada," *Journal of the Board of Agriculture* 22 (1915/16): 1061–1062.

61. Brenchley, *Weeds of Farm Land* (1920), and H. C. Long, *Weeds of Arable Land* (London: Ministry of Agriculture and Fisheries, 1929). Long's book was published in five parts in the *Journal of the Ministry of Agriculture* 35 (1928/29).

62. Great Britain, *Journal of the Ministry of Agriculture* 35 (1928/29): 210.

63. E. K. Woodford, "Weed Control — Its Status and Organisation in Great Britain," *Weeds* 8 (1960): 572.

64. Brenchley, *Weeds of Farm Land*, 1.

65. Elliot, 682.

66. Ibid., 683.

67. Manitoba, *Statutes*, 1906, 5-6 Edw.7, c.65; 1911, 1 Geo.5, c.42; 1916, 6 Geo.5, c.80.

68. Ibid., 1941–1942, 5-6 Geo.6, c.37.

69. Saskatchewan, *Statutes*, 1924, 14 Geo.5, c.40.

70. Alberta, *Statutes*, 1928, c.11.

71. Ibid., 1930, c.16.

72. Ibid., 1932, c.28.

73. Ibid., 1941, c.92.

74. Ibid., 1945, c.19.

75. Saskatchewan, *Statutes*, 1946, 10 Geo.6, c.61; 1949, 13 Geo.6, c.75.

76. *Country Guide*, February, 1946, 33. For a summary of the weed control activities of Alberta's Agricultural Service Boards up to the summer of 1949, see *Country Guide*, June, 1949, 14, 42–44.

77. For a brief history of the Manitoba Weeds Commission and its changing position within the government bureaucracy, see Joseph H. Ellis, 171, 470–472.

78. Saskatchewan, Department of Agriculture, *Annual Report*, 1921, 59; Alberta, Department of Agriculture, *Annual Report*, 1922, 49.

79. Alberta, Department of Agriculture, *Annual Report*, 1908, 97.

80. Saskatchewan, Department of Agriculture, *Annual Report*, 1909, 169.

81. Manitoba had relied exclusively on municipal noxious-weed inspectors ever since 1871 when noxious-weed legislation was first passed.

82. Saskatchewan, Department of Agriculture, *Annual Report*, 1918, 87.

83. Joseph H. Ellis, 155.

84. The *Country Guide* (Winnipeg), October, 1930, 5, and O. S. Longman, "Weed Control in Alberta," *Proceedings of the Associate Committee on Weeds* 5 (1939): 13.

85. Manitoba, Department of Agriculture and Immigration, *Annual Report*, 1913, 34.

86. Saskatchewan, Department of Agriculture, *Annual Report*, 1909, 171.

87. *The Nor'-West Farmer* (Winnipeg), December 5, 1911, 1407.

88. F. C. Nunnick, "Agricultural Survey, 1913," *Report of the Canadian Commission of Conservation* 5 (1914): 151–152.

89. Alberta, Department of Agriculture, *Annual Report*, 1925, 71.

90. Saskatchewan, Department of Agriculture, *Annual Report*, 1910, 130–131.

91. *Farmer's Advocate*, December 8, 1909, 1641.

92. Manitoba, *Statutes*, 1911, 1 Geo.5, c.42.

93. Saskatchewan, Department of Agriculture, *Annual Report*, 1913, 90.

94. *Nor'-West Farmer*, May 5, 1911, 553; Saskatchewan, Department of Agriculture, *Annual Report*, 1913, 91; and Alberta, Department of Agriculture, *Annual Reports*, 1914, 131; 1929, 30.

95. J. M. Manson, *Weed Survey of the Prairie Provinces*, National Research Council of Canada, Report 26, 1932, 22.

96. Alberta, Department of Agriculture, *Annual Report*, 1920, 35.

97. Ibid., 1933, 28.

98. Ibid., 1937, 17.

99. In 1912, for example, Saskatchewan weed inspectors served approximately 10,000 weed destruction notices and fifty-seven landowners were prosecuted under various sections of the provincial Noxious Weeds Act. Three decades later, Alberta's field crops commissioner reported that enforcement of his province's weed act had resulted in thirty court cases and twenty-five convictions over the course of the year (Saskatchewan, Department

of Agriculture, *Annual Report*, 1913, 72, and Alberta, Department of Agriculture, *Annual Report*, 1942, 13). These figures provide a good sense of the annual number of weed destruction notices served and prosecutions initiated under prairie noxious-weed legislation, although actual figures vary considerably from year to year.

100. *Country Guide*, October, 1930, 5.

101. Saskatchewan, Department of Agriculture, *Annual Reports*, 1927, 340; 1928, 64; 1930, 236–237.

102. Ibid., 1908, 169, 171.

103. Saskatchewan, Department of Agriculture, *Annual Report*, 1914, 96; Alberta, Department of Agriculture, *Annual Reports*, 1912, 132; 1915, 141.

104. Alberta, Department of Agriculture, *Annual Report*, 1917, 89.

105. Imperial Oil advertisement in *Nor'-West Farmer*, April 21, 1930, 2, and K. W. Neatby, *An Illustrated Guide to Prairie Weeds* (Winnipeg: The North-West Line Elevators Association, 1941).

106. Alberta, Department of Agriculture, *Annual Report*, 1917, 89.

107. Saskatchewan, Department of Agriculture, *Annual Reports*, 1925, 150; 1929, 17.

108. Alberta, Department of Agriculture, *Annual Report*, 1929, 30.

109. Saskatchewan, Department of Agriculture, *Annual Report*, 1906, 122.

110. Canada, Dominion Experimental Farms, *Annual Report*, 1909, 38.

111. Alberta, Department of Agriculture, *Annual Report*, 1921, 43; Saskatchewan, Department of Agriculture, *Annual Report*, 1921, 77.

112. Canada, Dominion Experimental Farms, *Report of the Superintendent at Brandon*, 1926, 56.

113. Ibid., 1926, 56; 1930, 71, and Canada, Dominion Experimental Farms, *Progress Report for Indian Head*, 1937–1947, 38.

114. Saskatchewan, Department of Agriculture, *Annual Reports*, 1930, 11; 1931, 16.

115. Ibid., 1937, 81; 1938; 90.

116. Alberta, Department of Agriculture, *Annual Report*, 1944, 20.

117. M. J. Tinline, "Crops, Rotation and Weed Control," *Dominion Experimental Farms Seasonable Hints–Prairie Edition* 40 (1928): 8; Bracken, 211.

118. *Country Guide*, April 1941, 14.

119. *Nor'-West Farmer*, January 20, 1916, 60A.

120. Ibid.
121. Ibid., February 5, 1924, 96.
122. Ibid.
123. Joseph H. Ellis, 496, and MacPherson and Thompson, 18.
124. Manson, 22.
125. Nunnick, "Agricultural Survey, 1913," 148; Saskatchewan, *Department of Agriculture*, Annual Report, 1928, 16.
126. A. Wenhart, "Recent Developments in Tillage Machinery," *Proceedings of the Western Canadian Weed Control Conference* 4 (1950): 141.
127. Manson, 19.
128. F. H. Read, "The Summer-Fallow," *Dominion Experimental Farms Seasonable Hints–Prairie Edition* 22 (1922): 10, and Bracken, 179.
129. *Grain Growers' Guide*, February 15, 1927, 20.
130. Joseph H. Ellis, 267, 268, 497.
131. MacPherson and Thompson, 14.
132. *Country Guide*, August 15, 1928, 23.
133. H. E. Wood, "Fifty Years of Weed Control in Western Canada," *Proceedings of the Western Canadian Weed Control Conference* 8 (1955): 3–4, and Isern, "The Discer," 80–81.
134. *Nor'-West Farmer*, April 20, 1917, 462.
135. Ibid.
136. *Nor'-West Farmer*, May 5, 1920, 663.
137. Timmons, 296. Rod weeders consist of a fixed or rotating bar which is drawn horizontally through the soil at a depth of about three inches.
138. *Nor'-West Farmer*, July 20, 1927, 9; Evan A. Hardy, "What's Wrong with Tillage Machines," *Proceedings of the Western Canadian Weed Control Conference* 3 (1949): 173.
139. *Grain Growers' Guide*, September 15, 1927, 15. For Barnes's own summary of his soil moisture research at the Dominion Experimental Station, Swift Current, see his article: "The Effect of Weeds on Soil Moisture," *Dominion Experimental Farms Seasonable Hints—Prairie Edition* 42 (1928): 8–9.
140. *Grain Growers' Guide*, September 15, 1927, 16.
141. *Country Guide*, November 1, 1928, 7. Champlin may have overestimated the speed at which farmers accept new ideas and discard the old. In 1934, for example, a columnist for the *Nor'-West Farmer* wrote that "the theory that a dust mulch conserves moisture has been one of the costliest mistakes

made in Western agriculture.... And sadly enough, it continues to be taught and preached from many quarters although it was definitely proven wrong some time ago" (*Nor'-West Farmer*, March, 1934, 3).

142. E. S. Hopkins and S. Barnes, *Crop Rotations and Soil Management for the Prairie Provinces*, Dominion Experimental Farms, Bulletin 98, New Series, 1928, 42.

143. Isern, "The Discer," 81.

144. For detailed discussions of the history and adoption of these implements, see Isern, "The Discer," 81–89, and Grant MacEwan, *Charles Noble: Guardian of the Soil* (Saskatoon: Western Producer Books, 1983).

145. *Country Guide*, December 1947, 25.

146. Ibid., May 1945, 32

147. Hardy, 171.

148. *Farmer's Advocate*, June 5, 1899, 287; May 1, 1907, 646; May 8, 1907, 690; May 15, 1907, 728.

149. *Grain Growers' Guide*, February 15, 1927, 20.

150. G. H. Hutton, "Fall Cultivation for the Eradication of Weeds and Conservation of Moisture," *Dominion Experimental Farms Seasonable Hints* 11 (1918): 10–11.

151. *Nor'-West Farmer*, July 6, 1925, 6.

152. Manson, 20.

153. Alberta, Department of Agriculture, *Annual Report*, 1929, 68.

154. Robert E. Ankli, H. Dan Helsberg, and John Herd Thompson, "The Adoption of the Gasoline Tractor in Western Canada," *Canadian Papers in Rural History* 2 (1980): 33, 35.

155. Ibid., 10, 35.

156. *Country Guide*, July 1944, 20.

157. *Nor'-West Farmer*, January 20, 1916, 60A.

158. Bracken, 361.

159. E. S. Hopkins, "Losses Caused by Weeds," *Proceedings of the Associate Committee on Weeds* 2 (1936): 31; McRostie et al., 5.

160. McRostie et al., 5.

161. Hopkins, "Losses," 34.

162. Alberta, Department of Agriculture, Field Crops Branch, *Weeds of Alberta: Their Identification and Control* (Edmonton: Department of Agriculture, 1941), 2.

163. Ibid., 6.

164. Ibid.

165. F. C. Nunnick, "Agricultural Surveys and Illustration Farms," *Report of the Canadian Commission of Conservation* 6 (1915): 214.

166. J. M. Thurston, "Wild Oats as Successful Weeds," in *Biology and Ecology of Weeds*, ed. W. Holzner and M. Numata (The Hague: Dr. W. Junk Publishers, 1982), 192–196.

167. Ibid., 197.

168. Ibid., 194, 196–197.

169. J. W. Robertson, "Work of the Committee on Lands," *Report of the Canadian Commission of Conservation* 3 (1912): 61.

170. Ibid.

171. Nunnick, "Agricultural Surveys and Illustrations Farms," 214.

172. Manson, 10; Alberta, *Weeds of Alberta*, 46, and Herbert Groh and C. Frankton, *Canadian Weed Survey: Sixth Report* (Ottawa: Department of Agriculture, 1947), 3–4.

173. F. C. Nunnick, "Agricultural Survey, 1912," *Report of the Canadian Commission of Conservation* 4 (1913): 157.

174. Robertson, 62.

175. *Country Guide*, November 1, 1928, 7.

176. Ibid., October 1, 1929, 5.

177. Alberta, Department of Agriculture, *Annual Report*, 1918, 105.

178. *Nor'-West Farmer*, June 5, 1919, 831.

179. *Farmer's Advocate*, September 29, 1909, 1305, and Clark and Fletcher, 171.

180. *Nor'-West Farmer*, March 20, 1911, 347.

181. Ibid., June 5, 1919, 831.

182. *Country Guide*, March 1, 1929, 5.

183. Ibid.

184. Ibid.

185. Alberta, Department of Agriculture, *Annual Reports*, 1910, 136; 1929, 30.

186. Manson, 10.

187. Ibid., 10–11.

188. *Country Guide*, July 1931, 5.

189. G. L. Godel, "Report on Weed Control Investigations Carried Out by the Saskatchewan Department of Agriculture," *Proceedings of the Associate Committee on Weeds* 5 (1939): 17; Saskatchewan, Department of Agriculture, *Annual Report*, 1947, 142.

190. McRostie et. al., 14–15.
191. *Country Guide*, July 1931, 23; Herbert Groh, *Canadian Weed Survey: First Report* (Ottawa: Department of Agriculture, 1942), 20.
192. Herbert Groh, "Turkestan Alfalfa as a Medium of Weed Introduction," *Scientific Agriculture* 21 (1940/41): 40.
193. George Batho, "The Most Serious Weed Problems of Manitoba," *Proceedings of the Associate Committee on Weeds* 3 (1937): 16; Alberta, Department of Agriculture, *Annual Reports*, 1939, 12; 1942, 15; Saskatchewan, Department of Agriculture, *Annual Report*, 1945, 69.
194. Alberta, Department of Agriculture, *Annual Report*, 1941, 11.
195. E. S. Hopkins, "Weed Projects on the Dominion Experimental Farms in the Prairie Provinces," *Proceedings of the Associate Committee on Weeds* 5 (1939): 10.
196. Alberta, Department of Agriculture, *Annual Report*, 1934, 63.
197. *Country Guide*, April 1931, 3.
198. Ibid.
199. Alberta, Department of Agriculture, *Annual Report*, 1940, 13.
200. W. D. Albright, "The Weed Problems of the Peace," *Proceedings of the Associate Committee on Weeds* 3 (1937): 13.
201. Herbert Groh, *Canadian Weed Survey: Fourth Annual Report* (Ottawa: Department of Agriculture, 1945), ii.
202. *Nor'-West Farmer*, February 5, 1924, 96.

Notes to Chapter 6

1. Canada, Dominion Experimental Farms, *Annual Report*, 1910, 281.
2. For a summary of the early history of herbicides, see Allan E. Smith and Diane M. Secoy, "Early Chemical Control of Weeds in Europe," *Weed Science* 24 (1976): 594-597.
3. Alberta, Department of Agriculture, *Weeds of Alberta: Their Identification and Control* (Edmonton: Department of Agriculture, 1941), 18.
4. Smith and Secoy, "Early Chemical Control," 596; E. Bourcart, *Insecticides, Fungicides and Weed Killers: A Practical Manual on the Diseases of Plants and their Remedies, for the Use of Manufacturing Chemists, Agriculturists, Aboriculturists and Horticulturists*, trans. Donald Grant (London: Scott, Greenwood and Son, 1913), 211, and Timmons, 297.

5. George P. Gray, "Herbicides," *Monthly Bulletin of the Department of Agriculture, State of California* 11 (1922): 264, and Voelcker, 767.

6. Canada, Dominion Experimental Farms, *Annual Report*, 1899, 193–196, and Ontario, Ontario Agricultural College, *Annual Report*, 1899, 3.

7. *Farmer's Advocate–Western Edition* (Winnipeg), July 19, 1905, 1083 and Alberta, Department of Agriculture, *Annual Report*, 1911, 135–136.

8. *Farmer's Advocate*, July 15, 1908, 980; Canada, Dominion Experimental Farms, *Annual Report*, 1910, 281; *Nor'-West Farmer* (Winnipeg), July 5, 1911, and Anstey, 293.

9. Canada, Dominion Experimental Farms, *Annual Report*, 1899, 193, and Alberta, Department of Agriculture, *Annual Report*, 1913, 70.

10. Clark and Fletcher (1909), and Bracken, 227.

11. Wilfred W. Robbins, Alden S. Crafts and Richard N. Raynor, *Weed Control: A Textbook and Manual* (New York: McGraw-Hill, 1942), 149. For supporting evidence, see Cates, 213 and George P. Gray, 265–267.

12. For the details of government funded testing, see Ontario, Ontario Agricultural College and Experimental Farm, *Annual Reports*, 1911, 51–53; 1913, 44–45; Saskatchewan, Department of Agriculture, *Annual Reports*, 1919, 84; 1925, 149, and Canada, Dominion Experimental Farms, Division of Botany, *Report of the Dominion Botanist*, 1926, 6–8.

13. J. Eaton Howitt, "Identification of Weeds and Weed Seeds and Methods of Eradication," in Ontario Agricultural and Experimental Union, *Annual Report*, 1911, 65.

14. *The Country Guide* (Winnipeg), March 1, 1930, 5.

15. The report that is credited with renewing interest in herbicides in North America is the Cornell University botanist, Alfred Alsander's "Chlorates as Plant Poisons," *Journal of the American Society of Agronomy* 18 (1926): 1101–1102.

16. W. H. Cook and A. C. Halferdahl, *Chemical Weed Killers: A Review, National Research Council of Canada*, Bulletin 18, 1937, 39–44; Alden S. Crafts, "Weed Control Research—Past, Present, and Future," *Weeds* 8 (1960): 537; and *Country Guide*, March 15, 1929, 17. German railways were regularly using chlorates by the early 1920s and the Canadian Pacific and Canadian National railways began using them in 1926 in western Canada.

17. Alberta, Department of Agriculture, *Annual Report*, 1928, 29, and *Nor'-West Farmer*, August 20, 1928, 8.

18. Canada, Dominion Experimental Farms, *Report of the Dominion Botanist*, 1929, 11; Joseph H. Ellis, 473; Saskatchewan, Department of Agriculture, *Annual Report*, 1930, 239; and Alberta, Department of Agriculture, *Annual Report*, 1929, 30.

19. *Nor'-West Farmer*, April 20, 1929, 25; May 20, 1929, 43; *Country Guide*, July 1, 1929, 36. I was unable to find any Atlacide ads after 1930 in either paper.

20. Manson, 4.

21. G. P. McRostie, et al., 4.

22. R. Newton, "Summary of Remarks by Dr. Newton," *Proceedings of the Associate Committee on Weeds* 2 (1936): 4.

23. Canada, Dominion Experimental Farms, *Report of the Superintendent at Brandon*, 1930, 17-18, 29–33, and Hopkins, "Weed Projects," 8.

24. Alberta, Department of Agriculture, *Annual Report*, 1929, 30, 94; 1930, 30, 97; 1932, 25; George L. Godel, "Some Considerations in Regard to Experiments with Chemical Herbicides," *Canadian Journal of Research* 7 (1932): 499–500; Godel, "Weed Control Experiments Conducted by the Saskatchewan Department of Agriculture," *Proceedings of the Associate Committee on Weeds* 1 (1935): 53; and Joseph H. Ellis, 473.

25. Manson, 3.

26. Alberta, Department of Agriculture, *Annual Report*, 1930, 98.

27. Ontario, Ontario Agricultural and Experimental Union, *Annual Report*, 1929, 56.

28. Batho, 17.

29. Alberta, Department of Agriculture, *Annual Report*, 1936, 27-28; Saskatchewan, Department of Agriculture, *Annual Report*, 1937, 76.

30. Alberta, *Weeds of Alberta*, 20; *Country Guide*, July 1944, 20; Alberta, Department of Agriculture, *Annual Report*, 1945, 18; and Crafts and Harvey, 307.

31. Alberta, Department of Agriculture, *Annual Report*, 1938, 18.

32. Saskatchewan, Department of Agriculture, *Annual Report*, 1946, 81, and Alberta, Department of Agriculture, *Annual Report*, 1945, 19.

33. *Country Guide*, February 1946, 33.

34. The total government outlay for Atlacide between 1940 and 1945 was $156,000, $131,000 of which was recouped from rural municipalities through sales to farmers (Ibid., 32).

35. Manitoba, *Statutes*, 1941–1942, 5-6 Geo.6, c.37.

36. Alberta, *Weeds of Alberta*, 18, and *Country Guide*, January 1944, 19.

37. For a summary of the history and development of 2,4-D in England and the United States, see Crafts and Harvey, 301-302; Sir John Russell, 441–443; and Gale E. Peterson, "The Discovery and Development of 2,4-D," *Agricultural History* 41, no. 3 (1967): 243–253.

38. *Country Guide*, October 1948, 8.

39. Alberta, Department of Agriculture, *Annual Report*, 1945, 18–19; Canada, Dominion Experimental Farms, *Progress Report for Brandon, 1937–1947*, 16; Canada, Dominion Experimental Farms, *Progress Report for Lethbridge*, 1937–1946, 21; and Joseph H. Ellis, 476.

40. *Country Guide*, March 1947, 11.

41. Ibid., March 1947, 11, 78.

42. A. M. Wilson, "The Third Western Weed Control Conference," *Proceedings of the Western Canadian Weed Control Conference* 3 (1949): 4. Tillage, cropping, and cultural control studies are complicated by the need to consider a wide range of variables (variations in weather, soils, weed populations, timing of tillage operations, etc.) and they take many years to bear meaningful results.

43. H. E. Wood, "Introductory Remarks," *Proceedings of the Western Canadian Weed Control Conference* 1 (1947): 5.

44. *Proceedings of the Western Canadian Weed Control Conference* 1 (1947): 1–4.

45. *Country Guide*, December 1947, 12.

46. Herbert Groh and Clarence Frankton, *Canadian Weed Survey: Fifth Report* (Ottawa: Department of Agriculture, 1946), i-ii.

47. H. E. Wood, "Introductory Remarks," *Proceedings of the Western Canadian Weed Control Conference* 2 (1948): 1.

48. *Country Guide*, May 1948, 33; December 1950, 26.

49. Joseph H. Ellis, 475.

50. The first 2,4-D ad in the *Country Guide* was placed in 1946 by Chipman Chemicals of Winnipeg. At this stage it was still being marketed as a chemical for lawn weed control. Similar ads can be found in most subsequent issues (*Country Guide*, June 1946, 28).

51. *Country Guide*, June 1948, 29.
52. D. D. Fraser, "Merchandising of Herbicides," *Proceedings of the Western Canadian Weed Control Conference* 4 (1950): 120.
53. *Country Guide*, December 1950, 26.
54. For accounts of typical weed-spraying demonstrations, see Saskatchewan, Department of Agriculture, *Annual Report*, 1947, 142; *Country Guide*, July 1944, 20; February 1946, 34; July 1946, 21–22; August 1947, 19.
55. F. E. Werry, "A Farmer Appraises 2,4-D," *Proceedings of the Western Canadian Weed Control Conference* 4 (1950): 124.
56. Fraser, 118.
57. H. E. Wood, "'Selling' Chemical Weed Control," *Proceedings of the Western Canadian Weed Control Conference* 4 (1950): 123.
58. Ibid., 120, 123.
59. Ibid., 121.
60. *Country Guide*, February 1948, 5.
61. Ibid.
62. Ibid., April 1949, 28.
63. Ibid., March 1950, 13. The development of low-volume spray nozzles in the late 1940s greatly reduced the amount of water needed to spray a field. In doing so, they decreased the number of filling and mixing operations and enabled farmers to cover their fields much faster.
64. Wood, "'Selling' Chemical Control," 121.
65. Ibid.
66. Ibid.
67. H. A. Friesen, "The Place of Cultural and Chemical Control Methods," *Proceedings of the Western Canadian Weed Control Conference* 8 (1955): 26, and Wood, "'Selling' Chemical Control," 122.
68. Crafts and Harvey, 291.
69. T. K. Pavlychenko, "Development of New Herbicides," *Proceedings of the Western Canadian Weed Control Conference* 4 (1950): 115. In Canada, 2,4-D was not available for testing until the following year.
70. Frankton, 4.
71. P. O. Ripley, "National Organization for Weed Control," *Proceedings of the Western Canadian Weed Control Conference* 8 (1955): 19.
72. Ibid.

73. P. O. Ripley, "Weed Control in Britain and Western Europe," *Proceedings of the Western Canadian Weed Control Conference* 3 (1949): 124.

74. Ibid., 125.

75. Timmons, 298.

76. Ibid., 299.

77. G. E. Jones, "Food Production in Canada: The Weed Scientists' Role," *Weed Science* 18 (1970): 545.

78. Orvin C. Burnside, "Weed Science: The Step Child," *Weed Technology* 7 (1993): 517.

79. Pavlychenko, 115–116.

80. Ibid., 116.

81. Mitich, 242.

82. Of the 275 weed abstracts published in the North Central Weed Conference Research Report for 1954, 133 were contributed by Canadian researchers (Ripley, "National Organization," 18).

83. C. J. Willard, "Where do We go from Here?" *Weeds* 1 (1951): 9.

84. Chester G. McWhorter and William L. Barrentine, "Research Priorities in Weed Science," *Weed Technology* 2 (1988): 3.

85. Mitich, 243.

86. Willard, 12.

87. Burnside, "Weed Science," 516.

88. Crafts and Harvey, 291.

89. Freed, 623.

90. P. O. Ripley, "Getting Experimental Work Done," *Proceedings of the Western Canadian Weed Control Conference* 7 (1953): 86.

91. Ibid., 83.

92. G. E. Jones, 545–546.

93. B. J. Gorby, "Whither the Wild Oat?", *Proceedings of the Western Canadian Weed Control Conference* 2 (1948): 73.

94. Ibid.

95. D. R. Lindsay, "Taxonomic and Genetic Studies on Wild Oats (*Avena fatua* L.)," *Weeds* 4 (1956): 1.

96. Ibid.

97. M. P. Sharma and W. H. Vanden Born, "The Biology of Canadian Weeds, 27. *Avena fatua* L.," *Canadian Journal of Plant Science* 58 (1978): 145.

98. Barrett, 256. For easily accessible, more in-depth discussions of this issue, see J. Glauninger and W. Holzner, "Interference between Weeds and Crops: A Review of Literature," in *Biology and Ecology of Weeds*, eds. W. Holzner and M. Numata (The Hague: Dr. W. Junk Publishers, 1982), 156–157, and A. J. Willis, "Ecological Consequences of Modern Weed Control Systems," in *Weed Control Handbook: Principles*, 8th ed., eds. R. J. Hance and K. Holly (Oxford: Blackwell Scientific Publications, 1990): 501–519.

99. A. Gordon Thomas, 40, 42.

100. Ibid., 42.

101. Alex, "Canada," 325.

102. L. M. Stahler, "What's New and What's Needed in Weed Control Research," *Proceedings of the Western Canadian Weed Control Conference* 2 (1948): 4.

103. Willis, 506.

104. Pierre Grignac, "The Evolution of Resistance to Herbicides in Weedy Species," *Agro-Ecosystems* 4 (1978): 377.

105. Ibid., 384.

106. Jodie S. Holt, "History of Identification of Herbicide-Resistant Weeds," *Weed Technology* 6 (1992): 615.

107. Ibid., 619.

108. Don Gayton, *The Wheatgrass Mechanism: Science and Imagination in the Western Canadian Landscape* (Saskatoon: Fifth House Publishers, 1990), 47. R. J. Aldrich, a USDA scientist and professor of agronomy at the University of Missouri, presents essentially the same argument in his book, *Weed-Crop Ecology*, 25.

109. Joseph A. Cocannouer, *Weeds: Guardians of the Soil* (New York: Devin-Adair, 1950), 56–58.

110. Glenn C. Klingman, "Who Will do the Research and Teaching," *Weed Science* 18 (1970): 541.

111. Ibid.

112. Aldrich, 1.

113. Glauninger and Holzner, 157.

114. See, for example: J. H. H. Eussen, "The Ecology of Pests: Weeds," *Protection Ecology* 4 (1982): 219–220; Aldrich, 8; B. R. Trenbath, "Weeds

and Agriculture: A Question of Balance," in *Studies on Plant Demography: A Festschrift for John L. Harper*, ed. James White (London: Academic Press, 1985), 172; and Navas, 171–172.

115. McWhorter and Barrentine, 4.
116. Burnside, "Weed Science," 518.
117. J. D. Fryer, "Recent Research on Weed Management: New Light on an Old Practice," in *Recent Advances in Weed Research*, ed. W. W. Fletcher (Farnham Royal, Engl.: Commonwealth Agricultural Bureaux, 1983), 181.
118. Wood, "Fifty Years of Weed Control," 6.
119. Ibid., 5.
120. Ripley, "National Organization," 20.
121. H. A. Friesen, 21.
122. Ibid., 23.
123. Ripley, "National Organization," 17.
124. A. Gordon Thomas, 35.
125. John H. Perkins, *Insects, Experts, and the Insecticide Crisis: The Quest for New Pest Management Strategies* (New York: Plenum Press, 1982), vi, and Dunlap, *DDT*, 240.
126. See, for example, Orvin C. Burnside, "Rationale for Developing Herbicide-Resistant Crops," *Weed Technology* 6 (1992): 621–625.

Notes to Conclusion

1. Wood, "Fifty Years of Weed Control," 5.
2. Federal seed laws, on the other hand, are far more effective because they help prevent weed problems from starting through encouraging the use of clean seed.
3. The traditional view of weed control's place in crop production schemes was that it "should be incidental and in connection with other farm operations in so far as possible" (Cates, 213).
4. Knobloch, 144.
5. Gerald Friesen, 338. Friesen does not deserve to be singled out for criticism as he is merely expressing the conventional views of Canadian agricultural historians such Vernon Fowke and George Britnell, to name but two.

Bibliography

Primary Sources

Alberta. *Statutes of Alberta*, 1906–1950.

Alberta. Department of Agriculture. *Annual Reports*, 1905–1950.

Alberta. Department of Agriculture. Field Crops Branch. *Weeds of Alberta: Their Identification and Control*. Edmonton: Department of Agriculture, 1941.

Albright, W. D. "The Weed Problems of the Peace." *Proceedings of the Associate Committee on Weeds* 3 (1937): 12–14.

Allardice, Robert Barclay. *Agricultural Tour in the United States and Upper Canada, with Miscellaneous Notices*. Edinburgh: William Blackwood and Sons, 1842.

Ålsander, Alfred. "Chlorates as Plant Poisons." *Journal of the American Society of Agronomy* 18 (1926): 1101–1102.

Bacon, Francis. *Sylva Sylvarum, or a Natural History in Ten Centuries*. London: Printed for W. Lee, 1628.

Banks, Sir Joseph. "A Short Account of the Cause of the Disease in Corn, called by Farmers the Blight, the Mildew, and the Rust." *Communications to the Board of Agriculture* 4 (1805): 399–406.

Barnes, S. "The Effect of Weeds on Soil Moisture." *Dominion Experimental Farms Seasonable Hints — Prairie Edition* 42 (1928): 8–9.

Batho, George. "The Most Serious Weed Problems of Manitoba." *Proceedings of the Associate Committee on Weeds* 3 (1937): 16–17.

Blackman, G. E. "Recent Developments in the Control of Weeds." *Journal of the Royal Horticultural Society* 73 (1948): 134–141.

Blith, Walter. *The English Improver Improved or the Survey of Husbandry Surveyed.* N.p., 1652.

Bourcart, E. *Insecticides, Fungicides and Weedkillers: A Practical Manual on the Diseases of Plants and their Remedies, for the Use of Manufacturing Chemists, Agriculturists, Aboriculturists and Horticulturists.* Translated by Donald Grant. London: Scott, Greenwood and Son, 1913.

Bracken, John. *Dry Farming in Western Canada.* Winnipeg: The Grain Growers' Guide, 1921.

Bradley, Richard. *The Country Gentleman and Farmer's Monthly Director.* 6th ed. London: Printed for D. Browne and T. Woodman, 1732.

Brenchley, Winifred E. "Useful Farm Weeds." *Journal of the Board of Agriculture* 25 (1918/19): 949–958.

———. *Weeds of Farm Land.* London: Longmans, Green and Co., 1920.

British American Cultivator (Toronto), 1842–1847.

Brodie, Patrick. "On the Destruction of Weeds." *Communications to the Board of Agriculture* 7 (1811): 64–69.

Buckman, James. "On Agricultural Weeds." *Journal of the Royal Agricultural Society of England* 16 (1855): 359–381.

Bulletin (Edmonton), 1945.

Burton, J. E. *Essay on Comparative Agriculture, or a Brief Examination into the State of Agriculture as it now Exists in Great Britain and Canada.* Montreal: Printed at the Montreal Gazette Office, 1828.

Caird, James. *English Agriculture in 1850–51.* 1852. Reprint, with a foreword by G.E. Mingay, London: Frank Cass and Co., 1967.

Campbell, Elmer G. "What is a Weed?" *Science* 58 (1923): 50.

Canada. *Statutes of Canada*, 1841–1950.

Canada. Department of Agriculture. Dominion Experimental Farms. *Annual Reports*, 1887–1923.

———. *Reports of the Superintendents*, 1920–1930.

———. *Progress Reports*, 1937–1946.

Canada. National Archives of Canada. Records of the Royal Canadian Mounted Police, Record Group 18, Vol. 1319, file 229-1894.

Canadian Agricultural Reader. Niagara: John Simpson, 1845.

Canadian Agriculturist (Toronto), 1849–1863.

The Canadian Who's Who. Toronto: The Musson Book Company Limited, 1910.

Cates, H.R. "The Weed Problem in American Agriculture." In *Yearbook of the United States Department of Agriculture,1917*, 205–215. Washington, D.C.: Government Printing Office, 1918.

Clark, George H. and James Fletcher. *Farm Weeds of Canada.* 2d ed. Ottawa: Department of Agriculture, 1909.

Claypole, E. W. "On the Migration of Plants from Europe to America, with an Attempt to Explain Certain Phenomena Connected Therewith." *Report of the Montreal Horticultural Society and Fruit Growers' Association of the Province of Quebec* 3 (1877): 70–91.

Cocannouer, Joseph A. *Weeds: Guardians of the Soil.* New York: Devin-Adair, 1950.

Cook, W. H. and A. C. Halferdahl. *Chemical Weed Killers: A Review.* National Research Council of Canada, Bulletin 18, 1937.

Country Guide (Winnipeg), 1928–1950.

Crafts, A. S. and W. A. Harvey. "Weed Control." *Advances in Agronomy* 1 (1949): 289–320.

Cresinus, C. F. "On the Agriculture of Canada, No.1–11." *Canadian Magazine and Literary Repository* 2 (1823): 329–331, 418–419, 503–507; 3 (1824): 97–101, 217–220, 481–484; 4 (1825): 1–6, 97–100, 193–196, 297–299, 406–409, 491–495.

Croil, James. "Lecture on Practical Agriculture, Delivered before the Dundas County Agricultural Society." *Transactions of the Board of Agriculture and of the Agricultural Association of Upper Canada* 3 (1859): 73–84.

Darlington, William. *American Weeds and Useful Plants.* 2d ed. New York: Orange Judd and Company, 1859 [1847].

Darwin, Charles. *The Variation of Animals and Plants Under Domestication*, 2 vols. American Ed. New York: Orange Judd and Co., 1868.

Dawson, Sir John W. *First Lessons in Scientific Agriculture.* Montreal: John Lovell, 1864.

De Schweinitz, Lewis D. "Remarks on the Plants of Europe which have become Naturalized in a More or Less Degree, in the United States." *Annals of the Lyceum of Natural History of New York* 3 (1832): 148–155.

Dewey, Lyster H. *The Russian Thistle.* United States Department of Agriculture, Farmers' Bulletin 10, 1893.

———. *Legislation Against Weeds*. United States Department of Agriculture, Division of Botany, Bulletin 17, 1896.

———. "Migration of Weeds." In *Yearbook of the United States Department of Agriculture, 1896*, 263–286. Washington, D.C.: Government Printing Office, 1897.

———. *Weeds and How to Kill Them*. United States Department of Agriculture, Bulletin 28, Second Revision, 1905.

Dickson, Adam. *A Treatise of Agriculture*, 2 vols., 2d ed. Edinburgh: Printed for A. Kincaid and J. Bell, 1765.

Ellis, William. *Chiltern and Vale Farming Explained*. London: Printed for Weaver Bickerton, 1733.

———. *The Modern Husbandman, or, the Practice of Farming*, 4 vols. London: Printed for T. Osborne and M. Cooper, 1744.

———. *Agriculture Improv'd: or, the Practice of Husbandry Display'd*, 2 vols. London: Printed for T. Osborne, 1745, 1746.

Evans, William. *A Treatise on the Theory and Practice of Agriculture*. Montreal: Fabre, Perrault and Company, 1835.

Farmer's Advocate–Western Edition (Winnipeg), 1890–1910.

Fergusson, Adam. *On the Agricultural State of Canada and Part of the United States of America*. Leith, Scotland: William Reid and Son, 1832.

Fitzherbert, Sir Anthony. *The Boke of Husbandry*. London: Printed by T. Berthelet, 1534.

Fletcher, James. *The Russian Thistle or Russian Tumble-Weed*. Ottawa: Government Printing Bureau, 1894.

———. *Weeds*. Department of Agriculture, Central Experimental Farm, Bulletin 28, 1897.

Fogg, John M. *Weeds of Lawn and Garden: A Handbook for Eastern Temperate North America*. Philadelphia: University of Pennsylvania Press, 1945.

Fraser, D. D. "Merchandising of Herbicides." *Proceedings of the Western Canadian Weed Control Conference* 4 (1950): 117–120.

Fream, William. *Canadian Agriculture–Part I. The Prairie*. London: William Clowes and Son, 1885.

French, Henry F. "Observations on English Husbandry." *Report of the Commissioner of Patents for the Year 1860*, 140–165. Washington, D.C.: GPO, 1860.

Friesen, H. A. "The Place of Cultural and Chemical Control Methods." *Proceedings of the Western Canadian Weed Control Conference* 8 (1955): 21–26.

Georgia, Ada E. *A Manual of Weeds*. New York: Macmillan, 1914.

Goff, E. S. *The Russian Thistle: A New and Dangerous Weed to Wisconsin*. Wisconsin Agricultural Experiment Station, Bulletin 37, 1893.

———. *Noxious Weeds*. Wisconsin Agricultural Experiment Station, Bulletin 39, 1894.

Godel, George L. "Weed Control Experiments Conducted by the Saskatchewan Department of Agriculture." *Proceedings of the Associate Committee on Weeds* 1 (1935): 52–53.

———. "Some Considerations in Regard to Experiments with Chemical Herbicides." *Canadian Journal of Research* 7 (1932): 499–519.

———. "Report on Weed Control Investigations Carried Out by the Saskatchewan Department of Agriculture." *Proceedings of the Associate Committee on Weeds* 5 (1939): 16–21.

Gorby, B. J. "Whither the Wild Oat?" *Proceedings of the Western Canadian Weed Control Conference* 2 (1948): 72–77.

Grain Growers' Guide (Winnipeg), 1908–1928.

Gray, Asa. "The Pertinacity and Predominance of Weeds." *The American Journal of Science and Arts* 18, Third Series (1879): 161–167.

Gray, George P. "Herbicides." *Monthly Bulletin of the Department of Agriculture, State of California* 11 (1922): 263–269.

Great Britain. *Statutes*, 1920, 10 and 11 Geo.5, c.76.

———. *Statutes of Northern Ireland*, 1909, 9 Edw.7, c.31.

Great Britain. Board of Agriculture and Fisheries. *Destruction of Charlock*. Leaflet 63, 1900.

———. "Weeds Act in the Isle of Man." *The Journal of the Board of Agriculture* 7 (1900/01): 245

———. *Weeds and Their Suppression*. Leaflet 112, 1904.

———. "Agricultural Education in the United States and Canada." *Journal of the Board of Agriculture* 17 (1910/1911): 912–915.

Grece, Charles F. *Essays on Practical Husbandry Addressed to the Canadian Farmers*. Montreal: Printed by William Gray, 1817.

Groh, Herbert. "A Survey of Weed Control and Investigation in Canada." *Scientific Agriculture* 3 (1922/23): 415–420.

———. "Turkestan Alfalfa as a Medium of Weed Introduction." *Scientific Agriculture* 21 (1940/41): 36–43.

———. *Canadian Weed Survey: First Report*. Ottawa: Department of Agriculture, 1942.

———. *Canadian Weed Survey: Second Annual Report*. Ottawa: Department of Agriculture, 1943.

———. *Canadian Weed Survey: Fourth Annual Report*. Ottawa: Department of Agriculture, 1945.

Groh, Herbert and Clarence Frankton. *Canadian Weed Survey: Fifth Report*. Ottawa: Department of Agriculture, 1946.

———. *Canadian Weed Survey: Sixth Report*. Ottawa: Department of Agriculture, 1947.

Hale, Thomas. *A Compleat Body of Husbandry*. London: Printed for T. Osborne, J. Shipton, J. Hodges, T. Trye, S. Crowder and H. Woodgate, 1756.

Hamilton County Agricultural Society. *The Western Agriculturist and Practical Farmer's Guide*. Cincinnati: Robinson and Fairbank, 1830.

Hansen, Albert A. *Canada Thistle and Methods of Eradication*. United States Department of Agriculture, Farmers' Bulletin 1002, 1918.

Hardy, Evan A. "What's Wrong with Tillage Machines." *Proceedings of the Western Canadian Weed Control Conference* 3 (1949): 171–174.

Harrison, F. C. *Some Common Ontario Weeds*. Toronto: Ontario Department of Agriculture, 1900.

Harrison, F. C. and William Lockhead. *Some Common Ontario Weeds*. Ontario Agricultural College and Experimental Farm, Bulletin 18, 1903.

Hayden, Ada. "The Story of Weed Seed Dissemination." In *The Weed Flora of Iowa*, edited by L. H. Pammel and Charlotte M. King, 561–574. Des Moines: Iowa Geological Survey, 1926.

Herald (Calgary), 1945.

Heresbach, Conrad. *Four Books of Husbandry*. Edited and translated by Barnabe Googe. London: Printed by Richard Watkins, 1577.

Hill, Thomas. *The Profitable Art of Gardening*. London: Printed by Henry Bynneman, 1579.

Holdich, Benjamin. "The Weeds of Agriculture." In *Hortus Gramineus Woburnensis*, 4th ed., George Sinclair, 299–362. London: Ridgways, n.d. [1825].

Home, Francis. *The Principles of Agriculture and Vegetation*. Edinburgh: Printed for G. Hamilton and J. Balfour, 1757.

Hopkins, E. S. "Losses Caused by Weeds." *Proceedings of the Associate Committee on Weeds* 2 (1936): 28–34.

———. "Weed Projects on the Dominion Experimental Farms in the Prairie Provinces." *Proceedings of the Associate Committee on Weeds* 5 (1939): 7–11.

Hopkins, E. S. and S. Barnes. *Crop Rotations and Soil Management for the Prairie Provinces*. Dominion Experimental Farms, Bulletin 98, New Series, 1928.

Howitt, J. Eaton. "Identification of Weeds and Weed Seeds and Methods of Eradication." In Ontario Agricultural and Experimental Union, *Annual Report*, 1911, 62–69.

———. *The Perennial Sow Thistle and Some Other Weeds Pests of 1908*. Ontario Agricultural College and Experimental Farm, Bulletin 168, 1908.

Hutton, G. H. "Fall Cultivation for the Eradication of Weeds and Conservation of Moisture." *Dominion Experimental Farms Seasonable Hints* 11 (1918): 10–11.

James, Charles C. *Agriculture*. Toronto: George N. Morang and Company, 1899.

Johnson, James. "Annual Address." *Transactions of the Board of Agriculture and of the Agricultural Association of Upper Canada, 1864 to 1868* 6 (1872): 21–29.

Johnston, James F. W. *Notes on North America: Agricultural, Economical, and Social*. Vol.1. Edinburgh: William Blackwood and Sons, 1851.

Journal (Edmonton), 1945.

Leader (Regina), 1894–1903.

Leighty, Clyde E. "Crop Rotation." In *Yearbook of Agriculture, 1938: Soils and Men*, 406–430. Washington, D.C.: Government Printing Office, 1938.

Lisle, Edward. *Observations in Husbandry*, edited by Thomas Lisle. London: Printed by J. Hughs for C. Hitch, L. Hawes, J. Rivington, J. Fletcher, W. Sandby and R. & J. Dodsley, 1757.

Litzenberger, S. C., A. H. Post and H. E. Morris. *Important Perennial Weeds in Montana: Their Identification and Control*. Montana State College Agricultural Experiment Station, Bulletin 426, 1945.

Long, Harold C. "The Identification and Eradication of Some Common Weeds, I." *Journal of the Board of Agriculture*, 18 (1911/12): 288–294.

———. "The Identification and Eradication of Some Common Weeds, IV." *Journal of the Board of Agriculture*, 19 (1912/13): 273–277.

————. *Weeds of Arable Land.* London: Ministry of Agriculture and Fisheries, 1929.

Longman, O. S. "Weed Control in Alberta." *Proceedings of the Associate Committee on Weeds* 5 (1939): 12–15.

Loudon, J. C. *An Encyclopedia of Agriculture.* London: Printed for Longman, Hurst, Rees, Orme, Brown and Green, 1825.

Macoun, John. *Manitoba and the Great North-West.* Guelph, Ontario: The World Publishing Co., 1882.

————. *Catalogue of Canadian Plants.* Part I. *Polypetalae.* Montreal: Dawson Brothers, 1883.

————. *Catalogue of Canadian Plants.* Part II. *Gamopetalae.* Montreal: Dawson Brothers, 1884.

Manitoba. *Statutes of Manitoba,* 1870–1950.

————. Advisory Board. *Our Canadian Prairies.* Toronto: C. Blackett Robinson, 1895.

————. *Prairie Agriculture.* Winnipeg: The Advisory Board of Manitoba, 189?

————. Department of Agriculture and Immigration. *Noxious Weeds and How to Destroy Them.* Winnipeg: Department of Agriculture and Immigration, 1897.

————. Department of Agriculture and Immigration. *Annual Reports,* 1900–1919.

Manson, J. M. *Weed Survey of the Prairie Provinces.* National Research Council of Canada, Report 26, 1932.

Markham, Gervase. *Markham's Farewell to Husbandry.* London: Published by M. F. for Roger Jackson, 1625.

Marshall, William. *Minutes of Agriculture.* London: Printed for J. Dodsley, 1778.

————. *The Rural Economy of Norfolk,* 2 vols. London: Printed for T. Caddell, 1787.

————. *The Rural Economy of Yorkshire,* 2 vols. London: Printed for T. Caddell, 1788.

————. *The Rural Economy of Glocestershire,* 2 vols. Glocester: Printed by R. Raikes for G. Nicol, 1789.

————. *The Rural Economy of the Midland Counties,* 2 vols. London: Printed for G. Nicol, 1790.

————. *The Rural Economy of the West of England,* 2 vols. London: Printed for G. Nicol, G. G. and J. Robinson, and J. Debrett, 1796.

Maxwell, Robert. *The Practical Husbandman.* Edinburgh: Printed by C. Wright and Company for the author, 1757.

McRostie, G. P., L. E. Kirk, G. Godel, W. G. Smith and J. M. Manson. *Weeds and their Control.* National Research Council of Canada, Report 27, 1932.

Mills, James and Thomas Shaw. *The First Principles of Agriculture.* Toronto: J. E. Bryant Co., 1890.

Michigan. Secretary of the State Board of Agriculture. *Annual Reports,* 1882–1949.

Morgan, Henry, ed. *The Canadian Men and Women of the Time: A Hand-book of Canadian Biography of Living Characters.* 2nd ed. Toronto: William Briggs, 1912.

Mortimer, John. *The Whole Art of Husbandry; or the Way of Managing and Improving Land.* 2d ed. London: Printed by J.H. for H. Mortlock and J. Robinson, 1708.

Morton, John C. *A Cyclopedia of Agriculture,* Vol. 2. London: Blackie and Son, 1855.

Muenscher, Walter C. *Weeds.* New York: The Macmillan Company, 1952 [1935].

Neatby, K. W. *An Illustrated Guide to Prairie Weeds.* Winnipeg: The North-West Line Elevators Association, 1941.

Newton, R. "Summary of Remarks by Dr. Newton." *Proceedings of the Associate Committee on Weeds* 2 (1936): 4–6.

Nicholson, John. *The Farmers' Assistant.* Albany, N.Y.: Printed by H. C. Southwick, 1814.

North-West Territories. *Ordinances of the North-West Territories,* 1878–1905.

Nor'-West Farmer (Winnipeg), 1886–1936.

Nunnick, F. C. "Agricultural Survey, 1912." *Report of the Canadian Commission of Conservation* 4 (1913): 151–158.

———. "Agricultural Survey, 1913." *Report of the Canadian Commission of Conservation* 5 (1914): 142–174.

———. "Agricultural Surveys and Illustration Farms." *Report of the Canadian Commission of Conservation* 6 (1915): 210–222.

Ontario. *Statutes of Ontario,* 1867–1950.

———. Ontario Agricultural and Experimental Union. *Annual Reports,* 1889–1938.

————. Ontario Agricultural College and Experimental Farm. *Annual Reports*, 1889–1934.

Ontario Agricultural Commission. *Report of the Commissioners and Appendices*. 5 vols. Toronto: C. Blackett Robinson, 1881.

————. *Canadian Farming: An Encyclopedia of Agriculture*. Toronto: Williamson and Co., 1889.

Oswald, W. L. and Andrew Boss. *Minnesota Weeds: Series II*. Minnesota Agricultural Experiment Station, Bulletin 139, 1914.

Pammel, L. H. *Weeds of the Farm and Garden*. New York: Orange Judd Company, 1911.

Pammel, L. H. and Charlotte M. King, eds. *The Weed Flora of Iowa*. Des Moines, Iowa: Iowa Geological Survey, 1926.

Panton, J. Hoyes. *Weeds*. Ontario Agricultural College and Experimental Farm, Bulletin 10, 1887.

————. *Weeds of Ontario*. Ontario Agricultural College and Experimental Farm, Bulletin 91, 1893.

Pavlychenko, T. K. "Development of New Herbicides." *Proceedings of the Western Canadian Weed Control Conference* 4 (1950): 114–117.

Pennsylvania Agricultural Society. *Memoirs of the Pennsylvania Agricultural Society*. Philadelphia: Published by J. S. Skinner, 1824.

Percival, John. "Weeds and Their Suppression." *The Journal of the Board of Agriculture* 10 (1903/1904): 461–467.

————. *Agricultural Botany: Theoretical and Practical*. 4th ed. New York: Henry Holt and Company, 1915.

Pieters, A. J. "What is a Weed?" *Journal of the American Society of Agronomy* 27 (1935): 781–783.

Pitt, William. "On the Subject of Weeding; or the Improvements to be Effected in Agriculture by the Extirpation of Weeds." *Communications to the Board of Agriculture* 5 (1806): 233–271.

Read, F. H. "The Summer-Fallow." *Dominion Experimental Farms Seasonable HintsCPrairie Edition* 22 (1922): 10–11.

Rennie, George. "On Weeding or Cleaning Land." *Communications to the Board of Agriculture* 7, part 2 (1813): 292–298.

Ripley, P. O. "Weed Control in Britain and Western Europe." *Proceedings of the Western Canadian Weed Control Conference* 3 (1949): 123–130.

————. "Getting Experimental Work Done." *Proceedings of the Western Canadian Weed Control Conference* 7 (1953): 82–88.

————. "National Organization for Weed Control." *Proceedings of the Western Canadian Weed Control Conference* 8 (1955): 16–20.

Robbins, Wilfred W., Alden S. Crafts and Richard N. Raynor. *Weed Control: A Textbook and Manual.* New York: McGraw-Hill, 1942.

Robertson, J. W. "Work of the Committee on Lands." *Report of the Canadian Commission of Conservation* 3 (1912): 56–64.

Ross, Alexander. *The Red River Settlement: Its Rise, Progress, and Present State.* London: Smith, Elder and Company, 1856.

Ryerson, Egerton. *First Lessons on Agriculture.* Toronto: Copp, Clark and Company, 1870.

Rykert, J. C. "Annual Address." *Transactions of the Board of Agriculture and of the Agricultural Association of Upper Canada, 1864 to 1868* 6 (1872): 138–147.

Saskatchewan. *Statutes of Saskatchewan,* 1906–1950.

————. Department of Agriculture. *Annual Reports,* 1906–1950.

Schmaltz, C. S. Rafinesque. "An Essay on the Exotic Plants, Mostly European, Which have been Naturalized and Now Grow Spontaneously in the Middle States of America." *Medical Repository* 2 (1811): 330–345.

Scribner, F. Lamson. *Weeds of Maine.* Augusta, Maine: Printed at the Kennebec Journal Office, 1869.

Shaw, Thomas. *Weeds and How to Eradicate Them.* Toronto: J. E. Bryant and Company, 1893.

Shaw, Thomas and C. A. Zavitz. *Weeds and Modes of Destroying Them.* Ontario Agricultural College and Experimental Farm, Bulletin 85, 1892.

Shirreff, Patrick. *A Tour Through North America; Together with a Comprehensive View of the Canadas and United States as Adapted for Agricultural Emigration.* Edinburgh: Oliver and Boyd, 1835.

Sinclair, Sir John. *An Account of the Systems of Husbandry Adopted in the More Improved Districts of Scotland,* 2d ed., 2 vols. Edinburgh: Printed by James Bellantyne and Company, 1813.

————. *The Code of Agriculture.* London: B. McMillan, 1817.

Spencer, Edwin Rollin. *Just Weeds.* New York: Charles Scribner's Sons, 1940.

Stahler, L. M. "What's New and What's Needed in Weed Control Research." *Proceedings of the Western Canadian Weed Control Conference* 2 (1948): 3–8.

Stephens, Henry. *The Book of the Farm*, 3 vols. Edinburgh: William Blackwood and Sons, 1844.

Stevens, O. A. *North Dakota Weeds*. North Dakota Agricultural Experiment Station, Bulletin 162, 1922.

———. "What is a Weed?" *Science* 59 (April 18, 1924): 360–361.

———. *Perennial Sow Thistle: Growth and Reproduction*. North Dakota Agricultural Experiment Station, Bulletin 181, 1924.

Tanner, Henry. *Report Upon Canada*. London: The Freemason Printing Works, 1883.

Tinline, M. J. "Crops, Rotation and Weed Control." *Dominion Experimental Farms Seasonable Hints–Prairie Edition* 40 (1928): 8–9.

Torrey, John and Asa Gray. *A Flora of North America*, 2 vols. 1838–1843. Reprint, New York: Hafner Publishing Company, 1969.

Tull, Jethro. *The New Horse-Houghing Husbandry: or, an Essay on the Principles of Tillage and Vegetation*. Dublin: Printed by Aaron Rhames, 1731.

———. *The Horse-Hoing Husbandry: or, an Essay on the Principles of Tillage and Vegetation*. London: Printed for the author, 1733.

Tusser, Thomas. *Five Hundreth Points of Good Husbandry*. London: Richard Tottell, 1574.

United States. Department of Agriculture. "Weeds." *Yearbook of the United States Department of Agriculture, 1897*, 95–96. Washington, D.C.: Government Printing Office, 1898.

United States. Secretary of Agriculture. *Reports of the Secretary of Agriculture, 1891–1949*. Washington, D.C.: Government Printing Office, 1891–1949.

Upper Canada. *Statutes of Upper Canada*, 1792–1859.

Voelcker, J. Augustus. "The Destruction of Charlock." *Journal of the Royal Agricultural Society of England*, 3rd Series, 10 (1899): 766–755.

Wade, John. "Annual Address." *Transactions of the Board of Agriculture and of the Agricultural Association of Upper Canada, 1860 to 1863* 5 (1864): 38–41.

Walter of Henley. "Husbandry (ca 1286)." In *Walter of Henley and other Treatises on Estate Management and Accounting*. Edited and translated by Dorothea Oschinsky, 308–385. Oxford: Clarendon Press, 1971.

Waugh, F. A. "Some Phases of Weed Evolution." *Science* 5, New Series (May 21, 1897): 789–791.

Wenhart, A. "Recent Developments in Tillage Machinery." *Proceedings of the Western Canadian Weed Control Conference* 4 (1950): 140–143.

Werry, F. E. "A Farmer Appraises 2,4-D." *Proceedings of the Western Canadian Weed Control Conference* 4 (1950): 123–128.

Whitcombe, Charles E. *The Canadian Farmer's Manual of Agriculture*. Toronto: James Adam and Company, 1874.

Wilson, A. M. "The Third Western Weed Control Conference." *Proceedings of the Western Canadian Weed Control Conference* 3 (1949): 4–5.

Wilson, H. K., L. M. Stahler, A. C. Arny, R. B. Harvey, A. H. Larson and R. H. Landon. *Battling Weeds on Minnesota Farms*. Minnesota Agricultural Experiment Station, Bulletin 363, 1942.

Wood, H. E. "Introductory Remarks." *Proceedings of the Western Canadian Weed Control Conference* 1 (1947): 5.

———. "Introductory Remarks." *Proceedings of the Western Canadian Weed Control Conference* 2 (1948): 1–2.

———. "'Selling' Chemical Weed Control." *Proceedings of the Western Canadian Weed Control Conference* 4 (1950): 120–123.

———. "Fifty Years of Weed Control in Western Canada." *Proceedings of the Western Canadian Weed Control Conference* 8 (1955): 1–6.

Worlidge, John. *Systema Agriculturae; the Mystery of Husbandry Discovered*. London: Printed for Thomas Dring, 1681.

Wright, John. "Experiments on Weeding Broad-cast Crops." *Communications to the Board of Agriculture*, 6, Part 2 (1810): 387–388.

Young, Arthur. *Rural Oeconomy: or, Essays on the Practical Parts of Husbandry*. London: Printed for T. Becket, 1770.

———. *A Six Months Tour Through the North of England*, 3 vols. Dublin: Printed for P. Wilson, J. Exshaw, H. Saunders, W. Sleater, D. Chamberlaine, J. Potts, J. Hoey Jr., J. Williams, W. Colles, J. Porter, C. Ingham and T. Walker, 1770.

Secondary Sources

Ainsworth, G. C. *Introduction to the History of Plant Pathology*. Cambridge: Cambridge University Press, 1981.

Aldrich, R. J. *Weed-Crop Ecology: Principles in Weed Management*. North Scituate, Mass.: Breton Publishers, 1984.

Alex, J. F. "Canada." In *Biology and Ecology of Weeds*, edited by W. Holzner and M. Numata, 309–331. The Hague: Dr. W. Junk Publishers, 1982.

————. *Ontario Weeds.* Toronto: Ontario Ministry of Agriculture and Food, 1992.

Anderson, Edgar. *Plants, Man and Life.* Boston: Little, Brown and Company, 1952.

Anderson, Wood P. *Weed Science: Principles.* St. Paul, Minnesota: West Publishing Company, 1977.

Ankli, Robert E., H. Dan Helsberg and John Herd Thompson. "The Adoption of the Gasoline Tractor in Western Canada." *Canadian Papers in Rural History* 2 (1980): 9–39.

Anstey, T. H. *One Hundred Harvests: Research Branch, Agriculture Canada, 1886–1986.* Ottawa: Supply and Services Canada, 1986.

Ashton, Floyd M. and Thomas J. Monaco. *Weed Science: Principles and Practices.* 3rd ed. New York: John Wiley and Sons, 1991.

Baker, Herbert G. "Human Influences on Plant Evolution." *Economic Botany* 26 (1972): 32–43.

————. "The Continuing Evolution of Weeds." *Economic Botany* 45 (1991): 445–449.

Barrett, Spencer C. H. "Crop Mimicry in Weeds." *Economic Botany* 37 (1983): 255–282.

Best, K. F. and G. I. McIntyre. "The Biology of Canadian Weeds. 9. *Thlaspi arvense* L." *Canadian Journal of Plant Science* 55 (1975): 279–292.

Blackwell, W. H. "The History of Russian Pigweed, *Axyris amaranthoides* (Chenopodiaceae, Atripliceae), in North America." *Weed Science* 26 (1978): 82–83.

Bowden, Peter J. "Agricultural Prices, Farm Profits, and Rents." In *The Agrarian History of England and Wales.* Vol. 4. *1500–1640,* edited by Joan Thirsk, 593–695. Cambridge: Cambridge University Press, 1967.

————. "Agricultural Prices, Wages, Farm Profits, and Rents." In *The Agrarian History of England and Wales.* Vol. 5.2. *1640–1750: Agrarian Change,* edited by Joan Thirsk, 1–118. Cambridge: Cambridge University Press, 1985.

Britnell, G. E. *The Wheat Economy.* Toronto: University of Toronto Press, 1939.

Britnell, G. E. and V. C. Fowke. *Canadian Agriculture in War and Peace, 1935–50.* Stanford: Stanford University Press, 1962.

Brown, Jonathan and H. A. Beecham. "Farming Practices." In *The Agrarian History of England and Wales.* Vol. 6. *1750–1850,* edited by G. E. Mingay, 276–296. Cambridge: Cambridge University Press, 1989.

Bubar, Carol J. and Ian N. Morrison. "Thomas K. Pavlychenko: Pioneer Weed Experimentalist." *Weed Science* 30 (1982): 434–440.

Bunting, A. H. "Some Reflections on the Ecology of Weeds." In *The Biology of Weeds*, edited by John L. Harper, 11–26. Oxford: Blackwell Scientific Publications, 1960.

Burnside, Orvin C. "Rationale for Developing Herbicide-Resistant Crops." *Weed Technology* 6 (1992): 621–625.

———. "Weed Science: The Step Child." *Weed Technology* 7 (1993): 515–518.

Chacón, J. C. and S. R. Gliessman. "Use of the 'Non-Weed' Concept in Traditional Tropical Agroecosystems of South-Eastern Mexico." *Agro-Ecosystems* 8 (1982): 1–11.

Chambers, J. D. and G. E. Mingay. *The Agricultural Revolution, 1750–1880.* London: B.T. Batsford Ltd., 1966.

Chancellor, R. J. and R. J. Froud-Williams. "A Second Survey of Cereal Weeds in Central Southern England." *Weed Research* 24 (1984): 29–36.

Crafts, Alden S. "Weed Control ResearchCPast, Present, and Future." *Weeds* 8 (1960): 535–540.

Cronon, William. *Changes in the Land: Indians, Colonists, and the Ecology of New England.* New York: Hill and Wang, 1983.

———. "Modes of Prophecy and Production: Placing Nature in History." *Journal of American History* 76 (1990): 1122–1131.

Crosby, Alfred W. *Ecological Imperialism: The Biological Expansion of Europe, 900–1900.* Cambridge: Cambridge University Press, 1986.

Danbom, David B. "The Agricultural Experiment Station and Professionalization: Scientists' Goals for Agriculture." *Agricultural History* 60, no. 2 (1986): 246–255.

Danhof, Clarence H. *Change in Agriculture: The Northern United States, 1820–1870.* Cambridge, Mass.: Harvard University Press, 1969.

De Wet, J. M. J. and J. R. Harlan. "Weeds and Domesticates: Evolution in the Man-Made Habitat." *Economic Botany* 29 (1975): 99–107.

Duncan, Colin A. M. "Legal Protection for the Soil of England: The Spurious Context of Nineteenth Century 'Progress.'" *Agricultural History* 66, no. 2 (1992): 75–94.

Dunlap, Thomas R. "Farmers, Scientists, and Insects." *Agricultural History* 54 (1980): 93–107.

————. *DDT: Scientists, Citizens and Public Policy.* Princeton: Princeton University Press, 1981.

Elliot, J. G. "The Contribution of Weed Science to Food Production in Great Britain." *Weed Science* 18 (1970): 681–686.

Ellis, Joseph H. *The Ministry of Agriculture in Manitoba, 1870–1970.* Winnipeg: Manitoba Department of Agriculture, 1970.

Ernle, Lord. *English Farming Past and Present.* 6th ed. London: Longmans, Green and Co., 1961 [1912].

Estey, Ralph H. "Publicly Sponsored Agricultural Research in Canada since 1887." *Agricultural History* 62 (Spring 1988): 51–63.

Eussen, J. H. H. "The Ecology of Pests: Weeds." *Protection Ecology* 4 (1982): 213–221.

Finberg, P. R. and Joan Thirsk, eds. *The Agrarian History of England and Wales.* 8 vols. Cambridge: Cambridge University Press, 1967-.

Forcella, Frank and Stephen J. Harvey. "Patterns of Weed Migration in Northwestern U.S.A." *Weed Science* 36 (1988): 194–201.

Fowke, Vernon C. *Canadian Agricultural Policy: The Historical Pattern.* Toronto: University of Toronto Press, 1947.

————. *The National Policy and the Wheat Economy.* Toronto: University of Toronto Press, 1957.

Frankton, Clarence. *Weeds of Canada.* Ottawa: Canada Department of Agriculture, 1955.

Frankton, Clarence and Gerald A. Mulligan. *Weeds of Canada.* Ottawa: Agriculture Canada, 1993.

Freed, Virgil. "Weed Science: The Emergence of a Vital Technology." *Weed Science* 28 (1980): 621–625.

Friesen, Gerald. *The Canadian Prairies: A History.* Toronto: University of Toronto Press, 1987.

Fryer, J. D. "Recent Research on Weed Management: New Light on an Old Practice." In *Recent Advances in Weed Research,* edited by W. W. Fletcher, 181–198. Farnham Royal, Engl.: Commonwealth Agricultural Bureaux, 1983.

Fussell, G. E. "Science and Practice in Eighteenth-Century British Agriculture." *Agricultural History* 43 (1969): 7–18.

————. "Agricultural Science and Experiment in the Eighteenth Century: An Attempt at a Definition." *Agricultural History Review* 24 (1976): 44–47.

————. *The Old English Farming Books.* Vol. 3. London: The Pindar Press, 1983.

Gade, Daniel W. "Weeds in Vermont as Tokens of Socioeconomic Change." *Geographical Review* 81 (1991): 153–169.

Gates, Paul W. *The Farmer's Age: Agriculture 1815–1860.* New York: Holt, Rinehart and Winston, 1960.

Gayton, Don. *The Wheatgrass Mechanism: Science and the Imagination in the Western Canadian Landscape.* Saskatoon: Fifth House Publishers, 1990.

Glauninger, J. and W. Holzner. "Interference between Weeds and Crops: A Review of Literature." In *Biology and Ecology of Weeds,* edited by W. Holzner and M. Numata, 149–159. The Hague: Dr. W. Junk Publishers, 1982.

Goddard, Nicholas. "The Development and Influence of Agricultural Periodicals and Newspapers, 1780–1880." *Agricultural History Review* 31 (1983): 116–131.

Godwin, H. "The History of Weeds in Britain." In *The Biology of Weeds,* edited by John L. Harper, 2–10. Oxford: Blackwell Scientific Publications, 1960.

Grigg, David. *English Agriculture: An Historical Perspective.* Oxford: Basil Blackwell, 1989.

Grignac, Pierre. "The Evolution of Resistance to Herbicides in Weedy Species." *Agro-Ecosystems* 4 (1978): 377–385.

Harlan, Jack R. *Crops and Man.* Madison, Wisc.: American Society of Agronomy and the Crop Science Society of America, 1975.

Harlan, Jack R. and J. M. J. De Wet. "Some Thoughts About Weeds." *Economic Botany* 19 (1965): 16–24.

Harper, John L. *Population Biology of Plants.* New York: Academic Press, 1977.

Haughton, Claire S. *Green Immigrants: The Plants that Transformed America.* New York: Harcourt Brace Jovanovich, 1978.

Hidden, Norman. "Jethro Tull I, II, and III." *Agricultural History Review* 37 (1989): 26–35.

Hill, Thomas A. *The Biology of Weeds.* London: Edward Arnold, 1977.

Holm, LeRoy. "The Role of Weeds in Human Affairs." *Weed Science* 19 (1971): 485–490.

Holt, Jodie S. "History of Identification of Herbicide-Resistant Weeds." *Weed Technology* 6 (1992): 615–620.

Holzner, W. "Concepts, Categories and Characteristics of Weeds." In *Biology and Ecology of Weeds,* edited by W. Holzner and M. Numata, 3–20. The Hague: Dr. W. Junk Publishers, 1982.

Hurt, R. Douglas. *Indian Agriculture in America: Prehistory to the Present.* Lawrence, Kansas: University of Kansas Press, 1987.

Isern, Thomas D. "Gopher Tales: A Study in Western Canadian Pest Control." *Agricultural History Review* 36 (1988): 188–198.

———. "The Discer: Tillage for the Canadian Plains." *Agricultural History* 62, no. 2 (1988): 79–97.

Jones, G. E. "Food Production in Canada: The Weed Scientists' Role." *Weed Science* 18 (1970): 545–546.

Jones, Robert L. *History of Agriculture in Ontario, 1613–1880.* Toronto: University of Toronto Press, 1946.

Kelly, Kenneth. "Wheat Farming in Simcoe County in the Mid-Nineteenth Century." *Canadian Geographer* 15 (1971): 95–112.

———. "Notes on a Type of Mixed Farming Practised in Ontario During the Early Nineteenth Century." *Canadian Geographer* 17 (1973): 205–219.

———. "The Impact of Nineteenth Century Agricultural Settlement on the Land." In *Perspectives on Landscape and Settlement in Nineteenth Century Ontario,* edited by J. David Wood, 64–77. Toronto: McClelland and Stewart, 1975.

Kendle, John. *John Bracken: A Political Biography.* Toronto: University of Toronto Press, 1979.

Kerridge, Eric. *The Agricultural Revolution.* London: George Allen and Unwin Ltd., 1967.

King, Lawrence J. "Some Early Forms of the Weed Concept." *Nature* 179 (1957): 1366.

———. *Weeds of the World: Biology and Control.* New York: Interscience Publishers, 1966.

Klingman, Glenn C. "Who Will do the Research and Teaching?" *Weed Science* 18 (1970): 541–544.

Knobloch, Frieda. *The Culture of Wilderness: Agriculture as Colonization in the American West.* Chapel Hill: University of North Carolina Press, 1996.

Lindsay, D. R. "Taxonomic and Genetic Studies on Wild Oats (*Avena fatua* L.)." *Weeds* 4 (1956): 1–10.

Lockhart, J. A. R., A. Samuel and M. P. Greaves. "The Evolution of Weed Control in British Agriculture." In *Weed Control Handbook: Principles,* 8th ed., edited by R. J. Hance and K. Holly, 43–74. Oxford: Blackwell Scientific Publications, 1990.

Long, W. Harwood. "The Low Yield of Corn in Medieval England." *Economic History Review* 32 (1979): 459–469.

MacDonald, Stuart. "The Diffusion of Knowledge among Northumberland Farmers, 1780–1815." *Agricultural History Review* 27 (1979): 30–39.

———. "Agricultural Improvement and the Neglected Labourer." *Agricultural History Review* 31 (1983): 81–90.

MacEwan, Grant. *Charles Noble: Guardian of the Soil.* Saskatoon: Western Producer Books, 1983.

Mack, Richard N. "Invasion of *Bromus tectorum* L. into Western North America: An Ecological Chronicle." *Agro-Ecosystems* 7 (1981): 145–165.

———. "The Commercial Seed Trade: An Early Disperser of Weeds in the United States." *Economic Botany* 45 (1991): 257–273.

MacPherson, Ian and John H. Thompson. "An Orderly Reconstruction: Prairie Agriculture in World War Two." *Canadian Papers in Rural History* 4 (1984): 11–32.

Marcus, Alan I. *Agricultural Science and the Quest for Legitimacy: Farmers, Agricultural Colleges, and Experiment Stations, 1870–1890.* Ames: Iowa State University Press, 1985.

McCallum, John. *Unequal Beginnings: Agriculture and Economic Development in Quebec and Ontario until 1870.* Toronto: University of Toronto Press, 1980.

McEvoy, Arthur F. "Toward an Interactive Theory of Nature and Culture: Ecology, Production and Cognition in the California Fishing Industry." In *The Ends of the Earth: Perspectives on Modern Environmental History,* edited by Donald Worster, 211–228. Cambridge: Cambridge University Press, 1988.

McInnis, R. M. "Perspectives on Ontario Agriculture, 1815–1930." *Canadian Papers in Rural History* 8 (1992): 17–127.

McMillen, Wheeler. "Father's War Against Weeds." *Agricultural History* 63, No.4 (1989): 72–75.

McNeil, J. "The Taxonomy and Evolution of Weeds." *Weed Research* 16 (1976): 399–413.

McRae, Andrew. "Husbandry Manuals and the Language of Agrarian Improvement." In *Culture and Cultivation in Early Modern England: Writing and the Land,* edited by Michael Leslie and Timothy Raylor, 35–62. Leicester: Leicester University Press, 1992.

McWhorter, Chester G. and William L. Barrentine. "Research Priorities in Weed Science." *Weed Technology* 2 (1988): 2–11.

Merchant, Carolyn. "The Theoretical Structure of Ecological Revolutions." *Environmental Review* 11 (Winter 1987): 265–274.

———. *Ecological Revolutions: Nature, Gender, and Science in New England.* Chapel Hill: University of North Carolina Press, 1989.

———. "Gender and Environmental History." *Journal of American History* 76 (1990): 1117–1121.

Mingay, G. E., ed. *The Agricultural Revolution: Changes in Agriculture 1650–1880.* London: Adam and Charles Black, 1977.

Mitich, Larry W. "Looking Back to See." *Weed Technology* 5 (1991): 238–243.

Moore, R. J. "The Biology of Canadian Weeds. 13. *Cirsium arvense* (L.) Scop." *Canadian Journal of Plant Science* 55 (1975): 1033–1048.

Mortimer, A. M. "The Biology of Weeds." In *Weed Control Handbook: Principles*, 8th ed., edited by R.J. Hance and K. Holly, 1–42. Oxford: Blackwell Scientific Publications, 1990.

Mulligan, G. A. and L. G. Bailey. "The Biology of Canadian Weeds. 8. *Sinapsis arvensis* L." *Canadian Journal of Plant Science* 55 (1975): 171–183.

Murray, Stanley N. "A History of Agriculture in the Valley of the Red River of the North, 1812 to 1920." Ph.D. diss., University of Wisconsin, 1963.

Muzik, Thomas J. *Weed Biology and Control.* New York: McGraw-Hill, 1970.

Nadeau, L. B. and W. H. Vanden Born. "The Root System of Canada Thistle." *Canadian Journal of Plant Science* 69 (1989): 1199–1206.

Navas, M. L. "Using Plant Population Biology in Weed Research: A Strategy to Improve Weed Management." *Weed Research* 31 (1991): 171–179

O'Mara, James. "The Seasonal Rounds of Gentry Farmers in Early Ontario: A Preliminary Analysis." *Canadian Papers in Rural History* 2 (1980): 103–112.

Ordish, George. *The Constant Pest: A Short History of Pests and Their Control.* New York: Charles Scribner's Sons, 1976.

Orwin, Christabel S. and Edith H. Whetham. *History of British Agriculture, 1846–1914.* London: Longmans, Green and Co., 1964.

Perkins, John H. *Insects, Experts, and the Insecticide Crisis: The Quest for New Pest Management Strategies.* New York: Plenum Press, 1982.

Peterson, Gale E. "The Discovery and Development of 2,4-D." *Agricultural History* 41, no. 3 (1967): 243–253.

Plant Protection Limited. *Common Farm Weeds Illustrated*. London: Butterworth's Scientific Publications, 1952.

Postles, David. "Cleaning the Medieval Arable." *Agricultural History Review* 37 (1989): 130–143.

Pritchard, Tom. "Race Formation in Weedy Species with Special Reference to *Euphorbia cyparissias* L. and *Hypericum perforatum* L." In *The Biology of Weeds*, edited by John L. Harper, 61–66. Oxford: Blackwell Scientific Publications, 1960.

Reaman, G. Elmore. *A History of Agriculture in Ontario*, 2 vols. Toronto: Saunders, 1970.

Richards, Stewart. "Agricultural Science in Higher Education: Problems of Identity in Britain's First Chair of Agriculture, Edinburgh 1790–c1831." *Agricultural History Review* 33 (1985): 59–65.

Riegert, Paul W. *From Arsenic to DDT: A History of Entomology in Western Canada*. Toronto: University of Toronto Press, 1980.

———."James Fletcher." In *Dictionary of Canadian Biography*. Vol. 13. Edited by Ramsay Cook, 347–348. Toronto: University of Toronto Press, 1994.

Ross, Alexander M. *The College on the Hill: A History of the Ontario Agricultural College*. Toronto: Copp Clarke, 1974.

Rossiter, Margaret W. *The Emergence of Agricultural Science: Justus Liebig and the Americans, 1840–1880*. New Haven, Conn.: Yale University Press, 1975.

———. "The Organization of Agricultural Improvement in the United States, 1785–1865." In *The Pursuit of Knowledge in the Early American Republic*, edited by A. Oleson and S. Brown, 279–298. Baltimore: Johns Hopkins University Press, 1976.

Rowe, J. Stan and Robert T. Coupland. "Vegetation of the Canadian Plains." *Prairie Forum* 9 (1984): 231–248.

Russell, Sir John. *A History of Agricultural Science in Great Britain, 1620–1954*. London: George Allen and Unwin Ltd., 1966.

Russell, Peter A. "Forest into Farmland: Upper Canadian Clearing Rates, 1822–1839." *Agricultural History* 57 (1983): 326–339.

Salisbury, Sir Edward. *Weeds and Aliens*. London: Collins, 1961.

Schlebecker, John T. *Whereby We Thrive: A History of American Farming, 1607–1972*. Ames: Iowa State University Press, 1975.

Sharma, M. P. and W. H. Vanden Born. "The Biology of Canadian Weeds. 27. *Avena fatua* L." *Canadian Journal of Plant Science* 58 (1978): 141–157.

Shepard, R. Bruce. "Walter Murray, Evan Hardy, and the American Presence at the University of Saskatchewan." *Agricultural History* 62, no. 2 (1988): 64–78.

Smith, Allan E. and Diane M. Secoy. "Early Chemical Control of Weeds in Europe." *Weed Science* 24 (1976): 594–597.

Sorensen, Conner. "The Rise of Government Sponsored Applied Entomology, 1840–1870." *Agricultural History* 62 , no. 2 (1988): 98–115.

Thirsk, Joan. "Farming Techniques." In *The Agrarian History of England and Wales.* Vol.4. *1500–1640,* edited by Joan Thirsk, 161–199. Cambridge: Cambridge University Press, 1967.

———. "Agricultural Innovations and their Diffussion." In *The Agrarian History of England and Wales.* Vol. 5.2. *1640–1750: Agrarian Change,* edited by Joan Thirsk, 533–589. Cambridge: Cambridge University Press, 1985.

———. "Making a Fresh Start: Sixteenth-Century Agriculture and the Classical Inspiration." In *Culture and Cultivation in Early Modern England: Writing and the Land,* edited by Michael Leslie and Timothy Raylor, 15–34. Leicester: Leicester University Press, 1992.

Thomas, A. Gordon. "Weed Survey System Used in Saskatchewan for Cereal and Oilseed Crops." *Weed Science* 33 (1985): 34–43.

Thomas, Keith. *Man and the Natural World: Changing Attitudes in England, 1500–1800.* London: Penguin Books, 1983.

Thomas, Lewis H. "A History of Agriculture on the Prairies to 1914." *Prairie Forum* 1 (1976): 31–46.

Thurston, J. M. "Wild Oats as Successful Weeds." In *Biology and Ecology of Weeds,* edited by W. Holzner and M. Numata, 191–199. The Hague: Dr. W. Junk Publishers, 1982.

Timmons, F. L. "A History of Weed Control in the United States and Canada." *Weed Science* 18 (1970): 294–307.

Trenbath, B. R. "Weeds and Agriculture: A Question of Balance." In *Studies on Plant Demography: A Festschrift for John L. Harper,* edited by James White, 171–183. London: Academic Press, 1985.

Tulloch, Catherine. "Pioneer Reading." *Saskatchewan History* 12, no. 3 (1959): 97–99.

Turner, Allan R. "Pioneer Farming Experiences." *Saskatchewan History* 8, no. 1 (1955): 41–55.

Weed Society of America. Terminology Committee. "Terminology Committee ReportCWeed Society of America." *Weeds* 4 (1956): 278–287.

Whetham, Edith H. "The Agriculture Act, 1920 and its Repeal — the 'Great Betrayal.'" *Agricultural History Review* 22 (1974): 36–49.

White, Richard. "Environmental History, Ecology, and Meaning." *Journal of American History* 76 (1990): 1111–1116.

Wicker, E. R. "A Note on Jethro Tull: Innovator or Crank?" *Agricultural History* 31, no. 1 (1957): 46–48.

Wilkes, Roger. "The Diffusion of Drill Husbandry, 1731–1850." In *Agricultural Improvement: Medieval and Modern*, edited by Walter Minchinton, 65–94. Exeter: University of Exeter, 1981.

Willard, C. J. "Where do We go from Here?" *Weeds* 1 (1951): 9–12.

Willis, A. J. "Ecological Consequences of Modern Weed Control Systems." In *Weed Control Handbook: Principles*, 8th ed., edited by R.J. Hance and K. Holly, 501–519. Oxford: Blackwell Scientific Publications, 1990.

Woodford, E. K. "Weed Control — Its Status and Organisation in Great Britain." *Weeds* 8 (1960): 561–572.

Worster, Donald. *Dust Bowl: The Southern Plains in the 1930s.* New York: Oxford University Press, 1979.

———. "Transformation of the Earth: Toward an Agroecological Perspective in History." *Journal of American History* 76 (1990): 1087–1106.

Young, James A. "The Public Response to the Catastrophic Spread of Russian Thistle (1880) and Halogeton (1945)." *Agricultural History* 62, no. 2 (1988): 122–130.

Index

A

Abel, P. M., 129
absinthe, 118
Advocate, 91
Agricultural Association of Upper Canada, 66, 70, 72
agricultural improvement: literature, 25, 37, 44; literature, British, 58–59; Ontario, 78
agricultural press. *See* farm press
agricultural reform: British movement for, 59; traditional agriculture, 23
agricultural reformers, xi, 23, 41, 55; Canadian, 59; Scottish, 9, 41
agricultural revolution, 9, 20, 27, 32
The Agricultural Revolution, 1770-1880 (Chambers and Mingay), 20
The Agricultural Revolution (Kerridge), 20
agricultural scientists. *See* scientists, agricultural
Agricultural Service Board Act of Alberta, 124
Agricultural Societies, 82, 97
agrochemical complex, xi
agronomists, 115
Agropyron repens (L.) Beauv. *See* quack grass
Alberta: Atlacide use, 157; poster campaign, 131; spending on weed inspection, 126; weed bulletins, 130; weed control demonstration plots, 133; weed law enforcement, 129; weed laws, 102
Alberta Department of Agriculture, 141; iron and copper spraying demonstrations, 153
Alberta's Agricultural Service Board Act, 125
Alberta's Field Crops Commissioner, 126

E

F

I

ignorance, 90; Ontario's farmers, 83; weed inspectors, 128

illustration farms, 133

immigrant plants, 65, 68, 70, 73, 77, 92, 106, 110–11, 147–48, 183; advantage, 93; aggressive European plants, 62; alien invaders from continental Europe, 21; alien species, 93; in Canada, 232n; freedom from predators and pathogens, 93; imported weeds, 55, 87–88, 93, 181; intruders, 57; invasions, 21; naturalization, 69; Ontario's weeds, 84; opportunistic, 182; success, 51, 74, 81, 107, 235n; success in West, 186; wild oats, 143; worst enemies of farmers, 112

immigrants, 78, 106. *See also* settlers; British, 181; competing groups of, 177; farmers, 53; from Ontario, 183; parallel streams, 97

Imperial Oil, 131–32

implements, xvii, 56, 110, 117; combine harvesters, 124; cultivators, 49, 138–39; discers, 137–38; disseminating weeds, 8; duckfoot cultivator, 137; farm implement industry, 159; harrows, 49, 86, 136–37; innovations, American, 116; manufacturers, 130, 164, 175, 187; moldboard plows, 140; new fallowing, 140; new techniques, 140; Noble Blade, 117, 138; one-way disc, 138, 140; plows, 30, 48–49, 137, 140; plows, disc, 136, 140; plows, improvements, 49; plows, moldbord, 136; rod weeders, 252n; spray machinery, 153; sprayers and dusters, 164; subsurface tillers, 138; threshing machines, 102; weeds and, 54

implements, animal-drawn, 28, 30

important weeds. *See* weeds, important

imported weeds. *See* immigrant plants

improvers. *See* agricultural improvers

Indian corn, 84

Indian Head, 118; lambs' quarters, 88; tumble mustard, 95

Indian Head Experimental Farm, 7, 79, 156

indigenous. *See* native

Injurious Weeds Regulation, 121

International Harvester, 130

Interprovincial Weed Train, 133

iron and copper sulphate sprays, 85, 224n; high cost, 153

iron sulphate, 152

Iva axillaris Pursh. *See* poverty weed

J

K

L

M

Mackay, Angus, 7, 87–88, 95
Maclean, H. S., 104
Macoun, John, 80, 86, 94
maize, 111
Manitoba, 106, 122, 147; Atlacide, 157; as colony of Ontario, 86; commercial
    agriculture, 86; copper sulfate tests, 153; cultivators, 137; fallows, 136; farmers
    of, 88; illustration farms, 133; laws and enforcement, 114; legislation, 124;
    Russian pigweed, 118; Russian thistle, 96; settlement boom, 86; sodium
    chlorate, 157; spending on weed inspections, 126
Manitoba Canada Thistle Act of 1871, 89
Manitoba Department of Agriculture, 98, 163
Manitoba Department of Agriculture and Immigration, 86–87, 97, 104
Manitoba Noxious Weed Act, 122
Manitoba Weeds Commission, 159–60, 163
Manitoba 1890 Noxious Weed Act, 89
A Manual of Weeds (Georgia), 119
manure, 32–34, 60, 72, 86, 88
Maritime provinces, 120
markets, xvi, 20, 73–74, 99–100, 108, 111, 142, 181; Ontario, 78, 84, 181–82
Markham, Gervase, 26, 44
Marshall, William, 24–25, 27–30, 36–37, 41, 59, 67
Massey-Harris, 139
Mayweed, 93
McKellar, Hugh, 104
McMillen, Wheeler, 113
MCPA (2-methyl 4-chlorophenoxyacetic acid), 169–70
Mennonite Reserve: Russian thistle, 96–97
Michigan, 118; noxious weed laws, 114
migration, southward: farmers, 117; plants, 117; technology, 117
milkweed, 57
Mills, James, 79, 83
Mingay, G. E., 20
Minnesota: noxious weed laws, 114; practices, 112; state agricultural experiment
    stations, 116
Minutes of Agriculture (Marshall), 37
mixed farming, x, 71, 78, 100, 110, 116, 149, 175, 186, 236n; Ontario, 181; and
    perennial sow-thistle, 145
moisture loss, 138
Montana weed bulletins, 117
More, Henry, 46
Morrill Land-Grant College Act, 1862, 115
Mortimer, John, 26

Q

S

U

V

W